Academic
Vocabulary in Use

50 units of academic vocabulary reference and practice

Self-study and classroom use

Michael McCarthy
Felicity O'Dell

CAMBRIDGE
UNIVERSITY PRESS

CAMBRIDGE UNIVERSITY PRESS
Cambridge, New York, Melbourne, Madrid, Cape Town, Singapore,
São Paulo, Delhi, Dubai, Tokyo

Cambridge University Press
The Edinburgh Building, Cambridge CB2 8RU, UK

www.cambridge.org
Information on this title: www.cambridge.org/9780521689397

First published 2008
3rd printing 2010

Produced by Kamae Design, Oxford

Printed in Dubai by Oriental Press

A catalogue record for this publication is available from the British Library

ISBN 978-0-521-68939-7 Edition with answers

Contents

Opinions and ideas

Functions

Reading and vocabulary

Reference

Acknowledgements

Authors' acknowledgements

The authors wish to thank their colleagues at Cambridge University Press, especially Martine Walsh, Caroline Thiriau and Nóirín Burke, whose wise expertise and support have been invaluable throughout this project. We are also very grateful for the thorough and useful input provided by Bernard Seal from Cambridge University Press New York. We thank Alison Silver for the professional job she carried out so efficiently in preparing the final manuscript for production and printing. Linda Matthews too deserves our thanks for organising the production schedules for the book.

We must also thank the lexicography and computational team at Cambridge University Press whose work with the Cambridge International Corpus, the Cambridge Learner Corpus and the CANCODE corpus of spoken English (developed at the University of Nottingham in association with Cambridge University Press), enabled us to make a fully corpus-informed selection of the academic vocabulary we focus on in these materials.

We acknowledge with gratitude the pioneering work on academic word lists done by Averil Coxhead. In planning this book we made considerable use of her lists at http://language.massey.ac.nz/staff/awl/index.shtml.

Also, as always, we thank our domestic partners for their patience and support during the writing of this book.

Michael McCarthy & Felicity O'Dell
Cambridge, April 2007

Publisher's acknowledgements

Development of this publication has made use of the Cambridge International Corpus (CIC). The CIC is a computerised database of contemporary spoken and written English which currently stands at over one billion words. It includes British English, American English and other varieties of English. It also includes the Cambridge Learner Corpus, developed in collaboration with the University of Cambridge ESOL Examinations. Cambridge University Press has built up the CIC to provide evidence about language use that helps to produce better language teaching materials.

The authors and publishers would like to thank all the ELT professionals who reviewed the material:

Sue Argent, Long Dalmahoy, Scotland; Jennifer Bixby, California, USA; Jane Bottomley, Manchester, UK; Cherry Campbell, California, USA; Anthony Cosgrove, London, UK; Rosie Ganne, London, UK; Ludmila Gorodetskaya, Moscow, Russia; Mark Krzanowski, London, UK; Joseph McVeigh, Vermont, USA; Julie Moore, Bristol, UK; Brendan Ó Sé, Cork, Ireland; Barbara Rooksen, Tilburg, The Netherlands.

The authors and publishers would like to thank the following for permission to reproduce copyright material in *Academic Vocabulary in Use*. While every effort has been made, it has not been possible to identify the sources of all the material used and in such cases the publishers would welcome information from copyright holders.

Cambridge University Press for the extracts on *p. 14* (3A second text) from *Mechanics 1 (International)* by Douglas Quadling, copyright © 2002; *p. 112* 'The World Wide Web' from *Telecommunications* by Stuart Kennedy, copyright © 2001; *p. 141* sentences from *Cambridge Advanced Learner's Dictionary,* reproduced by permission of Cambridge University Press; NewScientist for the extracts on *p. 25* (8.4) from *NewScientist,* 30 March 2006; *p. 113* 'The Human Brain' by Helen Philips, from *NewScientist,* 4 September 2006; *p. 114* 'Nanotechnology' by John Pickrell, from *NewScientist,* 4 September 2006, reproduced by permission of NewScientist Magazine; Scientific American for the extracts on *p. 27* (9.3) 'Shutting down Alzheimer's' by Michael S. Wolfe, from *Scientific American,* 5 May 2006; *p. 110* 'Good Friends' by Klaus Manhart, from *Scientific American,* April/May 2006, reproduced by permission of Scientific American Inc. All rights reserved; Nature for the extract on *p. 39* (15.4) from *Nature* Vol. 441, 4 May 2006, published by Nature Publishing Group; Indiana University for the extract on *p. 55* (23.4), copyright © 2004, the Trustees of Indiana University, reproduced by permission of Indiana University; the Wikipedia website for the extract on *p. 70* (31A) http://en.wikipedia.org/wiki/Main_Page; ResCen, Middlesex University for the text on *p. 78* (35B) from the Rescen Research website http://www.mdx.ac.uk/rescen/main_pages/profile.html, reproduced by permission of the Centre for Research into Creation in the Performing Arts (ResCen) at Middlesex University; Thomson Learning for the extract on *p. 111* 'Australia' from *World of Earth Science (Vol 1)* by K. Lee Lerner and Brenda Wilmoth (Editor), copyright © 2003, reprinted with permission of Gale, a division of Thomson Learning: www.thomsonrights.com; Legal Information Institute for the adapted text on *p. 115* 'International law: an overview' from the website www.law.cornell.edu/wex/index.php/international_law, copyright Legal Information Institute 1996–2007, reproduced by permission of Legal Information Institute.

Photographs

The publishers are grateful to the following for permission to reproduce copyright photographs and material:

p. 20 © Thomas Fricke/Corbis; *p. 36* © Robert E. Daemmrich/Stone/Getty Images; *p. 66* © John Henley/CORBIS; *p. 74* © age fotostock/SuperStock; *p. 76* © Helen King/Corbis; *p. 77* © Jerry Schatzberg/CORBIS; *p. 88* © image100/Corbis.

Illustrations

Kamae Design *pp. 35, 40, 44, 60, 61, 62, 63*

To the student and the teacher

Who is the book for?

This book is for anyone who wants or needs to learn the kind of English which is used in academic contexts. It deals with the kinds of language used in academic textbooks and articles as well as in lectures and seminars. It also presents vocabulary relating to being a student at a university or college in that it covers such topics as *Applications and application forms*, *Money and education* and *Academic courses* associated with university life. It will be particularly useful for students preparing for IELTS or any other examination aimed at assessing whether candidates' English is at a high enough level to study in an academic institution where English is the medium of instruction. It will be helpful for people who need to attend – or indeed give – lectures and presentations in English or to participate in international conferences. It will enable students who have to prepare assignments or write up a dissertation in English to do so in a much more natural and appropriate way.

What kind of vocabulary does the book deal with?

The book presents and practises the kind of vocabulary that is used in academic speech and writing regardless of which discipline you are concerned with. So it considers words and expressions like *concept*, *cast doubt on*, *put forward a theory* and *come to a conclusion*. It does not deal with the specialist vocabulary of any particular subject such as medicine or physics. Such specialist terms are often relatively easy to master – they will be explained and taught as you study the subject and these words may indeed sometimes be similar in English and your own language. However, it is the more general words used for discussing ideas and research and for talking and writing about academic work that you need to be fully familiar with in order to feel comfortable in an academic environment. Despite the fact that they are much more frequent than specialist words, these more general words are often felt to be more difficult to learn. It is, therefore, extremely useful to approach them in the systematic way suggested by this book.

One positive aspect of this kind of academic vocabulary is that there are relatively few differences depending on whether you are studying in London or New York, Delhi or Sydney, Johannesburg, Dublin, Wellington, Singapore or Toronto or indeed any other place where you may be using English for academic purposes. Academic English tends to be a truly international language and the units of the book focus on vocabulary that will be essential for you regardless of where you are studying now or may study in the future. There are some differences between the words used to describe people and places and these are highlighted in Units 18 and 19. References 3 and 4 also focus on some vocabulary and spelling variations. In the units of the book we use British English spelling conventions except when quoting texts which originally used American spelling.

Much of the vocabulary in the book is neutral in the sense that it is equally appropriate for both written and spoken contexts. We indicate those instances where a word or expression is too formal for use in speech or too informal for use in academic writing.

How was the vocabulary for the book selected?

The academic vocabulary focused on in this book was all selected from language identified as significant by the Cambridge International Corpus of written and spoken English and also the CANCODE corpus of spoken English developed at the University of Nottingham in association with Cambridge University Press. These enormous corpora include large collections of written and spoken academic text and so it was possible to identify language that is distinctive for academic contexts. We also made considerable use of the Cambridge Learner Corpus, a corpus of tens of thousands of learner scripts from students taking Cambridge ESOL exams all over the world. From this corpus we were able to learn what kinds of errors students taking, for example IELTS, were typically making.

In planning this book we made considerable use of Averil Coxhead's work on developing academic word lists. Her lists can be found at http://language.massey.ac.nz/staff/awl/index.shtml and we would highly recommend that students of academic vocabulary investigate this site.

How is the book organised?

The book has 50 two-page units. The left-hand page presents the academic vocabulary to be focused on in the unit. You will usually find examples of academic vocabulary presented in context with, where appropriate, any special notes about their meaning and usage. The right-hand page checks that you have understood the information on the left-hand page by giving you a series of exercises practising the language that was presented.

The units are organised into different sections. The first introductory section includes nine units which look at basic aspects of academic vocabulary such as what is special about academic vocabulary, key verbs and key quantifying expressions. The second section devotes seven units to how words typically combine with one another in academic English. The third section has six units focusing on aspects of life at academic institutions. The fourth section provides eight units discussing ways of talking about such things as numbers, time and cause and effect. Then we have seven units exploring aspects of opinions and ideas and finally there are thirteen units with a functional focus such as organising a text, comparing and contrasting and describing change.

Towards the end of the book you will find six reading texts relating to different academic disciplines with exercises based on the vocabulary in those texts. We hope that you will find these useful examples of how to use texts to expand your knowledge of academic vocabulary in English and would recommend that you read these texts and do the exercises on them even if they relate to an academic subject that is very different from your own.

There are six reference sections dealing with some key areas where we felt it would be useful for you to have lists of items that could not be presented as fully in the main body of the book, i.e. *Formal and informal academic words and expressions*; *Numbers, units of measurement and common symbols*; *British and North American academic vocabulary*; *Spelling variations*; *Word formation* and *Abbreviations*. Where appropriate, these reference sections provide space for you to add further examples of your own.

At the end of the book there is a Key with answers to all the exercises and an Index of all the key words and expressions, indicating the units where they can be found. The pronunciation is provided for standard British English.

How should I use this book?

We recommend that you work through the nine introductory units first so that you become familiar with key aspects of academic vocabulary and how best to study it. After that you may work on the units in any order that suits you.

What else do I need in order to improve my academic vocabulary?

You need a notebook or file in which you can write down all the academic vocabulary that you study in this book as well as any other words and expressions that you come across elsewhere. In your vocabulary notebook it is important to record such things as:

- examples of the word or expression in use
- typical word combinations – you might, for example, note down adjectives or verbs typically associated with a noun that you want to learn or nouns, adverbs or prepositions associated with a verb
- any special features of the word (e.g. is there anything special about its grammar or pronunciation, or is it particularly characteristic of either written or spoken English?).

You may also find it helpful to record such things as:

- any other information that might help you to learn the word (e.g. is it similar to any word in your own language, or does it, perhaps, share a root with a word that you already know?)
- any additional vocabulary that learning this word may help you to learn (e.g. does a verb have a related noun, or what is the opposite of an adjective?)
- any extended uses of the word being focused on (e.g. can it be used metaphorically, or does the same word have other meanings in the way that so many English words do?).

One very important aspect of learning vocabulary is to *organise* the words and expressions you meet; this will help you remember them better. You can do this in a number of ways. In recording words many learners find it helpful to include little diagrams such as *word bubbles*, for example:

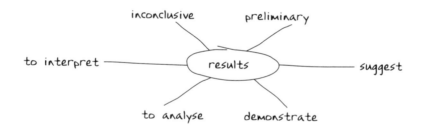

or *word forks*, for example:

You also need to have access to a good dictionary. We strongly recommend the *Cambridge Advanced Learner's Dictionary* as this provides exactly the kind of information that you need in order to be able to understand and use English vocabulary. Through its example sentences it provides you with the information you need about how the word is used in practice and which other words it typically combines with. The dictionary also helps you with difficult items such as phrasal verbs, for example, indicating whether the object can come before the particle (*set up the apparatus / set the apparatus up; go through a set of calculations*, but not *go a set of calculations through*). This dictionary is available as a book and on a CD-ROM and can also be accessed online at www.dictionary.cambridge.org. You will need a specialist dictionary relating to your own subject area as well. Your teacher may also be able to recommend other dictionaries for your specific needs.

As well as working through the units in this book you should read as much English as you can in the subject areas that are most relevant for you. If you are new to studying in English, you could start by reading a textbook aimed at students at a slightly lower level than you are at as far as the subject area is concerned; or you might prefer to read the latest articles in your field from a journal or the internet. If you have easy access to the web, then there is an enormous wealth of material available for you to study and learn from; many universities and other academic institutions have extensive websites, for example, as do professional organisations and journals.

So, good luck with your work in academic English. We hope that the materials in this book will help you to enjoy and to benefit fully from your studies. We hope you will be able to share ideas in a creative, exciting way with scholars from all over the world and we wish you the very best for a successful and rewarding academic life in English.

1 What is special about academic English?

A Everyday words and academic uses

Many words in academic English are the same as everyday vocabulary, but they are often also used with a slightly different meaning, which may be specialised.

everyday or academic use	meaning	academic use	meaning
Standards of **discipline** in schools have declined.	ability to control oneself or other people	Nanotechnology is a relatively new **discipline**.	area of study
Underline your family name on the form.	draw a line under it	The research **underlines** the importance of international trade agreements.	gives emphasis to
The lake was frozen **solid**.	not liquid or gas	We have no **solid** evidence that radiation has caused the problem.	certain or safe; of a good standard

B Vocabulary and academic style

- In writing, academics use many expressions which are neutral, but they also use rather formal expressions which are not common in everyday language. Knowing whether an expression is formal or just neutral is important.

neutral	more formal	neutral	more formal
in short, briefly, basically	in sum, to sum up	try	attempt
only	sole(ly)	mainly/mostly	primarily
almost / more or less	virtually	typical of	characteristic of

However, very **in**formal vocabulary may be used in *spoken* academic styles in classes and lectures. Learn to understand such language when you hear it but be careful not to use it in essays and written assignments. Here are some examples of teachers using informal language.
'OK. **Have a shot at** doing task number 3.' [more formal: Try/Attempt to do ...]
'**There's no way** schools can be held responsible for failures of government policy.' [more formal: Schools cannot in any way be held ...]

- Academic language tries to be clear and precise, so it is important to keep a vocabulary notebook (see page 8) and learn the differences between similar words, as well as typical word combinations (underlined here).
The building is a **prime example** of 1920s architecture. [excellent in quality or value]
The group's **primary concern** is to protect human rights. [main / most important]

C Noun phrases

Academic language puts a lot of information into noun phrases rather than spreading it out over a whole sentence. For example, instead of saying *Radiation was accidentally released over a 24-hour period, damaging a wide area for a long time*, an academic might say *The accidental release of radiation* over a 24-hour period caused *widespread long-term damage*. It is therefore important to learn the different forms of a word, for example:

noun	verb	adjective(s)	adverb(s)
accident		accidental	accidentally
quantity/quantification	quantify	quantitative/quantifiable	quantitatively/quantifiably

Finally, be aware of 'chunks' or phrases which occur frequently, and learn them as whole units. Examples: *in terms of, in addition, for the most part, in the case of*, etc. (See Unit 16.)

Exercises

1.1 Each word in the box can be used in two ways, one an everyday way, the other a typically academic way. Complete each pair of sentences using the same word for both sentences and making any necessary grammatical changes.

| generate | turn | solid | confirm | identify | underline | character | pose | nature | focus |

1 A She loves to _pose_ for photographs in front of her fabulous house.
  B The events _____ a threat to stability in the region.
2 A It was difficult to _____ the camera on the flower as it was so small.
  B We should _____ our attention on the most important issues.
3 A I called the airline and _____ my reservation.
  B The data _____ my hypothesis that animal-lovers enjoy better health.
4 A The power plant _____ electricity for the whole region.
  B This issue always _____ a great deal of debate among academics.
5 A The murderer was _____ from fingerprints discovered at the scene.
  B In this theory of history, progress is closely _____ with technology.
6 A She became interested in _____ conservation.
  B The first lecture in the series was on the _____ of human communication.
7 A Jim's a very interesting _____ . I hope you meet him.
  B The book attempts to explain the fundamental _____ of social life.
8 A I saw her _____ to her husband and whisper something in his ear.
  B Let us now _____ to the subject of town planning.
9 A He always _____ every new word when he's reading.
  B The study _____ the fact that very little research exists.
10 A The liquid became _____ as the temperature was lowered.
  B The study lacks _____ evidence and therefore its conclusions are doubtful.

1.2 Use more formal alternatives to the words in bold. Make any necessary grammatical changes.

1 The book is **mainly** concerned with the problem of policing the internet.
2 **Almost** every school in the county had reported problems with the new system.
3 The work of the Institute is not **only** devoted to cancer research.
4 **Basically,** we believe we have demonstrated a significant link between the two events.
5 We **tried** to find a new way of understanding the data.
6 The study is a **really good** example of the way sociologists collect their data.
7 The reaction is **typical** of the way large corporations keep control of their markets.
8 **There's no way** London can be compared to Sydney as a place to live and work.

1.3 Read the text and then answer the questions.

> The production of plastics depends heavily on petroleum, but a novel way of making plastics out of sugar could reduce our reliance on oil. The discovery that a chemical in sugar can be converted relatively easily into a substance similar in structure to the material obtained from petroleum has led to the claim that plastics could soon be produced cheaply using the new method.

1 Underline two verbs with adverbs after them which it would be useful to learn as pairs.
2 Underline two adverbs next to each other which it would be useful to learn together.
3 What are the noun forms of the verbs *produce, rely, discover* and *claim*?

2 Key nouns

This unit focuses on some frequent and important nouns in academic English. See also Units 10, 11 and 15.

A General nouns referring to ideas

example (with prepositions underlined)	comment
She wrote an article **on the subject of** class.	thing which is being discussed, considered or studied
The theme of the poem is emigration.	main subject of a talk, book, etc.
The students were given a list of **essay topics**.	used to refer to what one is studying or writing about
There was a lively debate on **the issue of** globalisation in the seminar yesterday.	subject/problem which people are thinking/talking about
Political **theory** is a popular undergraduate subject. Einstein's **theory of** gravitation has been questioned recently.	statement of the rules on which a subject of study is based or, more generally, an opinion or explanation
The **model of** climate change presented in the Stern Review seems to be becoming a reality.	a representation of something as a simple description which might be used in calculations
The book is called '**The Nature of** Intelligence'.	main characteristic of something
Human behaviour is based on **the principle of** least effort.	basic idea or rule that explains how something happens or works

B More specific nouns connected with ideas and phenomena

example (with prepositions underlined)	comment
Repetition is an important **aspect of** speech development in children.	one individual part of a situation, problem, subject, etc.
Automatic backup is a **feature of** the new software.	a typical quality of something
The political motives for the government's actions are **beyond the scope of** this essay.	range of a subject covered by a book, discussion, class, etc.
The study **revealed a pattern of** results which could be interpreted in either of two ways.	showed a regularly repeated arrangement
During 2005, the **number of** violent attacks increased to an alarming degree.	amount or level

C Nouns referring to ways of thinking, processes and activities

Read these titles of academic books and articles. Note the key nouns and their prepositions.

Micro-organisms in water: their **significance**[1] and **identification**[2]

Renewable energy: a critical **assessment**[3] of recent research

The Case[4] **for** Change: Rethinking Teacher Education. Towards a New **Approach**[5]

Perspectives[6] **on** Ecological Management: A study of public **awareness**[7] of river pollution

Citizens' **Views on** Healthcare Systems in the European Union

Epidemiological **research into**[8] asthma and allergic disease: establishing a standardised **methodology**[9]

[1] importance [2] ability to establish the identity of something [3] judgement of the amount, value, quality or importance of [4] arguments, facts and reasons in support of or against something [5] way of considering something [6] different particular or individual ways of considering something [7] having special interest in or experience of something, and so being well informed [8] **research** is often also used with the preposition on [9] a system of ways of studying something

 ERROR WARNING *Research* is uncountable. Don't say *They carried out some interesting ~~researches~~*. To make it plural you can just say 'studies', or 'research studies' or 'pieces of research'.

Exercises

2.1 Look at A. Choose the most appropriate noun to complete each sentence.

1 Environmental *topics / issues / principles* should be at the top of today's political agenda.
2 In the exam students had to choose three from a choice of ten essay *subjects / theories / topics*.
3 There are still people who are reluctant to accept Darwin's *model / topic / theory* of evolution.
4 The professor decided to take moral courage as the *issue / theme / model* for his inaugural lecture.
5 The London underground map is best understood as a *model / principle / topic* showing how the different stations relate to one another rather than a precise representation of their distances from each other.
6 The Peter *Issue / Principle / Theme* states that members of a hierarchical group will usually end up being promoted to the point at which they become incompetent.

2.2 There are six phrases containing errors underlined in this paragraph. Can you correct them?

> The study showed that local police can play an important role in crime prevention. It makes <u>a strong case of</u> boosting the numbers of community police officers although it warns against increasing police presence on the streets <u>at an alarming degree</u>. <u>Its methodological</u> was based on a range of interviews asking members of the public for <u>their views in</u> how best to prevent crime. Unfortunately, how to implement this recommendation was <u>out of the scope of</u> the study but at least it serves a useful purpose in <u>raising awareness to</u> the issue.

2.3 Look at these titles of academic books (A–H). Then match them to their subject areas (1–8).

A The Nature of Democracy	1 economics
B The Significance of Dreams	2 education
C The Features of Glaciated Landscapes	3 literature
D The Assessment of Language Skills	4 history
E An Approach to Free Verse	5 geography
F The Identification of Bees	6 psychology
G Perspectives on Modern Taxation	7 politics
H New Perspectives on Cleopatra	8 zoology

2.4 Match the beginning of each sentence with the most appropriate ending.

1 The study revealed a regular	scope of your research.
2 The research focuses on one particular	awareness of the problem.
3 The writer makes a powerful	issues facing the world today.
4 The writers take an original	into the environmental effects of nanoparticles.
5 Until recently there was little	approach to their theme.
6 I think you should broaden the	aspect of modern society.
7 To date, there has been little research	pattern of changes in temperature.
8 There are many important	case for restructuring parliament.

3 Key verbs

In this unit we look at some important verbs in academic English.

A Verbs for structuring academic assignments

Look at these tasks which students have been given. Note the key verbs.

Discuss some of the problems **involved**[1] in **investigating** attitudes to diet and health. Write a critical review of an investigation you have read about, or describe an investigation you yourself could **conduct**[2]. **Consider** the advantages and disadvantages of different methods.

Starting from rest, an aircraft accelerates to its take-off speed of 60 m s^{-1} in a distance of 900 metres. **Illustrate**[3] this with a velocity-time graph. **Assuming**[4] constant acceleration, **find**[5] how long the take-off run lasts. Hence **calculate**[6] the acceleration.

'The fact that nations agree to follow international law **demonstrates**[7] that we can **identify**[8] ideals that are trans-national and trans-cultural.' How far is this statement true? Critically **analyse** any recent event which **supports** or **challenges**[9] the statement.

Examine[10] how industrial growth has **affected** any two developing countries. **Provide**[11] statistical evidence where necessary and **include** a discussion of likely future trends.

[1] which are part of/included in [2] organise and do [3] draw something in order to explain something [4] accepting something to be true [5] discover by calculating (see 6) [6] judge the number or amount of something and adding, multiplying, subtracting or dividing numbers [7] show, make clear [8] recognise someone or something and say or prove who or what they are [9] questions whether it is true [10] look at or consider carefully and in detail [11] give

B More key verbs

These extracts from academic books contain other key verbs.

In **developing** methods to explain the significance of health status measures, one can **classify**[1] ways of **establishing**[2] quality of life into two main types.

The length of time spent on the tasks may **account for**[3] the decrease in motivation which **was seen**[4] in many of the participants.

The data **presented**[5] in Chapter 3 **showed**[6] that the age of the subjects was not the main factor.

Political theory **attempts**[7] to build bridges between different schools of political thought.

[1] divide things into groups according to their type [2] discover or get proof of [3] explain [4] see is often used in the passive in academic style [5] given [6] proved [7] (formal) tries

C Verbs which combine with noun forms of key verbs

Often in academic style, a verb + the noun form of the key verb is used.

verb	verb + noun	example
explain	give/provide/offer an explanation (of/for)	The model **provides an explanation** for the differences between the two sets of data.
explore	carry out an exploration (of)	Kumar **carried out an exploration** of music genius.
emphasise	place/put emphasis (on)	The hospital **puts** a lot of **emphasis** on training nurses.
describe	give/provide a description (of)	The book **gives a description** of modern Europe.

 The verbs *affect* and *effect* are different. *To affect* means to influence, *to effect* means to make something happen / to bring about. *The burning of fossil fuels has negatively **affected** the global climate. The procedure has been successful and has **effected** a return to normal functioning of the engine.* See Unit 30 for more on *affect* and *effect*.

Exercises

3.1 Match each verb from A in the box on the left with its synonym from the box on the right.

affect attempt calculate challenge demonstrate identify include investigate provide	compute distinguish give influence involve question show study try

3.2 Choose the best verb from B or C to complete these sentences. Put the verb into the correct form.

1 As can _____ from Table II, participation figures have been steadily falling since 1970.
2 Different authors have _____ for the President's actions in different ways.
3 Mendel attempted to devise a system for _____ the many different types of pea plant that he grew.
4 It is often most effective _____ your data in a chart or table.
5 The data we have collected _____ that there has been a downward trend with regard to job satisfaction over the last 50 years.
6 The aim of the research is _____ a new software application which will help aviation engineers design more sophisticated aircraft.
7 The archaeologists should be able to use carbon dating techniques _____ exactly how old the bones are.
8 Charles Darwin attempted _____ the existence of different species in terms of evolution.

3.3 Explain the difference between the sentences in each pair.

1 Greig's article supports Park's theory.   Greig's article challenges Park's theory.
2 Describe the new tax regulations.   Discuss the new tax regulations.
3 Lodhi provides new data.   Lodhi considers new data.
4 Titova conducted four sets of experiments.   Titova examined four sets of experiments.
5 Lee established why such changes occur.   Lee investigated why such changes occur.
6 Okaz assumed that the data were reliable.   Okaz proved that the data were reliable.
7 Illustrate the magnitude of the deceleration.   Find the magnitude of the deceleration.
8 The events effected economic development.   The events affected economic development.

3.4 Rewrite each sentence using the word in brackets and make any necessary changes to other words.

1 Erikson's theory explains the fluctuations in the figures for this period. (PROVIDES)
2 Bevan explored the relationship between family background and political ambition. (EXPLORATION)
3 The book describes the life and times of Abraham Lincoln. (DESCRIPTION)
4 Cheng's theory emphasises the importance of extensive reading in language acquisition. (PUTS)

3.5 In academic style, noun phrases can often be used instead of some of the key verbs. Complete each phrase with the appropriate noun. Use a dictionary if necessary.

1 investigate = conduct, carry out an _____ into/of
2 illustrate = provide an _____ of
3 analyse = provide, carry out an _____ of
4 affect = have an _____ on
5 attempt = make an _____ to/at
6 classify = make, provide a _____ of

> **FOLLOW UP** Using the tasks in A as a model, prepare some assignment topics for students studying any subject that you are familiar with.

4 Key adjectives

For any adjective it is useful to know whether it is typically followed by a specific preposition and whether it has any synonyms (adjectives with a similar meaning) or antonyms (adjectives of opposite meaning).

A Adjectives and prepositions

Here are some extracts from academic texts, with adjectives followed by *to* or *of*.

> Language development is conceived as **relative**[1] **to** one's own past performance, or relative to that of others.

> Some of the responses to the questionnaire were **specific**[4] **to** young male respondents. Others were **common**[5] **to** all the respondents.

> How can we make science **relevant**[2] **to** environmental policy? Poor communication between scientists and politicians is **characteristic**[3] **of** the situation today.

> We need to plan technologies which are **appropriate**[6] **to** the needs of small farmers. It was **typical of** the farmers in the study that they had a negative attitude to technology.

[1] true to a particular degree when it is being compared with other things [2] connected with what is happening or being discussed [3] (rather formal) typical of [4] only found in [5] belonging to or shared by two or more people or things [6] suitable or right for a particular situation or occasion

B Adjectives and their opposites

Look at this abstract from a dissertation on drug abuse. In most cases you can work out the meanings of the opposites (which follow each numbered adjective), based on the definitions.

> We cannot discuss drug abuse as an **abstract**[1] problem without considering **concrete** examples of abuse and their social consequences. Abuse is rarely a **simple**[2] issue; it usually results from a **complex** set of circumstances. Both **quantitative**[3] and **qualitative** research is necessary to gain a full picture of the situation. By combining research methods, we may obtain an **accurate** picture of the causes and results of abuse, in contrast with the **inaccurate** assessments which often result from purely quantitative studies. A **significant**[4] amount of fear and prejudice surrounds the notion of abuse, and the media have a role which is also not **insignificant** in promoting such fears. The dissertation concludes that **rough**[5] estimates of the number of drug addicts need to be made more **precise** by properly defining addiction.

[1] existing as an idea, not as a material object; opposite: existing in a form that can be seen or felt [2] having or made of only one or a few parts [3] based on numbers and statistics; opposite: usually research using non-number-based methods such as interviews, focus groups, etc. [4] important or noticeable [5] fairly correct but not exact or detailed; opposite: exact and accurate

C Other important, frequent adjectives and typical combinations with nouns

There was an <u>apparent</u>[1] <u>discrepancy</u> between the two sets of results.
We noted a <u>potential</u>[2] <u>problem</u> with the experimental design which we had to deal with first.
The <u>principal</u>[3] <u>cause</u> of the failure was a sudden temperature change.
The research used a <u>rigorous</u>[4] <u>methodology</u> which had been tested on many occasions.

[1] seeming to exist or be true [2] possible when the necessary conditions exist [3] first in order of importance [4] careful to look at or consider every part of something to make certain it is correct

 ERROR WARNING   Remember to say *typical of*, NOT *typical for*. Learn adjectives with the prepositions that often follow them, as in A.

Exercises

4.1 Look at A. Correct the preposition errors in these sentences.

1 A lengthy discussion of the advantages of solar power is not relevant with an essay that required you to focus on wind turbines.
2 It is typical to the disease for it to start with an itchy rash.
3 This methodology is not appropriate about the kind of research you are planning.
4 The use of original metaphors is characteristic from the writer's style.
5 Relative with previous attempts to explain the phenomenon, this interpretation is quite persuasive.
6 The dark hair and eyes are common for all people from the region.

4.2 Rewrite each sentence using the *opposite* of the adjective in italics.

1 Karlsson checked the figures and agreed with me that they were *accurate*.
2 The solution to the problem is a *simple* one.
3 Make *rough* calculations before you begin to write up your results.
4 The army played a *significant* role in events.
5 Hernandez prefers to discuss ideas in *abstract* terms.

4.3 Match the adjective on the left with the noun it often combines with on the right.

1 apparent   methodology
2 rigorous   problem
3 principal   discrepancy
4 potential   cause

4.4 Now use one of the combinations from 4.3 to complete these sentences.

1 There is an .... in your figures.
2 Management's refusal to listen to the workers' demands was the .... of the riots.
3 Lamaque devised a .... which has since been used successfully by many other researchers in the field.
4 We spotted a .... with our procedure and so we changed it in two areas.

4.5 Choose the best adjective from the box to complete these sentences.

qualitative   complex   potential   rigorous   specific

1 The plant is difficult to grow and needs very .... conditions to survive.
2 His tutor was critical of his work for not being .... enough.
3 In the past the northern tribes looked on the tribes of the south as .... enemies.
4 We chose a .... approach to our research and interviewed individuals personally.
5 A .... set of circumstances led to a civil war in 1897.

> **FOLLOW UP** When you come across any of the key adjectives from this unit in your reading, note it down in a phrase so you build up a set of useful phrases using the adjective.

5 Key adverbs

This unit deals with just some of the adverbs that are particularly frequent in an academic context. You will find more in other units throughout this book.

A Adverbs that compare

adverb	meaning	example
comparatively/relatively	in comparison with something else	Our sample was **relatively/comparatively** small.
especially/particularly	more than usual	The process was not **especially/particularly** difficult.
specially	more than usual (spoken English only) for a specific purpose	The exam was **specially** hard this year. We used **specially** designed equipment.
somewhat (opposite: considerably)	(slightly formal) a little, slightly	When we tested younger boys, we obtained **somewhat/considerably** different results.
primarily	mainly	Amir is **primarily** interested in bio-physics.
mostly/largely	almost completely (but not totally so)	The research was **largely/mostly** successful.
directly (opposite: indirectly)	without anything else being involved	The illness is **(in)directly** linked to poor housing.

B Adverbs that relate to numbers or time

There are **approximately** 20 varieties of bird in this species. [roughly, about]
There are **precisely** 48 different managerial posts in the company. [exactly]
Interviewees **frequently** misunderstood one of the questions. [often]
We **eventually** obtained the results we were hoping for. [in the end, after some time]
Ultimately we plan to repeat the experiment. [finally, after other things have been completed]

C Adverbs that relate to how things are stated

Hall's latest article **essentially**[1] differs from his earlier work in that it is **explicitly**[2] critical of the government. **Generally**[3], his disapproval of their policies was only conveyed **implicitly**[4] in his previous writing, but here he **specifically** condemns their handling of a number of issues.

[1] referring to its main characteristics; also **basically** [2] openly [3] usually, also **on the whole**
[4] not directly, suggested or implied rather than stated

D Adverbs that restrict or limit

merely = exactly and nothing more: *The medication will **merely** make the symptoms bearable; it will not cure the disease.*
simply Note that **simply** can have different meanings. *To put it **simply**, the risks of this approach would seem to outweigh its advantages.* [plainly] *The book presents difficult ideas **simply**, in a way appropriate for the **layman**.* [easily; someone who isn't a specialist in the field] *The exam results were **simply** dreadful.* [absolutely, without doubt]
hardly ever = almost never: *The tribe has **hardly ever** had contact with the outside world.*

Eventually means 'in the end'. It does not mean 'perhaps/possibly'.
*We will **perhaps/possibly*** (NOT ~~eventually~~) *discover life on other planets in the future.*
Eventually [in the end], *we were able to interview all 20 children involved in the test.*

Exercises

5.1 **Look at A and B. Explain the difference between the sentences in each pair.**

1 Heinrich's experiments were mostly successful.
  Heinrich's experiments were most successful.
2 The results were somewhat surprising given the circumstances.
  The results were especially surprising given the circumstances.
3 First-year students are directly affected by the new rules relating to tuition fees.
  First-year students are particularly affected by the new rules relating to tuition fees.
4 The study is primarily concerned with urban alienation.
  The study is ultimately concerned with urban alienation.
5 The team eventually obtained unpredicted results.
  The team frequently obtained unpredicted results.

5.2 **Choose the more appropriate adverb from the options.**

What you are saying is *essentially / merely* true. To put it *basically / simply*, there is *specially / basically* no significant difference between the two writers' theories. However, one of them writes in a *simply / precisely* dreadful style while the other has *eventually / possibly* a more impressive style than any other contemporary scientist.

5.3 **Change the sentences using adverbs which mean the *opposite* of the underlined ones.**

1 There were <u>roughly</u> 350 people living in the village in 1958.
2 Parents <u>seldom</u> complained that the school authorities failed to inform them of changes.
3 We investigated the problem and <u>initially</u> found some small errors in the calculations.
4 The temperature was <u>exactly</u> half a degree lower than the average.
5 Singh (1998) is <u>explicitly</u> critical of existing theories of economic growth.
6 Soil erosion is <u>specifically</u> caused by water or wind.
7 Senior citizens <u>almost always</u> use the internet to communicate with one another.
8 The disease is <u>directly</u> linked to environmental factors.

5.4 **Underline the adverbs in these texts. Then answer the questions.**

Marine conservationists are currently attempting to save the world's coral reefs. One plan is to literally glue the damaged reefs back together, using coral artificially raised in underwater labs. Reefs are increasingly under attack from human activity as well as from events occurring naturally, such as hurricanes and tsunamis. A recent UN report warns that 30% of the world's coral reefs have been completely destroyed or are severely damaged.

Scientists have recently discovered that ants can remember how many steps they have taken. By carefully shortening or lengthening the legs of ants, the team observed that short-legged ants apparently became lost and could not easily find their way home to the nest. Similarly, ants with longer legs typically travelled 50% further than they needed to and were also temporarily unable to find the nest. It seems ants can definitely count their steps.

1 Which adverb means 'in the same way'?
2 Find two pairs of adverbs that mean the opposite of each other.
3 Which adverb means the opposite of 'a long time ago'?
4 Which adverb means 'more and more'?
5 Which adverb could be substituted by *seriously*?
6 Which adverb means 'for a limited time'?

 FOLLOW UP Find an article of interest to you in your discipline and underline all the key adverbs. Then check that you understand their meaning.

6 Phrasal verbs in academic English

Although phrasal verbs occur most frequently in more informal spoken and written English, they are also not uncommon in an academic context. You will hear them used in lectures and will read them in serious journals. From this unit only **go/look back over** and **work out** are not appropriate for a formal written assignment.

A Phrasal verbs and one-word synonyms

Phrasal verbs often have one-word synonyms. These are usually of Latin origin and sound more formal than their phrasal verb equivalent but both are appropriate when writing or talking about academic subjects. Vary your language by using both.

phrasal verb	synonym	example
put forward (an idea/view/opinion/ theory/plan)	present	In her latest article Kaufmann **puts forward** a theory which is likely to prove controversial.
carry out (an experiment / research)	conduct	I intend to **carry out** a series of experiments.
make up	constitute	Children under the age of 15 **make up** nearly half of the country's population.
be made up of	consist of	Parliament is **made up of** two houses.
point out	observe	Grenne **points out** that the increase in life expectancy has led to some economic problems.
point up	highlight	The study **points up** the weaknesses in the current school system.
set out (to do something)	aim	In his article Losanov **sets out** to prove that ...
set out	describe	The document **sets out** the terms of the treaty.
go into	discuss	In this book Sergeant **goes into** the causes of the Civil War in some depth.
go/look back over	revise, review *	Please **go/look back over** this term's notes.
go through	check	**Go through** your calculations carefully.

* *Revise* is the BrE synonym and *review* the AmE synonym. (*Revise* in AmE only means to edit or change something to make it better; *review* is not used in BrE in the context of preparing for a test as focused on here.)

B Carrying out research

After completing her first degree in zoology Meena **went on to**[1] apply to graduate school. She wanted to **work on**[2] animal behaviour at a well-known institute in New Zealand. She **set up**[3] a series of experiments investigating how bees communicate. She has noticed some curious behaviour patterns but has not yet **worked out**[4] why her bees behave as they do. What she has observed seems to **go against**[5] current theories of bee behaviour. When she has completed all her research she will have to **write** it all **up**[6].

[1] do something after doing something else [2] study, work in the field of [3] prepared, arranged [4] come to a conclusion about [5] not be in agreement with [6] (of an important document) write in a final form

TIP Consult a good dictionary when you use phrasal verbs in your writing. For example, a good dictionary tells you when the object can be used before the particle (e.g. write <u>your results</u> up) and when it cannot (e.g. this goes against <u>current theories</u>).

Exercises

6.1 Rewrite the sentences replacing the underlined word in each sentence with a phrasal verb from A. Note that both versions of each sentence are equally appropriate.

1 We <u>conducted</u> a series of experiments to test out our hypothesis.
2 Before the test you should <u>revise</u> Chapters 7 and 8 of your textbooks.
3 In his article on the American Civil War Kingston <u>discusses</u> the reasons why the situation developed in the way it did.
4 Cole <u>presents</u> some fascinating theories on the development of language in his latest book.
5 The psychologist <u>observed</u> that it was very unusual for a young child to behave in this way.
6 Please <u>check</u> your work again carefully before handing it in.
7 In this article Simpson <u>aims</u> to prove that the Chinese reached America long before the Vikings.
8 Women now <u>constitute</u> over half the student population in most universities in this country.

6.2 Fill in the missing words in this paragraph.

As part of my MA I've been doing some research on language acquisition. I've been working (1) .... how young children learn their mother tongue. I've been carrying (2) .... some experiments to see how much reading to young children affects their language development. I've had a great supervisor who has helped me set (3) .... my experiments and she's also pointed (4) .... lots of interesting things in my data that I hadn't noticed myself. I'm busy writing my work (5) .... now and I think I should be able to put (6) .... some useful ideas. It's been really fascinating and I hope I may be able to go (7) .... to do a doctorate in the same field although I certainly never set (8) .... to do a PhD.

6.3 Match the beginning of each sentence with the most appropriate ending.

1 Feudal society was made	forward a convincing theory with regard to this question.
2 Carlson was the first to put	up the flaws in the school's testing methods.
3 Her results appear to go	out the solution to the algebra problem.
4 The investigation pointed	out a lot of basic information about all the world's
5 It took him a long time to work	countries.
6 The geography book sets	against what she had found in her earlier studies.
	up of clearly defined classes of people.

6.4 Answer these questions.

1 What sort of things might a scientist carry out?
2 If you want to study something in more depth, what might you go on to do after getting a first degree?
3 What do postgraduate students typically have to write up at the end of their studies?
4 What sort of things do good students regularly look back over?
5 What sorts of things do scholars typically put forward in their lectures or articles?
6 Why is it sensible to go through any maths calculations that you had to make as part of a research study before you draw any conclusions?

7 Key quantifying expressions

Quantifying expressions are important in academic English as it is often necessary to comment on figures or trends. You will find more useful language for talking about numbers in Units 25 and 26 and in Reference 2, which focuses on measurement.

A Number and amount

Learners of English often choose the wrong noun relating to quantity. For example, you say a **great** (not ~~large~~) **deal** (informal) or a **large/great amount** of an uncountable noun such as *money*, *interest* or *influence*. However, you say a **large number** of a plural noun such as *articles*, *books* or *words*. Both a *number* and an *amount* can be described as **small, considerable, substantial, significant, enormous, total, surprising, excessive** [too much/many], **fair** [quite a lot] and **reasonable** [acceptable].

B Other nouns relating to quantity

The size of our survey was relatively small-scale. We sent out 2,500 questionnaires **in total**[1]. Although a **couple**[2] of people did not respond, the **bulk**[3] of those sent questionnaires have completed them. The survey shows that, **as a whole**[4], the population is becoming more aware of the importance of recycling. Only **one of**[5] our respondents said that he recycled less than he used to.

[1] in all [2] two or three, a few [3] the majority [4] considered as a group rather than individually
[5] notice how *respondents* is in the plural; it is a common error to write a singular noun after *one of ...* (*respondents/surveys/conclusions*, etc.)

C Comparing numbers and quantities

expression	example	comment
exceeding	Results **exceeding** 5 cm were eliminated from the survey.	(formal) means higher than
in excess of	People who drive **in excess of** the speed limit will be fined.	means over, used mainly in official or legal writing
fewer and fewer / less and less	**Fewer and fewer** people are staying in the same job throughout their lives. Young people are becoming **less and less** interested in politics.	a steadily declining/decreasing number of, decreasingly
more and more	There is **more and more** interest in the topic. People are becoming **more and more** aware of the environment.	a steadily increasing amount of, increasingly
more or less	The experiment was **more or less** a success.	(slightly informal) means mostly or approximately
no fewer than	**No fewer than** 200 people responded.	used to suggest the number was unexpectedly large

ERROR WARNING
Note the significant difference between **few** and **a few** and between **little** and **a little**. *Few* [Not many] *people enjoy X's music.* **A few** [Some] *people enjoy it.* We had **little** [not much] *response to our survey.* We had **a little** [some] *response to our survey.* In other words, **few/little** has a more negative tone than **a few / a little**.

Exercises

7.1 Complete the sentences using the correct forms of the words in italics.

1 In a _____ number of cases, there was no reaction at all to the drug. *surprise*
2 The analysis demanded an _____ amount of computer time. *exceed*
3 _____ numbers of birds inhabit the lake during the winter. *consider*
4 The course requires a _____ amount of prior knowledge of computers. *reason*
5 The survey took a _____ amount of research time and costs were high. *substance*
6 The two dams can hold in _____ of two cubic kilometres of water. *exceed*
7 In _____, 12 areas of the Southern Indian Ocean are now closed to deep-sea fishing. *totality*
8 Groups _____ four people were considered too large for the experiment. *exceed*
9 No _____ than 2,000 new computer viruses are created every year. *few*
10 In a _____ number of cases, surface damage was noticed. *signify*

7.2 The sentences below are typical of spoken English. Replace the underlined words to make them sound more appropriate for a written assignment.

1 The bulk of our work is concerned with carbon emissions.
2 We have noticed that fewer and fewer students are joining the course.
3 Our team spent a fair amount of time getting funding for the research.
4 In a couple of cases, we could not find any reason for the outbreak.
5 We spent a great deal of time on the project.
6 As you repeat the experiment, use less and less water each time.

7.3 Read the text and answer the questions.

> For some years now, scientists have been using a powerful new machine to recreate the conditions that existed at the birth of the universe. The machine generates a massive number of hot, dense, bursts of matter and energy, simulating what happened in the first few microseconds of the beginning of the universe. After no more than ten microseconds, the particles of matter joined together, like water freezing into ice, forming the origin of more or less everything we see in the universe today.

1 Which expression explains how long scientists have been using this machine?
2 Which expression tells us how many bursts of matter and energy the machine generates?
3 Which time period does the machine simulate?
4 Which expression states how long it was before the particles of matter joined together?
5 Which expression in the last sentence means *approximately*?

7.4 Rewrite the paragraph using the *opposites* of the underlined words or expressions.

> There have been a small number of studies investigating the impact of email on interpersonal communications. None of the studies has been large-scale but they suggest some interesting trends in patterns of email use. From one of the older studies it seems that more and more people send in excess of 50 emails daily. Moreover, it appears that a substantial number of senior citizens use email a lot more frequently than younger people do.

 FOLLOW UP Find five quantifying expressions from one of your textbooks and write your own sentences using them.

8 Words with several meanings

A Set

Many words in English have more than one meaning. The word **set**, for example, is one word with a particularly large number of distinctly different meanings. As our focus is academic English, some key uses of **set** are illustrated by these examples.

a) Set the instruments to zero. [get something ready so it can be operated]
b) I would like to set some ground rules for the course. [establish]
c) The decision set a number of changes in motion. [caused to be in a stated condition]
d) We must set a time for our next meeting. [arrange]
e) Concrete sets as it cools. [becomes solid]
f) The students entered the room and immediately set to work. [started work]
g) The condition is associated with a particular set of symptoms. [group]
h) We have a number of set books to study in our literature class. [that must be studied]

B More academic meanings for familiar words

Here are some more words which in an academic context may have a different meaning from those you are familiar with from your knowledge of general English.

word	academic meaning(s)	example
accommodate (verb)	change to allow something to fit in	He had to adapt his theory to **accommodate** new information.
contract (verb)	shorten, become smaller	As the metal cools it **contracts**.
occur (verb)	exist	Some valuable minerals **occur** naturally in these rocks.
reference (noun)	author or book mentioned in a piece of writing to show where information was found	You must provide a list of **references** at the end of your assignment.
revolution (noun)	complete turn (e.g. of a wheel)	Time is measured by the **revolution** of the earth around the sun.
structure (noun)	way in which parts of a system or object are organised or arranged	The **structure** of this element is particularly complex.

C Words with several different academic meanings

Many academic words have specific meanings according to their discipline. **Channel**, for example, has specific meanings in electronics, linguistics, biology, physics and geography. So you will, of course, need a specialist dictionary for your own subject.
Other words, e.g. **issue** and **point** have several generally important academic meanings.
The writer **takes issue with** Kwame's interpretation. [raises arguments against]
In your essay you should address a number of key **issues**. [topics]
Have you seen the latest **issue** of the *Malaysian Medical Journal*? [edition]
Jackson raises some interesting **points** in his article. [opinions, ideas, information]
The writer takes a long time to get to the **point**. [most significant part]

 TIP If you come across a word that you think you know but it does not seem to make sense in that context, check to see whether it has another distinct meaning. If so, write it down with both (or all) its meanings in your vocabulary notebook.

Exercises

8.1 Which meaning given in A does *set* have in these examples?

1 If you don't set to work immediately you won't finish the task by the end of term.
2 Before we start I'd like everyone to set their watches to precisely the same time.
3 Professors will set a date for the submission of assignments relating to their own courses.
4 We expected the mixture to set quickly but it had not hardened by the morning.
5 Before leaving the area, the retreating army set the farm buildings on fire.
6 The engine's performance has set a new fuel consumption record.
7 During the first semester, music students have to study a number of set pieces.
8 There are a whole set of issues that need to be discussed.

8.2 Choose a word from B to complete each sentence. Change the form if necessary.

1 When you are doing research it is sensible to keep good records of all your .... as it can be difficult to locate sources later.
2 This medical condition is most likely to .... in fair-skinned people.
3 In first gear the engine makes ten .... for every .... of the wheels.
4 *Wealth*, the theme of the anthology, is general enough to .... a wide variety of approaches.
5 The .... of society in Ancient Rome can be said to resemble that of the modern USA.
6 They carried out an experiment to check whether the gold .... or expanded under a range of different conditions.

8.3 Which word could fit in each of these sets of phrases?

1 discuss the following ....
underline the key ....
make some thoughtful ....

2 to .... a precedent
a .... of exercises
a .... book

3 take .... with
the latest .... of the *New Scientist*
a controversial ....

4 a .... of communication
the English ....
to .... one's energies into

8.4 Read this text about some new medical software. For each underlined word give the meaning in the text and one other meaning. Use a dictionary to help you if necessary.

A simulator showing how outbreaks of infection might spread around the world would be of great assistance in the struggle to <u>contain</u> such diseases. Researchers at the World Health Organization <u>maintain</u> that to effectively confront emerging infectious diseases, they need a significant amount of computing power. A global epidemic simulator would mimic climate simulators which <u>monitor</u> the movement of weather systems. It would <u>record</u> where disease outbreaks <u>occur</u>, where they are heading and, crucially, would allow scientists to test out virtual mitigation <u>measures</u> to see which might work best on the ground.

8.5 Jokes are often based on words having several meanings. Explain this joke.

A neutron goes into a bar, orders a drink and asks how much it will be.
The barman replies: 'For you, sir, no charge.'

FOLLOW UP Look at a textbook on an academic subject of special interest to you. Look for some of the words in this unit and decide which meaning they have in your text.

9 Metaphors and idioms

A metaphor is a way of using language which describes something by indirectly comparing it to something else with similar characteristics. For example, you might say an academic 'attacks' or 'demolishes' someone's theory or argument, just as an army can attack an enemy or workers can demolish a building. If a metaphor is used so often that the original force of the comparison is lost then it may be called an idiom. For example, people often use the idiom 'I'm snowed under with work at the moment'. Originally this was a metaphor based on the idea of a great deal of work having the characteristics of 'snow' (deep, overwhelming everything else and making movement difficult). However, this expression has been used so frequently that it no longer gives people a mental picture of snow.

A Metaphors and idioms referring to light and darkness

The present experimental data may **shed (new) light on**[1] the formation of the planets.
Views on depression have changed **in (the) light of**[2] recent studies of the brain.
Novelists, poets and essayists often use history to **illuminate**[3] their understanding of human behaviour. The book provides an **illuminating** discussion of how languages change.
Animal models can be used to **elucidate**[4] basic principles of the developmental origins of adult diseases.
The report revealed the **glaring**[5] discrepancy between patients' needs and what the health service can offer them, and **highlighted**[6] the need for a new approach.
The report **shines a light on**[7] the questions surrounding child care and provides crucial data.
Substance abuse continues to destroy individuals and communities, and researchers **remain in the dark**[8] about what can ensure successful recovery from addiction.
The book dealt with economic policy **in the shadow of**[9] the Civil War of 1994–1999.

[1] provide an explanation for it which makes it easier to understand. We can also say *cast* or *throw* light on [2] because of [3] show more clearly something that is difficult to understand [4] explain or make clear (from the Latin *lucidus* meaning 'clear') [5] something bad that is very obvious (*to glare* means to shine too brightly) [6] emphasised something important [7] focuses on [8] continue in a state of not knowing something [9] in a situation where something bad has happened or is happening

B Metaphors and idioms referring to war and conflict

Look at these extracts from lectures where the speakers use such metaphors and idioms.

'Critics **opposed to** D.H. Lawrence **attacked** his novels on various grounds, both trivial and important. But despite the apparent diversity of opinion, Lawrence's critics were **united** on what they saw as several serious problems.'

'In the last two poems we see the poet becoming increasingly detached from the material world, **retreating**[1] more into his own mind than before.'

'Parents and teachers need to **maintain a united front**[3] on the question of bad conduct at school.'

'It's useful at the present time to look at Japan's experience in **the battle against** air pollution, and it's **a battle** no nation can afford to **lose**.'

'Lawsuits can certainly affect the value of a company, and firms need strategies to combat the **onslaught**[2] of lawsuits.'

'In the last ten years or so, children have been **bombarded with**[4] increasing amounts of violence in the media.'

[1] going back [2] a very powerful attack [3] remain united in their opinions and agree on how to act [4] forced to experience, subjected to

Exercises

9.1   Choose a word from the box to complete each sentence.

elucidate	glaring	highlights	illuminate	light
remained	shadow	shed	shine	

1 The results of the investigation .... a light on the pressures of the global economy on farmers in developing countries.
2 Until recently, scientists have .... in the dark as to the causes of the disease, but a recent breakthrough promises to .... new light on the problem.
3 Our whole notion of time and space has changed in the .... of recent developments in physics.
4 These communities have lived for decades in the .... of poverty and social deprivation.
5 The collapse of the bridge .... the need for a more rigorous analysis of the effects of constant traffic movements.
6 The team carried out a series of experiments in an attempt to .... the mysterious processes at work in the organism.
7 The article helps to .... for the ordinary reader some of the more difficult references in Shakespeare's plays.
8 The professor found some .... errors in one student's calculations.

9.2   Rewrite these sentences using metaphors of conflict instead of the underlined words.

1 Scientists <u>who don't agree with</u> this theory have recently attacked its basic assumptions.
2 Governments need to <u>remain in complete agreement</u> on the issue of economic migrants.
3 Nowadays, we <u>get a huge number of</u> advertisements every time we watch TV or open a magazine.
4 G. J. Franklin has recently <u>moved away</u> from the view that economic processes cannot be altered, and is now moving towards a different approach.
5 The <u>efforts</u> against crime <u>will fail</u> without police and community cooperation.
6 The protests were a response to the devastating <u>sudden large number</u> of trade restrictions on small producers.

9.3   Look at this text and underline key words and phrases which construct the main metaphor: 'the human brain is a computer'.

Shutting down Alzheimer's

The human brain is a remarkably complex organic computer, taking in a wide variety of sensory experiences, processing and storing this information, and recalling and integrating selected bits at the right moments. The destruction caused by Alzheimer's disease has been likened to the erasure of a hard drive, beginning with the most recent files and working backward. As the illness progresses, old as well as new memories gradually disappear until even loved ones are no longer recognized. Unfortunately, the computer analogy breaks down: one cannot simply reboot the human brain and reload the files and programs. The problem is that Alzheimer's does not only erase information; it destroys the very hardware of the brain, which is composed of more than 100 billion nerve cells (neurons), with 100 trillion connections among them.

FOLLOW UP   Look at some of the textbooks you use. Can you find any examples of metaphors or idioms there relating to light and darkness or war and conflict?

10 Nouns and the words they combine with

Nouns often combine with specific verbs, for example *carry out research*, *pay attention*, or with specific adjectives, for example *medical research*, *undivided attention*.

A Adjective + noun

noun	adjectives that often combine with it	example
contact	useful, valuable, personal, constant, close, frequent, intermittent[1]	I made some **useful contacts** at the conference.
debate	considerable, heated[2], intense, public, animated[3]	After the lecture there was a **heated debate**.
element [= factor]	crucial, decisive, fundamental	Timing is a **crucial element** of the experiment.
elements [= parts]	conflicting, contrasting, constituent[4]	There are **conflicting elements** in the artist's work.
energy	excess, sufficient, nuclear	Wind turbines create **sufficient energy** for the town's needs.
phenomenon	common, isolated, natural, recent, universal	Such anti-social behaviour is a **recent phenomenon**.
results	conflicting, (in)conclusive, unforeseen[5], preliminary[6], encouraging, interim[7]	Our **preliminary results** were **encouraging**.
role	decisive, challenging, conflicting, influential, key, pivotal[8]	Student activists played a **pivotal role** in the riot.
sample	random, representative	A **representative sample** of the population was surveyed.
in … terms	absolute, broad, relative, general, practical, economic	People are better off **in economic terms**.
way	alternative, efficient, fair, practical, convenient, proper, acceptable	It is important to treat your research subjects in a **fair way**.

[1] from time to time [2] strong, often angry [3] lively [4] that combine to make something
[5] not expected [6] first [7] temporary [8] important

B Noun + verb

Most of the nouns in the table above are also strongly associated with specific verbs.

You can **come into contact with** someone or something or you can **establish, maintain, break off** or **lose contact**.

Academics may **engage in debate** or **contribute to a debate**. You talk about the **debate surrounding** an issue.

You can **combine, differentiate** or **discern** [recognise] **the elements** of a chemical compound.

You **consume** [use], **conserve, generate** [create], **save** or **waste energy**.

Phenomena emerge or **occur** and students will try to **observe, investigate** and then **explain** those phenomena.

Academics **collect, collate** [organise] and **publish** their **results**. Sometimes **results** are **questioned** or **invalidated** [shown to be wrong]. Occasionally they are even **falsified**!

Roles may be **defined** or **strengthened**. People or factors can **play a role** or **take on a role**.

You can **take** or **provide** or **analyse a sample**.

You can **discover, devise** [think up], **work out** or **develop a way** to do something.

TIP Whenever you notice a noun that seems to be key as far as your own studies are concerned, write it down with the adjectives and verbs it is typically associated with.

Exercises

10.1 Answer these questions about the adjective + noun combinations in the table in A.

1 Put these types of contact in order of frequency – *frequent, constant, intermittent*.
2 Which of these is a *representative sample* and which is a *random sample*: a sample chosen by chance, a sample chosen as typical of the population as a whole?
3 Which adjective describes the opposite of a *common phenomenon*?
4 Would you be pleased if you did some research and got *inconclusive results*?
5 What adjective other than *key* can be used with *role* to give a similar meaning?
6 Which suggests that there is more energy – *excess* or *sufficient energy*?
7 Can you name three people who play an *influential role* in a child's development?
8 If two of the four *constituent elements* of most language exams are reading and speaking, what are the other two?

10.2 Fill in the gaps in these sentences with a verb from B. Change the form where necessary.

1 I first _____ into contact with Abdul when I started my doctoral research in 1987.
2 The country _____ so much energy that we don't _____ enough to meet all our needs.
3 The space race _____ an important role in post-war politics.
4 In her research project Diana _____ the phenomenon of extra-sensory perception but she was not able to come to any significant conclusions.
5 Although Hans's rivals attempted to _____ his results, they met with no success.
6 Green's poetry successfully _____ elements from a number of different traditions.

10.3 Match the beginning of each sentence with the most appropriate ending.

1 It took the team a long time to devise   surrounding the issue of global warming.
2 During the war we had to break   a blood sample for analysis.
3 There has been a lot of heated debate   the role of project leader.
4 Ian Hartmann was invited to take on   to the debate on cloning.
5 Part of my role was to collate   off contact with colleagues abroad.
6 The doctor wanted me to provide   seems to be emerging.
7 Scientists all over the world contributed   the key elements in a graph.
8 A new and unexpected phenomenon   a way to solve their problem.
9 Using shading helps to differentiate   the results of our experiments.

10.4 Choose the best word from the box to fill each of the gaps.

conflicting	crucial	define	discern	engaging
heated	interim	maintaining	practical	proper
publish	random	taking		

1 She obtained her results by _____ a _____ sample of the population.
2 Before we go any further we must _____ each of our roles more precisely.
3 We must decide what is the _____ way to proceed, in _____ terms.
4 The group succeeded in _____ contact long after they had all left college.
5 My trip to Africa was the _____ element in my decision to work in conservation.
6 Specialists in the field of bio-engineering have been _____ in _____ debate on this issue for some time.
7 I am told that Smythe is about to _____ some _____ results.
8 Professor Powell was able to _____ some _____ elements in different accounts of the incident.

11 Adjective and noun combinations

This unit focuses on a number of adjective + noun combinations which are particularly frequent in academic contexts.

A Adjectives suggesting importance

adjective	comment	some of the nouns it frequently goes with
important	**significant** can convey the same meaning and both adjectives often go with these nouns	aspect, contribution, difference, implications, point, question, reason, element
significant	can also mean large in size and as such goes with these nouns	increase, reduction, number, proportion
major	the opposite, **minor**, also often goes with these nouns	role, changes, problem, factor, issue, concern, difference, theme, contribution, point
enormous/ considerable	**enormous** can mean very large or very important; **considerable** means large or of noticeable importance (i.e. slightly less strong than enormous)	amount, expansion, number, range, diversity, difference, variation, extent, degree, impact, power, influence, significance, interest
particular	means special	interest, attention, significance, importance, concern

Note that a feature of academic writing is that it often uses an adjective + noun phrase to suggest importance of some kind instead of just using an adjective, e.g. *Marx's contribution is of **particular significance*** instead of *Marx's contribution is <u>very significant</u>*.

B Adjectives suggesting frequency

Widespread means that something happens in many places or among many people. It often combines with such nouns as *belief, acceptance, support, opposition, assumption, use*. For example, *There is **widespread support** for government policy in urban areas.*

Common can mean frequent. With this meaning it often combines with such nouns as *experience, practice, use, concern*. For example, *It is increasingly **common practice** for UK teenagers to take a gap year before entering university.*
Note that *common* can also mean 'shared' and as such it combines with *knowledge, ground, feature, interest*. For example, *There is much **common ground** between the two writers.*

Specific means relating to one thing and not to things in general. It often combines with *context, information, case, type, form, purpose, characteristics, conditions, example*. For example, *The reaction occurs only under **specific conditions**.*

C Other useful adjective and noun combinations

Inevitable is often used with words relating to results or changes such as *consequence, outcome, collapse, decline, conflict, effect, developments*. [unavoidable]

Explicit combines with words relating to how things are presented, e.g. *reference, statement, comparison, account, mention*. [clear and exact, communicated directly]

Relevant combines with words relating to evidence of different types, e.g. *data, documents, information, details, factors*. [connected with what is being discussed]

Exercises

11.1 Look at these statements about some academics. Complete each sentence with an appropriate adjective or noun. There may be more than one answer.

1 Davison did a considerable _____ of research into earthquake prediction.
2 Rawlinson drew _____ attention to the problem of energy consumption.
3 Werner's work had an enormous _____ on the way we design bridges today.
4 A _____ proportion of Thomaz's work was devoted to international law. Three of her five books were on the subject.
5 Prestyn made only a _____ contribution to modern psychology, but it was an interesting one, nonetheless.
6 Baklov's work has some extremely _____ implications for our work today.

11.2 Rewrite the sentences using adjectives from the opposite page instead of the words in bold.

1 There is opposition among students **in many places** to the idea of longer semesters.
2 The destruction of the riverbank will cause a decline **which is bound to happen** in the numbers of small mammals.
3 School standards are a concern **which occurs frequently** among parents nowadays.
4 Nowhere in the article does the author make mention **in a direct, clear and exact way** of the 20 cases which were never resolved.
5 There is very little ground **which is shared** between the two ways of addressing the problem.
6 The paper is too general and lacks examples **which relate only to individual things**.

11.3 Make sure you know the noun forms of these adjectives. Write them in the table. Use a dictionary if necessary.

adjective	noun	adjective	noun
significant		important	
relevant		valuable	
interesting		useful	
frequent		broad	

11.4 The sentences below came from lectures. Adapt them for use in an academic article by replacing the phrases in bold. In each case use an adjective from the box combined with a noun from 11.3 to make a phrase like *of great interest*.

huge	high	enormous	great	considerable

1 Johnson's work is **very relevant** for any student of medical engineering.
2 The research will be **very valuable** to anyone interested in economic planning.
3 It was an event **which was terribly important** in the history of Latin American politics.
4 Partich's book is an **extremely broad** work.
5 Sorlan's book was a **very significant** work in the development of political theory.
6 This software will be **quite useful** in the analysis of large amounts of numerical data.
7 The method she outlines is **very interesting** to anyone investigating sleeplessness.
8 'You know' is an expression which is **very frequent** in informal spoken English.

12 Verbs and the words they combine with

A How verbs combine with other words

You should note a number of things about verbs in an academic context, in particular:

- any nouns often used with the verb and whether the noun goes before or after the verb, for example, **the research/theory is based on, to pose a problem/question/threat**
- any adverbs often used with the verb, for example, **mainly/partly/loosely based**
- any prepositions following the verb, for example, **to base** something **on** something else
- if the verb is often used in the passive, for example, **be based on, be associated with**.

verb	nouns	adverbs	examples
base (on)	research, theory, story, hypothesis	mainly, partly loosely	The **story was loosely based on** a true event which occurred in 1892. The **theory is mainly based on** the writer's initial study.
associate (with)	word, idea, theory, term	generally, commonly, invariably	A decrease in consumer spending is **generally associated with** fears of instability. The **word is commonly associated with** youth culture.
discuss	idea, problem, issue, question, topic, theme	at length, briefly, thoroughly	Wilson and Crick (1965) **discuss the problem at length**. Sim's article **discusses the issue thoroughly**.
establish	relationship, connection	firmly, clearly, conclusively	Geologists have been unable to **firmly establish a connection** between the two types of fossils. Lopez **conclusively establishes a relationship** between the two phenomena.
examine	facts, evidence, effects, aspects	briefly, critically, thoroughly	We shall now **briefly examine the evidence** for the existence of dark matter. Our aim is to **thoroughly examine the effects** of stress.
demonstrate	existence, need, effects, importance	clearly, convincingly	The study **clearly demonstrates the importance** of support for dementia sufferers. Harvey's work **convincingly demonstrates the need** for a new approach to the problem.
identify (with) (often used in passive)	causes, factors, issues, properties, needs, approach, origin	correctly, clearly, closely	This **approach is closely identified with** the work of H. Crowley during the 1950s. The article **clearly identifies the factors** influencing the decision to go to war.

B More verbs in combination with nouns, adverbs and prepositions

- **pose** – This **inevitably poses a question concerning** the stability of society. Parks **poses a challenge to** Kahn's theory.
- **suggest** – The most recent results **strongly suggest a different interpretation** of the situation. The article **suggests a new approach to** the problem.
- **list** – Here I **simply list the main hypotheses/causes/features/characteristics**; they will be examined in detail below.
- **refer** – The book **refers frequently/specifically/in passing to** the 1956 economic crisis.
- **observe** – This is due to the **changes/trends/differences we observed** earlier.

Remember, we say *based on*, NOT ~~based in~~. We *discuss a problem / an issue*, NOT *discuss ~~about~~ a problem / an issue*.
Note any verb + preposition combinations that differ from those of your first language.

Exercises

12.1 Choose the most appropriate adverb for the verb in bold, and add it to the sentence. Note the word order used on the opposite page.

1 Paulson's research **demonstrated** the need for a new approach to the study of stress.
invariably   convincingly   closely

2 As was **observed**, there is a strong correlation between house prices and inflation.
closely   critically   earlier

3 In the study of language, 'tense' **refers** to the coding of time in the form of the verb.
specifically   strongly   briefly

4 Classical liberal economics **is identified** with the theories of Milton Friedman.
thoroughly   closely   conclusively

5 Chapter 1 **discusses** the main issues, but they are dealt with in greater detail in Chapter 2.
closely   simply   briefly

6 To date, no research exists that **establishes** a connection between behaviour, personality traits, and leadership traits.   firmly   thoroughly   critically

7 SENTA is a computer programming language **based** on Logo.
strongly   slightly   loosely

8 Social research techniques were applied to **examine** the effects of the policy on the poor.
strongly   mainly   critically

12.2 Complete each sentence with a suitable noun. There may be more than one answer.

1 Here we list again the main _____ of the present study and show which have been proven and which have been rejected.
2 The graph enables us to observe recent broad _____ in mortality rates.
3 The researchers concluded that it is still difficult to identify the _____ of the time-related changes in human beings that we call ageing.
4 A seminar was held to discuss the _____ of children's rights in the light of the Convention on the Rights of the Child.
5 Wu demonstrated the _____ for a comprehensive plan in preparation for a pandemic.

12.3 Complete each sentence with three possible nouns. Use a dictionary if necessary.

1 These figures lead me to suggest an alternative (1) _____ (2) _____ (3) _____ .
2 It is clear that these developments pose a new (1) _____ (2) _____ (3) _____ .
3 Before we reach any conclusion, it is important to examine the (1) _____ (2) _____ (3) _____ .

12.4 Underline useful verb + adverb combinations in this text.

The world is facing a looming water crisis. Disputes over allocation have steadily increased in the last decade, and demand has grown rapidly. Water is likely to generate the same degree of controversy in the 21st century as oil did in the 20th. If we take no action now, new conflicts are likely to occur periodically around the world. At the moment, instead of seeking solutions which directly address multiple needs, countries focus a little too narrowly on local issues and typically opt for expensive and inferior solutions. What is needed are decisions which can be quickly implemented and a debate which will seriously consider more than the short term needs of individual states.

12.5 Use one of the combinations you underlined in 12.4 to complete each sentence.

1 Various measures were introduced last year to _____ the issue of identity theft.
2 The justice system needs to _____ the impact of a prison sentence on offenders.
3 The number of university applications has been _____ over the last 50 years.
4 The article _____ on one angle of the problem rather than taking a broad view.
5 The suggested measures should be _____ to avoid further problems.

13 Prepositional phrases

Notice the prepositional phrases in the texts below.

A A book review

The *Guide to the Semi-Colon in English* was written by Keith Pedant **in conjunction with**[1] a team of researchers at Boardham University. **In comparison with**[2] previous works on the semi-colon, this is a very substantial volume. **In addition to** the main text there are a number of appendices. These are **to some extent**[3] the most useful parts of the book as, **in line with**[4] modern linguistic practice, they provide a wealth of real data. **In spite of**[5] its potentially dry topic, the book contains many fascinating examples, in the sections dealing with the history of the semi-colon **in particular**. **With the exception of**[6] the final chapter, this book may be of some interest to the general reader as well as the specialist but **on the whole**[7] is mainly for those who have a professional interest in punctuation marks.

[1] working together with [2] same meaning as **in contrast to** [3] notice also **to a greater/lesser/ certain extent** [4] following, same meaning as **in accordance with** [5] despite, not prevented by [6] not including (NB NOT ~~except~~) [7] generally

B A talk to a genealogy club

Chairperson: Now, **at this stage**[1] in the proceedings it's my pleasure to introduce our speaker tonight, Dr Anna Klein, the country's leading family history specialist. Anna, I'd like to welcome you **on behalf of**[2] all our members.

Anna Klein: Thank you. My own interest in the subject came about **as a result of** discovering some old letters in the attic at home. I found them **by chance**[3]. They'd been written by some relatives who'd emigrated to Canada a hundred years or so before and for me, as a ten-year-old then, they were **by far**[4] the most exciting things I had ever read. They were, **for the most part**[5], extremely well-written and, **from then on**, I was determined to learn as much as I could about my family. **In other words**[6], I had started out on my genealogical journey. **In some ways**, I was very lucky. I was able to collect quite a bit of key family information **on the basis of** the old letters and this enabled me to track down some relations living in Montreal. They, **in turn**, provided some contacts with Australian cousins and so it continued. **In the process**, I've learnt a great deal, not only about my own family, but also **in terms of**[7] how to approach tracing one's family. **In most respects**[8] it's been a thoroughly enjoyable adventure though there have been some difficult moments …

[1] now, also **at this point** [2] representing (NB NOT ~~on the part of~~) [3] accidentally [4] very much [5] generally [6] to express something differently, often more simply [7] as far as (how to approach …) was concerned [8] considering most aspects of the experience

ERROR WARNING Note that **on the one hand** and **on the other hand** are used to contrast two different ways of looking at an issue. *On the one hand flying is much more convenient than going by train, but **on the other hand**, train travel is often much more interesting.*

Exercises

13.1 Complete the prepositional phrases as used in these press announcements.

1 Professor Soltero said that, ... line .... government guidelines, the researchers had consulted local people.

2 A spokesperson for the drug company said that, ... stage, it is too early to make strong claims about the drug.

3 Dr Leiman said that while .... the .... hand the government wanted to encourage research, ... the .... hand they were reducing funding for universities.

4 .... addition .... a new building on the campus, the team will receive a very generous grant to conduct their research.

5 .... the exception .... one study in 1986, no major research had been carried out till now, Dr Peters stated.

6 Professor Karpal said that, ... the basis .... her studies so far, she was optimistic that a cure for the disease would be found.

7 Lauren Charles said that, ... whole, social conditions had improved since the report, especially .... terms .... jobs and housing for the poorer sectors.

8 The Professor said that he was delighted to accept the award .... behalf .... the whole university.

13.2 Match the beginning of each sentence with the most appropriate ending.

1 The conclusions are fair in   some ways it was sheer luck.
2 Dr Carr's team got the grant, in   conjunction with an American project.
3 We had little money to spare; in   comparison with other articles in the series.
4 We need people's personal data, in   spite of being the smallest team to apply.
5 We made an important discovery; in   most respects, though some are questionable.
6 This latest paper is quite short in   other words, we were underfunded.
7 The Indian study was carried out in   particular their parents' history of illnesses.

13.3 Read this paragraph about the discovery of dinosaurs. In each sentence there is one error in the use of a prepositional phrase. Correct each error.

A bone discovered on chance in the 17th century was the beginning of the search for dinosaurs. From then in, scientists and the public have been fascinated by these creatures. In accordance to beliefs at that time, the initial discovery was thought to be the bone of a human giant. However, in 1824, a scientist, William Buckland, calculated that the bone belonged to a 12-metre, flesh-eating reptile and named it *Megalosaurus*, on the process giving us the first of the wonderful list of exotic names for dinosaurs. The 17th century discovery had, on turn, led to a series of further finds around that time. All these at a greater or lesser extent confirmed Buckland's theories. For far the biggest dinosaur discovered to date was probably over 40 metres long. To the most part, dinosaurs ranged from the size of a chicken to that of a giraffe. At most respects, what we know about their habits is still very limited. What we do know is at least on some extent based on pure speculation.

FOLLOW UP Use a dictionary to find an example sentence using each of these phrases: *on the one hand, on the other hand, on behalf of, with the exception of, except.* Write them out and then add one more sentence for each one relating to your own academic discipline.

14 Verbs and prepositions

A Verbs with *on* – sentences from academic articles

Chapter 1 of Huang's book **focuses on** violent human behaviour.
Sura's article **draws on** data gathered over a period of ten years. [uses in support of his/her case]
The introduction to the book **comments** briefly **on** a case study carried out in Brazil.
In this section I **concentrate on** the economic aspects of immigration.
The book **is based on** a number of studies carried out during the 1990s. [often used in passive]
The method used by Scanlon **relies on / rests on*** two basic principles. [*(formal) is based on]

B Verbs with *to* – teachers talk to students

We **assigned**[1] the tasks randomly **to** the experimental group and the control group to see how the subjects would **react to** the different problems.

Malaria poses a major health risk to people who **are exposed to** infection where malaria is common. In 1997, 13% of deaths among children **were attributed to**[2] malaria in one area in Zaire.

OK, let's **turn to** the more difficult cases that I mentioned earlier. How should a doctor **respond to** a patient who doesn't **consent to** treatment when it seems to be essential?

We can't really say that an increase in inflation of two per cent **amounts to**[4] an economic crisis, and I **refer** here **to** some recent stories in the media which are highly exaggerated and which can **be traced to**[5] a deep misunderstanding of how inflation operates.

When you're planning a questionnaire, you should always **attend to**[3] design issues such as the number of questions and how clear they are.

[1] give a particular job or piece of work to someone [2] say or think that something is the result of something (often used in passive) [3] deal with, give one's attention to [4] be the same as something, or have the same effect as something [5] discover the origin of something by examining how it has developed (often used in passive)

C Other prepositions

	verbs	examples
with	associate, provide, couple, equip	Note: In the active voice, as in the first example, this group of verbs follows the pattern verb + object + preposition + complement. Note also that these verbs are often used in the passive, as in the second example. We try to **equip** our laboratories **with** the latest technology. Heart disease **is** often **associated with** unhealthy life styles.
from	depart, benefit, emerge, exclude	In this book, Herne **departs from** his earlier theory. [takes a different view] Some of the data **were excluded from** the final analysis.
of	write, speak, convince, dispose	Abuka **writes/speaks of** the early years of industrial development. [both are rather formal] We must **convince** people **of** the need for water conservation.
for	account, search, call, argue	Lung cancer **accounted for** 20% of deaths in men. [formed the total of] Hopper (1987) **argues for** a new approach to English grammar. [opposite: **argue against**]

ERROR WARNING
The verbs *emphasise* and *stress* are used without any preposition (NOT ~~on~~). *The study* **emphasises/stresses** *the need for more controlled experiments to back up the conclusions.*
Divide is followed by *into* (NOT ~~divide in~~). *The subjects* **were divided into** *three groups.*

Exercises

14.1   **Put the words in the right order to make sentences. Use the punctuation to help you.**

1 period. / focuses / the changes / The article / on / the / the post-war / economy / US / in / in
2 commented / student's / inconsistencies / a / The professor / of / in the / essay. / on / number
3 conducted / The / is / last / based / a series / theory / of / five / on / years. / over the / experiments
4 on / assistants. / The / research / relies / work / conducted by / professor's / experiments / his
5 is / are / very / your / your / studies / important / concentrate / to / over. / on / until / It / exams
6 was / The / draw / some / to / primary / on / only recently / become / have / available. / writer / sources / which / able

14.2   **Put these verbs in the right box.**

account	argue	assign	associate	attribute	benefit	call	consent	convince
depart	dispose	equip	exclude	provide	react	refer	search	write

for	from	of	to	with

14.3   **Now choose one of the word + preposition combinations from 14.2 to complete each sentence. Change the form of the verb if necessary.**

1 The lecturer _____ us _____ a number of very good writers on the subject.
2 Traffic accidents _____ most hospital admissions at the weekend.
3 The poets John Keats and Lord Byron are closely _____ the English Romantic Movement.
4 Remember to _____ carefully _____ all waste material.
5 Most people believe that they would _____ enormously _____ having more job security.
6 My parents tried to _____ me _____ the advantages of studying abroad.
7 I have been _____ an article on this topic for ages.
8 Our experiments _____ us _____ the data we needed to prove our hypothesis.
9 The head of department _____ the lecturer's request for leave of absence.
10 Mary Raskova _____ very movingly _____ her experiences in Rwanda.

14.4   **Correct the sentences. All of them have errors connected with prepositions.**

1 The course leader divided her students in five groups.
2 They had to trace everyone who had been exposed for the infection.
3 At the moment we have too few nurses attending at too many patients.
4 Excellent teaching coupled for first-class research have made this a successful college.
5 The country emerged off the crisis as a much stronger power.
6 Joe got an interest in politics from his uncle who often spoke over his days as a senator.
7 The government called to an investigation into the explosion at the nuclear reactor.
8 In your speech don't forget to emphasise on the advantages of studying here.

15 Nouns and prepositions

A Groups of related nouns sharing prepositions

Sometimes groups of nouns with related meanings share the same prepositions.

nouns	preposition(s)	example
book, article, essay, lecture, dissertation, project, assignment	about, on	In 1978, Da Silva published a **book about**[1] the history of emigration. She wrote a **dissertation on**[2] teenage slang in New York.
research (see also B), investigation, inquiry	into	Kelly (1969) conducted an **investigation into** the origins of international terrorism.
analysis, examination, exploration (see also B), study	of	The article offers an **analysis of** the potential impact of the H5N1 Avian Flu virus.
problem, difficulty	of, with	He gave a lecture on the **problem of** global warming. One **difficulty with** this approach is that a set of results may allow different interpretations.
reason, motivation, rationale (see also B)	for	Economists have recently questioned the **rationale for** government spending.

[1] and [2] *about* tends to be used for more general subjects; *on* is frequently used for more specific, detailed works, although both may be found in both uses

See also the notes on prepositions after nouns in Unit 44.

B Nouns commonly associated with particular prepositions

You can also learn the nouns which most frequently come before a particular preposition. Some of these are in A above. The following examples are all titles of academic articles.

nouns	preposition	example
look, attempt, point, age	**at**	An **attempt at** integration of economic and psychological theories of consumption
changes, differences, increase, decrease	**in**	Gender **differences in** risk-taking in financial decision-making
insight, inquiry, research, investigation	**into**	An **investigation into** sleep characteristics of children with autism
work, research, influence, emphasis, effect	**on**	Genetic **influence on** smoking – a study of male twins
basis, idea, part, lack, exploration, means	**of**	A computerised clinical decision support system as a **means of** implementing depression guidelines
need, reason, basis, case, preference	**for**	Assessing organisational culture: the **case for** multiple methods
relation, approach, response, attention	**to**	Communicating with strangers: an **approach to** intercultural communication
attitude, tendency, move, progress	**to/towards**	**Progress towards** sustainable regional development
principle, rationale, assumptions, logic	**behind**	Questioning the **assumptions behind** art criticism
relationship, difference, distinction	**between**	The **relationship between** educational technology and student achievement in mathematics

Exercises

15.1 Fill in the missing prepositions. In questions 4 and 5, more than one answer is possible.

1 One difficulty .... the class questionnaire was that some students had already left the course and could not be contacted.
2 She wrote a dissertation .... wild flower conservation in Finland in the 1990s.
3 The book is an exploration .... the origins of the economic crisis of 1997.
4 The rationale .... the present research is the need to better understand the process of agreement in international law.
5 Research .... spoken language has been considerably assisted in recent years by the availability of computerised databases or 'corpora'.
6 Prippen's (1984) book was an inquiry .... the foundations of nationalism.
7 What is Kazuo Matsui's book .... ? Have you read it?
8 He did a study .... the problem .... side-impact automobile collisions.

15.2 Correct the mistakes in the use of prepositions in these sentences. There may be more than one mistake per sentence.

1 Her dissertation produced some interesting insights to how young children develop a visual sense of the world and the age in which development is most noticeable.
2 The reason of the unwillingness of the people involved in the demonstration to be interviewed was fear of being arrested later.
3 Hierstat's approach at the analysis of solar phenomena is different from that of Donewski. He questioned the assumptions under much of the previous research.
4 Changes of the rate of growth of the cells were observed over time.
5 A lack in funding led to the cancellation of the project, and social scientists blamed the negative attitude of the government on social science research.
6 Jawil's article puts great emphasis into the need of more research and argues the case of greater attention on the causes of poverty rather than the symptoms.

15.3 Using a dictionary if necessary, match each noun with the preposition that usually follows it.

Nouns: attitude difference effect emphasis insight preference
principle rationale reason relationship tendency

Prepositions: behind between for into on to/towards

15.4 Underline typical academic noun + preposition combinations like those on the opposite page.

The possible ecological effects of climate change are often in the news, as is the matter of whether the potential impact can be predicted. New work on a migratory[1] bird, the pied flycatcher, takes things a stage further by showing how a climate-related population decline was actually caused. Timing is key. Over the past 17 years flycatchers declined strongly in areas where caterpillar[2] numbers (food for the nestlings[3]) peak early, but in areas with a late food peak there was no decline. The young birds arrive too late in places where caterpillars have already responded to early warmth. Mistiming like this is probably a common consequence of climate change, and may be a major factor in the decline of many long-distance migratory bird species.

[1] which travels to a different place, usually when the season changes [2] small, long animal with many legs which develops into a butterfly [3] young birds

16 Fixed expressions

If we look at a corpus of academic texts, we see that certain chunks of language occur very frequently in spoken and written contexts. This unit looks at some of the most useful ones.

A Number, quantity, degree

Look at these comments written by a college teacher on assignments handed in by her students. Note the expressions in bold.

> A good paper. It's clear you've spent **a great deal of** time researching the subject and you quote **a wide range of** sources.
> Grade: B

> Some good points here but it's not clear **to what extent** you're aware of all the issues involved. Global trade affects nations **in a variety of ways**.
> Grade: C

> I think you've misunderstood the topic **to some extent**. You've written **in excess of**[1] 3,000 words on areas that are not entirely relevant. Let's talk.
> Grade: F

[1] more than

B Generalising and specifying

In this class discussion, the students make fairly general statements, while the teacher tries to make the discussion more specific.

Marsha: Well, I think **on the whole** parents should take more responsibility for their kids.

Teacher: Yes, **with respect to**[1] home life, yes, but **in the case of** violence, surely the wider community is involved, isn't it? I mean, **for the purposes of** our discussions about social stability, everyone's involved, aren't they?

Marsha: Yes, but **in general** I don't think people want to get involved in violent incidents, **as a rule** at least. They get scared off.

Teacher: True. But **as far as** general discipline **is concerned**, don't you think it's a community-wide issue? I mean discipline **as regards**[2] everyday actions, **with the exception of** school discipline. What do you think, **in terms of** public life, Tariq?

Tariq: I think the community **as a whole** does care about crime and discipline and things, but **for the most part** they see violence as something that is outside of them, you know, not their direct responsibility.

Teacher: OK. So, let's consider the topic **in more detail**[3], I mean **from the point of view of** violence and aggression specifically in schools. Let's look at some extracts from the American Medical Association's 2002 report on bullying. They're on the handout.

[1] or **in respect of**, or (more neutral) **with regard to** [2] another neutral alternative to 1 [3] or (more formally) **in greater detail**

C Linking points and arguments

The increase in house sales is **due to the fact that** inflation fell in 2004. **At the same time**, tax rate reductions were beginning to have an effect.

Joslav used an eight-point scale in the questionnaire, **as opposed to**[1] a four-point one, **by means of which** he showed that attitudes covered a very wide range, **in the sense that** the results were spread very evenly over all eight points.

It's very difficult to interpret these data. **Be that as it may**[2], there is some evidence of a decline in frequency. **For this reason**, we decided to repeat the experiment.

In addition to surveying the literature on population movements, we also reviewed work carried out on family names in five regions.

[1] rather than [2] a typical academic way of saying 'although I accept that this is true'; more common in speech than in writing

Exercises

16.1 Choose one of the expressions in A to fill in the missing words in this feedback to a student from one of her teachers.

You have had a very good term (1) .... You have done (2) ....
work and have also taken part in (3) .... social activities. Your sporting
activities may have interfered with your studies (4) .... but you
still managed to write (5) .... 5,000 words for your end-of-term
assignment, which, I am pleased to report, was of a high standard.

16.2 Use the words in the box to form eight different phrases that are useful for academic discussions.

a	as	as	at	be	for	for	general	in
in	it	may	most	of	on	part	reason	rule
same	terms	the	the	the	that	this	time	whole

....
....
....
....

16.3 From the point of view of meaning, which expression in each set doesn't belong, and why?

1 in general, by means of which, as a rule, on the whole
2 as regards X, as far as X is concerned, with the exception of X, with respect to X
3 as a whole, in addition to, for the most part, in general

16.4 Choose the best expression to complete each sentence.

1 .... our discussion, I'd like to focus on the US context.
  A For the purposes of   B In the sense that   C From the point of view of
2 There is some evidence of an improvement in the economy but, ... , there
  is unlikely to be much change before next year.
  A for this reason   B as a rule   C be that as it may
3 I'd like to consider education .... industry.
  A in the case of   B from the point of view of C with the exception of
4 I'm not sure .... you agree with Qian's theory.
  A by means of which   B to what extent   C as regards
5 We will now discuss the development of the Surrealist Movement ....
  A on the whole   B to some extent   C in more detail

16.5 Complete these sentences in any logical way.

1 I enjoy watching most sports with the exception of ....
2 A poor relationship between parents and children is often due to the fact that
  ....
3 I love reading English novels as opposed to ....
4 In your first year of graduate school you have to take an end-of-year exam in addition to
  ....
5 It was a very useful course in the sense that ....

17 Applications and application forms

Here we look at applying for a place at a UK college or university. Institutions following the US system have different processes, which are usually described on their web pages.

A Getting information

Read this information about preparing an application for postgraduate study.

> **What should I do first?**
> Do all you can to learn about the **careers**[1] that will be open to you after studying – and what **qualifications** you will need in order to get the job you want.
>
> **What qualifications do I need for postgraduate study?**
> A first degree **is required** to study at postgraduate level.
> The specific **entry requirements** for each course of study are listed on the individual course pages.
> If needed, **clarification**[2] may **be sought**[3] from the department you are applying to.
> Your performance in previous schooling is very important to your application **profile**[4].
>
> **What are the requirements for international students?**
> In addition to the general admission requirements, international applicants must **submit**[5]:
> * A **transcript**[6] of university courses and grades, translated into English, and
> * Results of the International English Language Testing System (IELTS) or Test of English as a Foreign Language (TOEFL), unless you have received **English-medium**[7] education for at least one year. Applicants must have a minimum IELTS score of 6.5 or a TOEFL score of 580.
>
> **Are any grants**[8] **or scholarships**[9] **available for international students?**
> Visit our International Office pages for details.

[1] the job or series of jobs that you do during your working life [2] making something clear by giving more details or a simpler explanation [3] past participle of *seek*: 'to look for' [4] overall character of the application [5] give something for a decision to be made by others [6] official document listing courses completed and grades received [7] where all the classes are taught in English [8] money given specially by the government to a person to enable them to study [9] money given by a school, college, university, etc. to pay for the studies of a person with great ability

B The application process

Look at this email from Tania to Liam. Tania is applying to study at Wanstow University.

> Hi Liam,
> At last I've **filled in** my application form and sent it off. It took ages. As well as all my personal details they wanted the names of two **referees**[1], **financial guarantees**[2], and I had to attach a **personal statement** saying why I wanted to go to Wanstow. Anyway, the **deadline**[3] is next Friday, then the website said they'd take about six weeks to **process**[4] the application after they **acknowledge**[5] it, then I might be **called for**[6] an interview. By that time the **references** have to be in. I'm just hoping that because I'm a **mature student**[7] I might have a good chance of being **offered a place** – Wanstow has a lot of mature students and they have a strong **equal opportunities policy**[8]. The **fees**[9] are pretty high, but I can get a **student loan**[10] if I **get in**[11].
> Love, Tania

[1] person who knows you and who is willing to describe and, usually, praise you, to support your application [2] formal acceptance of financial responsibility and ability to pay (e.g. proof of a bank account) [3] final date by which something must be done [4] deal with documents officially [5] say that they have received it, NOT accepted it [6] asked to attend [7] a student at a college or university who is older than the usual age [8] principle of treating all people the same, regardless of sex, race, religion, etc. [9] amount of money paid for a particular service [10] money which must be repaid when one has completed one's studies [11] (informal) if I am accepted and given a place

Exercises

17.1 Read the text in A and answer a potential student's questions about the university.

1 Is it possible to do a postgraduate degree without having been to university before?
2 Where can I get more information about what qualifications I need for a specific course?
3 Will they want to know about my university grades?
4 When is an IELTS or TOEFL score not needed?
5 What IELTS score should applicants have?

17.2 Match the first half of the word combination on the left with the second half on the right.

personal	financial	seek	student		opportunities	score	student	degree
equal	mature	application	first		form	competition	guarantee	
minimum	tough				statement	clarification	loan	

17.3 Why does the university want each of these things? Answer in full sentences using, where possible, some of the vocabulary from the opposite page.

1 the names of two referees
2 financial guarantees
3 a personal statement
4 a transcript of courses taken and grades
5 a minimum TOEFL or IELTS score

17.4 Number the actions to show the order in which they usually happen for a prospective student.

.... wait for the application to be processed
.... find an appropriate course
.... attend an interview
.... attach a personal statement to the form
.... decide on what career they would like to do
.... be offered a place
.... be called for an interview
.... ask referees if it is all right to put their names on the application form
.... check that they fulfil the necessary entry requirements
.... fill in an application form

17.5 Complete the missing words in this email with words from the opposite page. The first letter of each word is given to help you.

Hi Miles,
I'd love a c................ as an international lawyer and am really hoping I can
g................ in to Wanstow University to do a p................ g................ course in
law there. I've f................ in all the necessary forms and just hope that my academic
p................ will be good enough for them. I think I fulfil all their e................
r................ but who knows! It took me ages to get the t................ of my college
g................ , etc. translated but I managed to get everything in by the d................ .
So now I just have to wait to see if they c................ me for an interview or not. Fingers
crossed!
Lucia

FOLLOW UP Look at the website of any English-speaking university that interests you. What information do they provide about applying to that university? Make a note of any other useful vocabulary you find there.

A Places

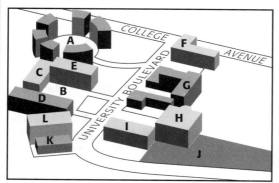

Key
A **Halls of residence**[1]
B University Square, staff car park
C **Administration**[2] Building
D Arts **Faculty**[3] Building
E **Great Hall**[4]
F University Health Centre
G University Bookshop, Cafeteria and visitors' car park
H University Library
I **Student Union**[5]
J Sports grounds
K **School**[6] of Engineering
L Arts **Lecture Theatre**[7]

[1] a college building where students live [2] the main offices of the university, often shortened to 'admin' [3] a group of departments or schools (see 6) in a college which specialise in a particular group of subjects [4] a large hall where graduation ceremonies and other important events are held [5] a building specially used by students to meet socially; the term also refers to the organisation of students which arranges social events and offers other services [6] part of a college or university specialising in a particular subject or group of subjects [7] a large hall with rows of seats, where lectures are held

B People, structures and activities

Dr Ward, Adviser to International Students, is giving an introductory session for new international postgraduate students in the Department of English Language at Wanstow.

Dr Ward: Let me tell you about the staff. The Head of Department is **Professor**[1] Bradley. He will be giving some of the postgraduate **seminars**[2] as well as giving some of the first-semester **lectures**[3]. Then there are two **Senior Lecturers**[4]. They'll be handling lectures and **tutorials**[5]. Then there are six **lecturers**[6] – they're all listed in your information pack. You'll also meet our **Research Assistant**, Angela Gorski, and there are four **research students** doing PhDs. Each of you will be given a personal **tutor**[7], who will be one of us. If you want to talk to any of us, our **office hours** are on the noticeboard and on the web page. Any questions?
Student: Is the personal tutor the same as our dissertation **supervisor**[8]?
Dr Ward: No. You'll be given a supervisor when you choose your dissertation topic. He or she'll supervise you during the spring **semester**[9] and the summer **vacation**[10]. Your personal tutor looks after your general academic welfare. You can also talk to a **student counsellor**[11] if you have any personal problems, and there's also a **postgrad rep**[12].

[1, 4] and [6] **professor** is the most senior academic title; **senior lecturers** are below professors in academic rank, and **lecturers** are below senior lecturers [2, 3] and [5] **seminars** consist of a teacher and a group of students meeting to study and discuss something; **lectures** are more formal events where larger groups of students listen and take notes; **tutorials** are usually smaller groups where students discuss their work with a teacher [7] teacher who works with one student or a small group [8] teacher with responsibility for a particular student [9] the university teaching year is normally divided into two semesters; the word **term** is also often used for the periods when students are in residence at a university [10] period when universities or colleges are closed; the word **holiday** is also used by students [11] someone trained to listen to students and give them advice about their problems [12] (informal) short form of *postgraduate representative* (someone who acts officially for that group of students)

Exercises

18.1 Look at A. Which building must students go to if they want to:

1 speak to a lecturer in the history department?
2 find information about student clubs?
3 visit someone who is living in the student accommodation?
4 enquire about payment of fees?
5 attend a graduation ceremony?
6 listen to a talk about English literature?
7 see a doctor?
8 borrow a book?

18.2 Read the text in B and answer the questions.

1 Are there likely to be more people in a seminar or a tutorial?
2 Who is the academic who guides a postgraduate student through their dissertation?
3 What word is used for the holiday period between university terms or semesters?
4 What is the difference between a personal tutor and a student counsellor?
5 What is the difference between a postgrad rep and a student counsellor?

18.3 Fill in the missing words in this email with words from the opposite page.

Hi Mum,
I've settled in well here at Wanstow. I like my room in this hall of _____ . I went to my first _____ this morning – it was on research methodology – and there were hundreds of students there. The _____ was very good – it was Professor Jones, our head of _____ . Tomorrow I'll have my first _____ – that'll be just me and one other student. We'll be discussing what we have to get done by the end of the _____ . I need to try to think some more about the topic for my _____ . When that is finalised I'll be assigned a _____ . I'll be expected to see him or her at least once a week during their office _____ . I hope I'll like him or her. You hear some awful stories!
Daisy

18.4 Put the words in the box into the correct category.

cafeteria	counsellor	lecture	lecturer
librarian	library	postgrad rep	professor
research assistant	research student	seminar	sports centre
sports grounds	tutor	tutorial	lecture theatre

people	place	event

FOLLOW UP Are universities/colleges in your country roughly based on a similar system to the UK one, or are there important differences? Make sure you can describe the main features in English. If your country's universities/colleges are more similar to the US system, study Unit 19.

19 Systems compared: the US and the UK

In US universities, many of the words for people and places are the same as those used in the UK (see Unit 18), but there are some differences.

A Terms with different meanings in US and UK university systems

US example	meaning/comment	UK example	meaning/comment
Are you **faculty** or student?	If you are *faculty*, you are a member of the academic staff.	The **faculty** will have to come to a decision on this.	*Faculty* refers to a group of departments (see Unit 18) with similar interests.
The grading **rubric** for term papers has been revised.	A *rubric* is a set of criteria or guidelines which tells how an assignment will be graded or scored.	Some students misread the exam **rubric** and didn't answer enough questions.	Instructions on an exam paper or in a textbook as to *how* a task must be done.
I went to **college** in St Louis. I attended Washington **University**. I took some fascinating courses at **college**.	The word *college* in American English refers broadly to the undergraduate experience, whether it is at a two-year community college, a four-year college, or a large state university in the US. A specific institution can be a college (granting undergraduate degrees only) or a university (granting undergraduate and graduate degrees).	She went to **university** in Scotland. She graduated from **university** in 1996.	In British English, *university* refers to the undergraduate experience. In both American and British English, no article is used before *college* or *university* in these examples.
Her brother went to **school** at Harvard.	*School* is often used to mean *university*. A common question is 'Where did you go to school?' meaning 'Where did you go to college?'	I went to **school** in London, then I went to university in Bristol.	Refers to primary or secondary education; *school* can also refer to a university department which covers several different teaching areas (e.g. School of English and Journalism).

B Different US terms

I wonder who should be on my **PhD committee**[1]. My **advisor**[2] suggested Dr Fry and Dr Roe. I have a lot of studying to do. I have my **comps**[3] in two weeks.

Let's meet in Harley **Commons**[4] at 7.30 pm, and we can study for tomorrow's **quiz**[5], OK?

It was tough being a **freshman**[6] because I wasn't used to such difficult **finals**[7], but life got a bit easier when I became a **sophomore**[8]. It was easy enough as a **junior**[9], but then it got tough again when I was a **senior**[10].

As a **graduate student**[11], I get to attend seminars with some of the top people in my field. The **fraternity**[12] and **sorority**[13] houses are all round the edge of the campus.

[1] a group of teachers who advise a PhD student [2] equivalent of the UK *supervisor* (see Unit 18) [3] short for *comprehensive examinations*, subject-area tests required of graduate students in some areas of studies [4] area where students can meet socially and eat in dining halls [5] short test on areas which have been taught [6] new, first-year undergraduate (also used in the UK) [7] final examinations at the end of the semester [8] second-year student, from the Greek *sophos*, wise, and *moros*, dull [9] third-year student [10] fourth-year student [11] student with a bachelor's degree (e.g. BA, BS) who is enrolled in a master's degree programme, equivalent of *postgraduate* student in the UK [12] a social organisation for male students [13] a social organisation for female students

Exercises

19.1 Look at A. Who is more likely to be speaking – a British person or an American? Why?

1 Only faculty can eat here.

2 All professors use the same rubric for grading term papers.

3 I went to school at Millintown, where I got my masters and PhD.

4 My department is within the Faculty of Engineering.

5 The rubric required students to answer all three questions on the exam paper.

19.2 Put these levels of student in an American university in order of seniority, starting with the first-year student. Explain what kind of student each term refers to.

graduate student   junior   freshman   senior   sophomore

19.3 Are the following statements true or false? If false, explain why they are incorrect.

1 An advisor is someone who helps American students with their emotional problems.
2 Women usually join a fraternity.
3 Finals means a student's last semester at university or college.
4 A PhD committee is a group of graduate students.

19.4 Use the clues to complete the crossword.

Across
1 Sometimes used to refer to college or university in the US
2 A short test of material that has been taught
3 Test to assess whether a student knows subject material required for a graduate degree
4 A social organisation for female students
5 A fourth-year student in the US

Down
6 A second-year student
7 A general word meaning academic staff in the US

20 Academic courses

A Course descriptions

Look at this extract from a UK university's web pages. American websites may use different terms.

Diploma/MA in English Language and Culture

* *Qualification:* **Diploma**[1] or MA. **Duration**: One year full-time or two years part-time. The course is a 180-**credit**[2] course, consisting of 120 credits of **core**[3] and **elective**[4] **modules**[5] plus a 60-credit dissertation module. Core modules are **obligatory**. **Candidates** not wishing to **proceed** to the MA may **opt for**[6] the Diploma (120 credits without dissertation).

* *Course description:* The course covers all the major aspects of present-day English language and culture. Topics include grammar, vocabulary, language in society, literature in English (for a full list, see the <u>list of modules</u>). Elective modules only run if a minimum of ten students **enrol**[7]. The modules consist of a mixture of **lectures**, **seminars**, **workshops** and **tutorials**[8].

* *Assessment*[9]*:* A 3,000-word **assignment**[10] must be submitted for each core module. Elective modules are assessed through **essays**, **projects** and **portfolios**[11]. The **word limit** for the dissertation is 12,000 to 15,000 words.
  Candidates must achieve a pass grade in all four core modules (20 credits each), plus 40 credits in elective modules (minimum of 30 credits in the English department plus 10 **optional** credits from modules offered by other departments), and, for MA, must pass the dissertation module (60 credits).
  Candidates who achieve a grade average of 70% or more over all modules may be **eligible**[12] for a **distinction**[13].

---

[1] a qualification between a bachelor's degree and a master's degree [2] unit which represents a successfully completed part of a course [3] most important parts of a course of study, that all students must do [4] which are chosen [5] one of the units which together make a complete course taught especially at a college or university [6] choose [7] put one's name on an official list of course members [8] see Unit 18 for the meaning of these; a workshop is a meeting to discuss and/or perform practical work in a subject [9] judgements of the quality of students' work [10] a piece of written work [11] a collection of documents that represent a person's work [12] having the necessary qualities or fulfilling the necessary conditions [13] a special mark given to students who produce work of an excellent standard

B Other aspects of courses

Dr Ward is holding a question-and-answer session for new MA students.

Reza: Can we **defer**[1] the dissertation if we can't stay here during the summer?

Dr Ward: Yes, you can defer for a year, but don't forget, if you do go home, you won't be able to have face-to-face **supervisions**[2].

Simon: Are the **in-sessional**[3] language courses compulsory?

Dr Ward: No. Most of you did the **pre-sessional**, which is the most important. But there are good in-sessional courses you can **sign up for**, especially the **EAP**[4] writing course.

Angela: If we get the MA, can we go on to do a PhD immediately?

Dr Ward: Not automatically. You have to show you can do PhD standard work first anyway, and then **upgrade**[5] to the PhD programme after a year or so.

[1] delay until a later time [2] individual meetings with the teacher who is responsible for the student's dissertation [3] courses held during the main teaching semesters; pre-sessional courses are held before the main teaching semesters begin [4] English for Academic Purposes [5] become officially registered for the higher degree

---

 When addressing someone with a PhD, always use their family name, e.g. *Excuse me, Dr Lopez*. Only medical doctors can be addressed simply as *Doctor*, without using their family name.

Exercises

20.1 Answer the questions about the text in A.

1 How long does the Diploma or MA course take if you study full-time?
2 How many credits is a dissertation worth?
3 What is special about core modules?
4 What is the difference between doing a Diploma and an MA?
5 How many students are required for an elective module to run?
6 How long do assignments have to be?
7 What kinds of classes do the students get?
8 On what kinds of work are they assessed?
9 What is the maximum number of words allowed in a dissertation?
10 What do students have to do to get a distinction?

20.2 Complete the missing words in this email from a student to a friend.

Diploma	dissertation	in-sessional	MA	module	PhD	project	sign

Hi Erika,

How are things going with you? I'm sorry not to have written to you sooner but I've been desperately busy with the linguistics (1) _____ I have to do for the elective (2) _____ I'm taking this term. It's really interesting and I think I might decide to do my final (3) _____ on a similar topic. At first I was only planning to do the (4) _____ but now I've decided to have a go at an (5) _____ . I might even (6) _____ up for a (7) _____ if they'll have me! PhD students are usually offered some language teaching on the (8) _____ EAP courses they run for foreign students, so it would be useful for my CV for the future.

Shoshana

20.3 Choose the correct word to complete each sentence.

1 I started out doing an MA but then decided to *upgrade / defer* to a PhD.
2 Students whose first language is not English usually have to attend a(n) *in-sessional / pre-sessional* language course before their main classes start.
3 Only six students have *enrolled / opted*, so the MEd programme will not run this year.
4 Most students decide to *sign / proceed* to the MA after completing their Diploma course.
5 Core modules are *obligatory / optional*.
6 When I was doing my PhD I had monthly one-to-one *seminars / supervisions*.
7 I won't be able to finish the dissertation this year, so I'll have to *opt / defer* till next year.
8 *Assessment / Assignment* consists of a three-hour end-of-module exam.

20.4 Complete the table below. Use a dictionary to help you if necessary.

verb	noun	adjective
opt		
		obligatory
	supervision +	
	assessment +	–
–		eligible

Compare your own course, or one you hope to do, with the course described in A in terms of duration, modules and assessment.

21 Study habits and skills

A Time management

West Preston University has a web-based self-assessment questionnaire on time management.

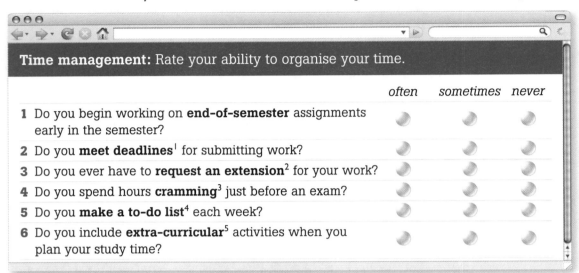

	often	sometimes	never
1 Do you begin working on **end-of-semester** assignments early in the semester?			
2 Do you **meet deadlines**[1] for submitting work?			
3 Do you ever have to **request an extension**[2] for your work?			
4 Do you spend hours **cramming**[3] just before an exam?			
5 Do you **make a to-do list**[4] each week?			
6 Do you include **extra-curricular**[5] activities when you plan your study time?			

[1] complete your work by the official final day or time [2] ask for more time beyond the deadline [3] try to learn a lot very quickly before an exam [4] make a list of things you should do [5] outside of the subjects one is studying

B Study habits and problems studying

Here are some students' comments about study habits and problems associated with studying.

'I try to **prioritise**[1] the most difficult or urgent task first, when I feel more motivated.'
'I'm a slow reader. I need to improve my **reading speed**. I find **revision** before exams really difficult. I can only **revise** for about two hours at a time. **My mind starts to wander**[2].'
'I always try to **review**[3] my **lecture notes** within 24 hours of the time I took them. I do need to improve my **note-taking**.'
'I use tricks to **memorise** things, like **mnemonics**[4] and **visualising**[5]. I try to **brainstorm**[6] the topic and draw **mind maps**[7] before I write a first **draft**[8] of an essay.'
'I know **rote learning**[9] isn't very fashionable nowadays, but I find it useful to learn some things **by heart**[10], especially lists of things.'
'I try to make a **study plan** each semester – but I never manage to keep to it!'
'I always try to get the books I need from the library on **long-term loan**. **Short-term loan** is never long enough, even though you can sometimes extend it for 24 hours.'
'In an exam I make **rough**[11] notes for each question, otherwise my mind just **goes blank**[12].'

[1] decide which things are the most important so that you can deal with them first [2] I start thinking of things not connected to my studies [3] read or study again [4] e.g. a very short poem or a special word used to help you remember something [5] forming an image in your mind [6] think of a lot of ideas very quickly before considering some of them more carefully [7] diagram or drawing showing how different ideas on a topic are related [8] text containing all the main ideas but not in a fully developed form [9] (often used with a negative association) learning something so you can repeat it from memory, rather than understand it [10] in such a way that you can say it from memory [11] not exact or detailed; approximate [12] you cannot remember a particular thing, or you cannot remember anything

Exercises

21.1 Match the first part of the word combination on the left with the second part on the right.

meet	to-do	extra-curricular	study
time	long-term	lecture	note-
request	first	rote	draw

activities	an extension	loan	draft
deadlines	learning	plan	management
mind maps	list	taking	notes

21.2 Complete each sentence with a word combination from 21.1.

1 I always try to _____ but this time I'm afraid I'm going to have to _____ . If only I could stick to the _____ I make at the beginning of every semester!
2 You should show the _____ of your essay to your tutor before you do any more work on it.
3 Helena missed the class but she borrowed the _____ from a friend.
4 Some people find it more helpful to _____ when they are studying than to take traditional notes.
5 This is an incredibly useful book. Fortunately, I've been able to take it out of the library on _____ .
6 Students who are working part-time as well as studying have to be particularly good at _____ .
7 Some students get distracted from their studies by all the _____ which most universities offer.
8 I always make a _____ when I'm getting ready to go on a trip.
9 _____ is often considered a very old-fashioned way of learning nowadays.
10 _____ is very important during lectures; you can't remember everything.

21.3 Answer these questions about study habits.

1 Can you think of an example of a mnemonic?
2 If you were brainstorming some good study habits, what would you write down?
3 In your opinion, what sorts of things are useful to learn by heart?
4 When do you start cramming before an exam?
5 Does your mind ever wander when you are studying? If so, what do you start thinking about?
6 Have you ever experienced your mind going blank during an exam?
7 Do you try to prioritise certain types of work? Which types?
8 Why is it a good idea to make rough notes before answering an exam question?

21.4 Here are some more useful words relating to study habits. Say in your own words what each expression in bold means. Use a dictionary to help you if necessary.

> ## University Library: Notice to all undergraduates
>
> Undergraduates are reminded that all books **on loan** must be **returned** by noon on June 30th, 2008. **Overdue** items will **incur** a fine of 50 cents per day. Failure to clear fines and overdue books may result in loss of **borrowing rights**. Additional regulations apply to **inter-library loans** (see the University Library web pages).
>
> University **Librarian**

 Ask some of your fellow students about their study habits using the questions from the questionnaire on the opposite page.

22 Online learning

A   What is online learning?

What makes studying online different from **face-to-face** study is that it uses the internet as the primary **means of communication**. Learning is often organised through a **virtual learning environment (VLE)**[1]. This provides discussion areas and **links** to **readings** and other **resources** as well as letting students **submit assignments**[2] **electronically** and take **quizzes** online. Online courses are often **collaborative**[3] with students **posting messages**[4] for each other to read and working together to **construct knowledge**[5]. As a result students in **virtual**[6] **classrooms** develop a sense of being part of an **online community** and feel much less isolated than they might in traditional **distance courses**[7]. The teacher's role is to **set appropriate tasks**, to **moderate**[8] discussions and to **provide feedback**[9]. Teachers may also conduct **online tutorials**[10].

[1] software that allows staff and students to interact (e.g. WebCT or Blackboard) [2] hand in essays or other work [3] involve students working together [4] making a contribution to an online discussion [5] build up understanding of the topic [6] online [7] courses where the student studies at home using materials sent by the academic institution [8] gently control, by asking questions and encouraging learners to make connections [9] comment on students' work [10] teaching sessions for individuals or small groups of students

B   Key terms

term	meaning	word combinations
hybrid/blended course	a course that combines both online and face-to-face (f2f) teaching and learning	enrol on a hybrid/blended course take/do a hybrid/blended course
a (mailing) list	online discussion group managed through a software program – each message or contribution is sent to a common email, then forwarded to all members	post a message to a list subscribe to a list[1] unsubscribe from a list[2]
discussion forum	area of website or VLE where you can post a message for other participants to read and reply to	participate / take part in a discussion forum
username	form of your name the software recognises and so lets you go further – it can be case-sensitive[3]	enter your username
a thread	an ordered row of comments in a discussion forum on a specific topic	start a new thread contribute to a thread follow a thread

[1] join a list [2] leave a list [3] the use of upper and lower case letters must exactly match what was entered as the username when setting up the account [upper case = capital letters]

C   Netiquette [rules for effective online communication]

- Reread your message before **hitting send**.
- Use an appropriate **subject header**.
- In a mailing list '**lurk** before you leap', i.e. observe the conventions others use before joining a discussion yourself.
- Obey the **KISS** principle (Keep it Short and Simple).
- Don't **flame** other posters. [be very rude to other members of an online group]

 TIP Could you do well as an online student? Read the profile of a virtual student at www.virtualstudent.com/html/profile.html. Note any useful vocabulary there.

Exercises

22.1 Look at A and fill in the gaps in this email from a student on an online course.

> Hi Jean,
>
> My online course is brilliant. We use Moodle which is VLE software – that means (1) .... learning environment. You get to know the other students well even though the web's our only (2) .... of communication. I really feel I'm part of an online (3) .... It's also great as you don't have to go to the library – all the readings and other (4) .... are online and there are (5) .... to them in Moodle – just click and you've got them. We work in groups – the teacher sets various collaborative (6) .... and then provides (7) .... on our work. We have to take a (8) .... every week but it's just a set of easy multiple-choice questions. At the end of the course we have to (9) .... a big assignment. Anyway, it's really fun.
>
> Ellen

22.2 Match the first part of the expression from the left-hand box with the second part on the right.

construct	post	from a mailing list	a new thread
enrol	start	in a discussion group	knowledge
enter	subscribe	the send button	messages
hit	take part	to a mailing list	your username
moderate	unsubscribe	discussions	on a hybrid course

22.3 Now choose word combinations from 22.2 to complete these sentences. Change the verb form where necessary.

1 When you log on you will be asked to .... and password.
2 A long time ago I .... for marine engineers. I don't want to receive messages from it any more but now I can't remember how to ....
3 I really enjoy .... for language teachers and yesterday I .... about teaching grammar online.
4 I decided to .... as I thought it would be good to experience a course with both online and face-to-face elements.
5 You will save yourself a lot of embarrassment if you get into the habit of always rereading what you've written before .... and ....
6 Online instructors must be good at .... so students can work together to ....

22.4 Answer these questions.

1 How would you feel if someone flamed you? Why would you feel like that?
2 Are your computer usernames and passwords case-sensitive?
3 Why do you think the KISS principle is important for online posts?
4 Is lurking online a good or a bad thing? Why?
5 Why is it important to choose subject headers carefully?
6 Have you any experience of being in a virtual classroom? What was it like?

 FOLLOW UP Use an online search engine (such as Google or Yahoo!) to do a search on *online courses* + the subject you are interested in. Click on one of the links it finds. Note any interesting vocabulary relating to online study that you find on that site.

23 Sources

A Referring to source materials

Look at these extracts where the writers are talking about their sources. Although these writers occasionally use 'I', many academic departments advise against doing this in writing if possible.

> This paper begins with **a review of the literature on**[1] patient communication. **The medical literature suggests** that patients with serious illnesses tend to communicate poorly, especially if the disease is not considered by the patient to be particularly threatening.

[1] a summary and evaluation of all the important works written on a particular subject

> This essay **draws its data** from the most important **primary source**[2] of information on manufacturing in Nigeria: the Central Bank of Nigeria. I shall **make reference**[3] to this source throughout this essay. Several recent **secondary sources**[4] were also **consulted**.

[2] an original document or set of documents giving information about a subject [3] slightly more formal alternative to *refer to* [4] books or articles about a subject, not original documents

> For this project, I consulted the county **archives**[5] in an attempt to explain why there were so many deaths in 1846 and 1847. These proved a **valuable resource**. I also **surveyed the literature on**[6] agricultural production during the 1840s. However, I only directly **cite**[7] those works which are particularly relevant in **the present study**.

[5] a collection of documents of historical importance [6] searched for all the important works, summarised and evaluated them [7] refer to for illustration or proof

> An **extensive body of literature**[8] **exists** on the effects of wildfires[9]. Wildfires have burned across the western United States for centuries, but their effects are not fully known or **documented**[10]. The present study **draws primarily on**[11] the work of Gordon (1996).

[8] also 'body of knowledge'; note how it combines with *extensive* and *exist* [9] fires starting naturally, not caused by human action [10] written about [11] uses information mainly from

> **As noted**[12] in a recent report, Australia has been at the forefront of developments in e-learning. This success **is often attributed to**[13] Australia's geographical position, but the factors **catalogued**[14] in the report reveal a more complex picture.

[12] given special mention [13] people often say that this is the cause [14] recorded, listed

B More ways of referring to sources

Beeching's **seminal**[1] work **laid the foundations**[2] for the field of functional analysis. Keynes's ideas **were set out**[3] in his book, *The General Theory of Employment, Interest and Money*, published in 1936. This work changed the way we look at how economies function. **Elsewhere**[4], Keynes claimed to be developing classical economic theory.
Design of compact heat exchangers **is dealt with** in **Appendix** A of the report, **treated**[5] separately from the **main body**[6] of the report.

[1] important and original work from which other works grow [2] created the first ideas from which a major set of ideas grew [3] gave all the details of his ideas, or explained them clearly (especially used about writing) [4] in another work by him [5] more formal version of *deal with* [6] the main part

Exercises

23.1 **Match the beginning of each sentence with the most appropriate ending.**

1 The letters proved to be a valuable   study, which focuses on metals only.
2 An extensive body of literature   body of the book; they are in the appendix.
3 Newspapers are a good primary   the literature on intellectual property rights.
4 The data are not given in the main   exists on human to animal communication.
5 Plastics are not dealt with in the present   source for the period 1980–1985.
6 The thesis begins with a review of   resource for the study of the poet's life.

23.2 **Rewrite the sentences using the word in brackets.**

1 The article refers to the work of Hindler and Swartz (1988). (MAKES)
2 Schunker's book was a useful critique for understanding the pre-war period. I also consulted original government papers. (SECONDARY)
3 Tanaka's book uses data from several Japanese articles on galaxy formation. (DRAWS)
4 In a different paper, Kallen reports on his research into cancer rates among farm workers. (ELSEWHERE)
5 Han consulted the documents of historical importance in the Vienna Museum. (ARCHIVES)

23.3 **Complete the table. Use a dictionary if necessary. Do not fill in the shaded boxes.**

noun	verb	adjective	adverb
	attribute		
document			
	consult		
		primary	
catalogue			
foundation			
note			
	suggest		
		extensive	
	cite		

23.4 **Look at this advice about plagiarism [pronounced /ˈpleɪdʒˀrɪzˀm/, the serious offence of using other people's work while pretending it is your own, without clearly acknowledging the source of that information] given to students by an American university. Underline words and phrases which mean:**

1 Expressing the same message in different words
2 Things known by everyone
3 Stating that one has obtained one's information from that source
4 Direct repetition of what someone has written or said
5 Stating that you have benefited from someone's work

> ### How can students avoid plagiarism?
> To avoid plagiarism, you must give credit by acknowledging your source whenever you use:
> → another person's idea, opinion, or theory;
> → any facts, statistics, graphs, drawings – any pieces of information – that are not common knowledge;
> → quotations of another person's actual spoken or written words; or
> → a paraphrase of another person's spoken or written words.

24 Facts, evidence and data

Being able to use the vocabulary in this unit well will help you avoid repetition in your writing.

A Countable or uncountable nouns

Fact is a countable noun and **evidence** is uncountable – you can refer to one **piece of evidence** or to the **body of evidence** [large amount of evidence].

Some people consider **data** as a plural noun – *these data show an unexpected trend* – while others consider it as uncountable – *this data differs from last year's. This is a particularly interesting piece/item of data*. The tendency is increasingly to use **data** as an uncountable noun but you will see both forms and may use it whichever way you prefer yourself.

B Words often used with facts, evidence and data

Researchers try to **establish the facts**. They hope that **the facts will bear out**[1] or **support their hypothesis**. Most carefully **check their facts** before **presenting** them to others although there are, of course, dishonest people prepared to **distort**[2] **the facts** in order to claim that their facts are **interesting, relevant**[3], **undeniable** or **little-known**.

[1] confirm [2] change [3] connected to the topic being discussed

Notice how *fact* is also often used in sentences like the following:
It is hard to **account for the fact that**[4] share prices rose over this period.
The problem **stems from the fact that**[5] there is a basic conflict of interests.
The lecturer **drew attention to the fact that**[6] the economy was starting to improve.

[4] explain why [5] has arisen because [6] emphasised that

Researchers may **look for, collect, examine** and **consider evidence**. The **evidence** they collect may **point to** or **suggest** a conclusion. If the evidence is **growing** or **widespread** it may serve to **support** a theory. In writing up their research they aim to **provide** or **offer** sufficient evidence to support their theories. They are happy if the evidence they find is **convincing** or **powerful** and are less happy if the evidence is **flimsy**[7] or **conflicting**[8]. They are pleased if **new evidence comes to light**[9] or **emerges** and if they find **abundant**[10] evidence. They may talk about finding **hard evidence**[11].

[7] not strong [8] contradictory [9] becomes known, see Unit 9 [10] plenty of [11] evidence which is reliable and can be proven, used mainly in spoken in English

The data is	reliable[12]. comprehensive[13]. accurate. empirical[14].	You	obtain organise analyse data. interpret record	Data	suggests reflects indicates something. shows demonstrates

[12] can be trusted [13] full, complete [14] based on observation rather than theory

C Giving examples

You often need to **give** or **provide an example** to **illustrate the facts** you're presenting. A good example can be described as **striking, clear, vivid, illuminating** or **telling**. Sometimes, particularly in written English, the word **instance** is used as an alternative to **example**. *There is a striking instance of the author's use of metaphor in the final poem. We shall now analyse one specific instance of this problem.* **Say** can be used in informal English instead of *for example. Try and finish writing the report by, say, next Friday.*

> **TIP**
> There are many verbs in English which can be spelt either *-ise/-yse* or *-ize/-yze* depending on whether the writer is using British English or American English spelling. See Reference 4.

Exercises

24.1 Fill the gaps in this extract from a university seminar on forest conservation. Some students are questioning aspects of a presentation given by Sandra, one of the group. The first letter of each missing word is given to help you.

Aidan: I enjoyed your presentation, and you've e_____ some interesting facts about the loss of forests year on year, and it's u_____ that tropical forests are in danger. But I think the evidence you o_____ for your claim that sustainable forest exploitation is failing is very f_____ and not very c_____ at all. We need to c_____ a lot more data. Right now there's a lot of c_____ evidence, so we can't say for certain that it's not working.

Sandra: If you want h_____ evidence, just look at the International Tropical Timber Organisation, and read their latest report. Their evidence d_____ that only three per cent of tropical forests are being managed properly.

Petra: Well, I've read the ITTO report, and actually it d_____ attention to the fact that their previous report had found only *one* per cent of forests were properly managed, so you may be d_____ the facts a little by just looking at one year. And also, there's a lot of l_____-k_____ work being done with local people to encourage them to conserve the forests, so you could say there's g_____ evidence that things are getting *better*.

Dr Li: Hmm, I don't think we're going to agree on this. I think, as usual, it's a question of how you i_____ the data. Thanks, anyway, for your presentation, Sandra.

24.2 The sentences below are correct. Vary them by substituting the words in bold for words or expressions with similar meanings.

1 The data **show** that the drug education project has been successful.
2 The data in the latest study are more **complete** than in the earlier one.
3 This is the most interesting **piece** of data in the whole thesis.
4 What a **clear** example this is of the power of the human mind!
5 Unfortunately, the facts do not **bear out** the hypothesis.
6 We cannot **explain** the fact that attitudes are more negative now than five years ago.
7 The problem **arises** from the fact that the software was poorly designed.
8 The article **gives** examples of different methods which have been used over the years.
9 New evidence has **emerged** that the cabinet was not informed of the Minister's decision.
10 We need to **examine** the evidence before we can reach a conclusion.
11 The evidence suggesting that sanctions do not work is **plentiful** and **very strong**.
12 A considerable **amount** of evidence now exists, but we always try to **get** more.
13 We have a lot of **observed** data which suggest the problem is on the increase.
14 This is a clear **example** of how conservation can benefit local people.

24.3 One word in each sentence does not fit the sentence. Which is it?

1 Thorsen's aim was to *establish / check / bear out / present* the facts.
2 The evidence *suggests / points to / supports / emerges* a different conclusion.
3 Lopez *collected / reflected / obtained / recorded* some fascinating data.
4 The writer provides some *growing / telling / striking / illuminating* examples.
5 The evidence Mistry presents is *convincing / flimsy / vivid / conflicting*.

 FOLLOW UP Look at any text from your discipline and see what words are used with *facts*, *data* and *evidence*. Are they the same as the ones in this unit? Note any different ones.

25 Numbers

A Types of numbers

Numbers in a group together may be called a **series** or **set of numbers**. If the order in which they occur is significant then they may be called a **sequence of numbers**. 1, 4, 9, 16, 25 is a sequence of numbers, for example – it represents the numbers 1 to 5 **squared**.

1, 3, 5, 7 … = **odd numbers**; 2, 4, 6, 8 … = **even numbers**; 2, 3, 5, 7, 11 … = **prime numbers**. The highest number in a group is the **maximum** and the lowest is the **minimum**. *The room holds a **maximum** of 50 and we won't run the class without a **minimum** of 12 students.*

An **approximate** number is one which is roughly correct but is not the **precise** or **exact number**. *Look at the figures and work out in your head what the **approximate** answer is likely to be. Then use a calculator to find the **exact number**.*

An **aggregate** is a number reached by totalling a set of numbers = the **total**. *The **average** mark achieved in the exam is calculated by taking the **aggregate** of all the marks and dividing by the number of exam entries.*

A **discrete** number or unit is something which is separate and cannot be divided into smaller numbers or units of the same thing. The opposite of discrete is **continuous**. A bag of apples, for example, could be considered as consisting of discrete items whereas apple sauce could be considered – by mathematicians, at least – as continuous.

A **constant** number or quantity is one that does not change. *In the experiment we **varied** [changed] the amount of water in the beaker but kept the amount of salt added **constant**.* A **random number** is one chosen by chance, i.e. it is not predictable.

B Working with numbers

The word **figure** is often used to refer to the symbol used for a number. *Write the total number in words and **figures**.*
Verbs that are frequently used with the word **number** include **calculate** [work out] a number, **estimate**[1] a number, round a number up/down[2], **total** [add up] a set of numbers. Numbers can also **tally**[3]. *My figures don't seem to **tally** with yours.* You can also **deduct** [take away, subtract] one number from another number.

[1] make a rough guess at   [2] make a **fraction**, e.g. $\frac{1}{6}$ or 0.78 into the nearest **whole number**
[3] match, agree

Values and **variables** are also useful terms when working with numbers. **Values** are individual numbers in a set of data. *The graph shows the temperature **values** for different months of the year.* **Variables** are characteristics that can take on different values for different members of a group or set being studied. *In investigating living standards you must take key **variables** such as social provision and cost of living into account.*

The **incidence** of something refers to how frequently it occurs. *The **incidence** of twins in the population is growing.* When talking about numbers, **magnitude** simply refers to the size of something, whereas in other contexts it indicates large size or importance. *Write down the numbers **in order of magnitude**, beginning with the smallest.*

When **making calculations** in, say, an exam, it is often a good idea to make an **estimate**[4] first of what the answer is likely to be. Then you will see if your final answer is **in the right area**[5] or not. Exam candidates are also often advised to **show their workings**[6] so that the marker can see how they **arrived at their answer** and they may get credit for their method even if the final answer is incorrect.

[4] rough guess   [5] approximately the same   [6] leave all their calculations on the page

Exercises

25.1 **Answer these questions.**

1 What is five squared?
2 What is the next prime number after 19?
3 How is this sequence of numbers created? 3, 9, 27, 81
4 What is the aggregate of this set of test marks? 6, 8, 9, 5, 6, 7
5 If you round up 6.66, what number do you have?
6 $\frac{7}{9}$ and 4 – which is a whole number and which is a fraction?
7 In your country is tax automatically deducted from employees' earnings?
8 Is an accountant pleased or displeased if figures that he/she is checking tally?

25.2 **Dr Syal is advising one of his dissertation students who is interested in pollution in road tunnels. Complete the conversation. You are sometimes given the first letter to help you.**

Dr Syal: You could c＿＿＿＿＿ the total number of private cars that use the tunnel each week, based on the day-to-day figures, and get an a＿＿＿＿＿ figure for how much carbon they're all emitting.

Melissa: How p＿＿＿＿＿ would that figure have to be?

Dr Syal: Oh, it doesn't have to be exact, you just need to e＿＿＿＿＿ more or less what the total pollution will be. Then you can check to see if those figures t＿＿＿＿＿ with the figures that have already been published for similar tunnels. And the figure won't be c＿＿＿＿＿ of course; it'll go up and down depending on lots of factors such as weather conditions, average speed, etc.

Melissa: But can we say if the figures will be true for the future too?

Dr Syal: Well, we do know that the traffic growth has been c＿＿＿＿＿ over the past ten years; it hasn't ever gone down, so I think you can make some useful predictions.

Melissa: Should I present each daily total as a d＿＿＿＿＿ item or can I just put them all together into one figure for each week?

Dr Syal: A weekly total is fine, and you can ＿＿＿＿＿ it up or ＿＿＿＿＿ to the nearest 100.

Melissa: Right, OK. Thanks so much for your help.

25.3 **Rewrite these spoken sentences so that they are more appropriate for writing, using the word in italics in an appropriate form.**

1 There were fewer car accidents last year. *incidence*
2 We made a rough guess at what the final figure might be. *estimate*
3 The graph shows the results from the lowest to the highest. *magnitude*
4 A computer program helped us work out the significance of the different variables. *calculate*
5 Taking x away from y will help you arrive at the correct answer. *subtract*
6 The results from the first experiment were not the same as those we got from the repeat experiment. *tally*

25.4 **Fill in the gaps in this advice a maths lecturer is giving her students.**

In the exam, don't forget to show all your (1) ＿＿＿＿＿ as we want to see how you (2) ＿＿＿＿＿ at your results. Make your (3) ＿＿＿＿＿ very carefully – you'd be amazed at how many people submit answers that are hardly even in the right (4) ＿＿＿＿＿ . And please write legibly – we must be able to distinguish all your (5) ＿＿＿＿＿ ! When doing graphs, plot your (6) ＿＿＿＿＿ carefully and if asked to describe an experiment don't forget to take all significant (7) ＿＿＿＿＿ into account. Good luck!

FOLLOW UP Find some examples of the use of numbers in your own subject area. Note down some interesting phrases or sentences.

26 Statistics

A Basic statistical terms

Notice the key vocabulary in these three short texts about statistics.

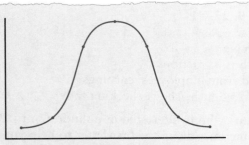

A **normal distribution** of data means that most of the examples in a **set of data** are close to the average, while relatively few examples tend to one extreme or the other. Normally distributed data shown on a chart will typically show a **bell curve**. It will often be necessary to work out the extent to which individuals **deviate**[1] **from the norm**[2] and to calculate the figure that represents **standard deviation**[3].

Six children are 7, 8, 8, 8, 11 and 12 years old. Their **average** age is 9 years old (the **sum** of their ages divided by six). The **mode** (the most frequent value) is 8. The **median** is 9.5 (the **halfway point** between the two **extremes** of the **range**).

Statisticians are often concerned with working out **correlations**[4] – the extent to which, say, left-handedness **correlates with** intelligence. They must ensure that any data they collect is **valid**, i.e. that it is measuring what it claims to measure – all the subjects in the **sample**[5] must be appropriately and accurately assessed as left- or right-handed, for example. The figures must also be **reliable**, i.e. they would be **consistent**[6] if the measurements were repeated. Usually, statisticians hope that their calculations will **show/indicate a tendency**, e.g. that left-handed people will be shown to be **significantly**[7] more intelligent than right-handed people.

[1] differ [2] the average [3] average difference from the norm [4] connections, often as cause and effect [5] the subjects of the experiment or group representing the total population measured [6] the same [7] noticeably

B A probability[1] problem

Notice the vocabulary in this problem from a statistics textbook.

Sue picks a card **at random**[2] from an ordinary pack of 52 cards. If the card is a king, she stops. If not, she continues to pick cards at random, without replacing them, until either a king is picked or six cards have been picked. The random **variable**[3], C, is the total number of cards picked. Construct a **diagram** to illustrate the possible **outcomes**[4] of the experiment, and use it to calculate the **probability distribution**[5] of C.

[1] likelihood of something happening [2] by chance [3] number or element of a situation that can change [4] results [5] assessment of probabilities for each possible value of C

C Other useful nouns for talking about statistics

In a class of 8 women and 4 men, what **proportion**[1] are male? Answer: one third
In the same class what is the female to male **ratio**[2]? Answer: 2:1
The figures show a **trend**[3] towards healthier eating habits.
The study investigates the increase in the **volume**[4] of traffic on the roads.

[1] number compared with another number [2] relationship between two numbers showing how much bigger one is [3] change in a particular direction [4] amount, quantity

ERROR WARNING We say 10 **per cent** (NOT ~~the 10 per cent~~ or ~~10 percentage~~) of students got an A for their exam but the **percentage** of students achieving an A has increased.

Exercises

26.1 Complete the sentences.

1 The six subjects who took the test scored 24, 22, 16, 16, 16, and 14 points out of 30. The .... was 16. The .... score was 19 and the .... score was 18.
2 The .... of all donations to the charity in 2003 was $3,938. The smallest donation was $10 and the largest was $130. Most were around the .... point of $60.
3 Each questionnaire item asked respondents to choose one of a .... of six options, with the two .... being 'very dissatisfied indeed' and 'completely satisfied'.

26.2 Use the correct form of the words in the box to complete this text.

distribute	trend	significant	probable	random	correlation	outcome	vary

Life insurance companies base their calculations on the laws of .... , that is they assess the likely .... , given the different .... such as age, sex, lifestyle and medical history of their clients. The premiums are therefore not chosen at .... but are carefully calculated. The .... of ages at which death occurs and causes of death are studied to see if they .... with other factors to be taken into account in setting the premiums. Naturally, the companies also monitor social .... and react to any changes which might .... affect mortality rates.

26.3 Answer the questions.

1 There are 12 male students and 6 female students in the class. What is the **ratio** of males to females? And what **proportion** of the class is male?
2 If I am collecting data on course choices among second-year undergraduates and my **sample** is too small, what exactly do I need to do?
3 If my data show that students have a **tendency** to choose the type of clothing their friends choose, does it mean that they always, often or rarely choose similar clothes?
4 If I repeat the same experiment three times and the results are not **consistent,** is my method **reliable**?
5 If 20 out of 200 students fail an exam, what **proportion,** in percentage terms, failed?
6 If the **average score** in a test is 56, and Barbara scores 38, by how many points has she **deviated from the norm**?
7 If the **volume** of court cases increases, what changes: the type of case, the size of each case or the total number of cases?
8 What does **standard deviation** tell us? (a) What the standard of something is, (b) what the norm is, or (c) what the average difference from the norm is?
9 If a general survey of teenage eating habits asks questions about what teenagers eat for breakfast and lunch, is the survey likely to be **valid**?
10 Here is a graph showing how many students got scores within each 10-mark band in a biology test. Are the scores **normally distributed**? What is the shape of the graph called?

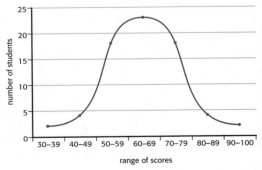

FOLLOW UP What kinds of statistical data are likely to be discussed in your discipline? Find a relevant chart, graph or table and write about it using some terms from this unit.

27 Graphs and diagrams

A Types of diagrams

 pie chart  bar chart  histogram

Number	Amount
1	10
2	5
3	20

table

cross-section

flowchart

Diagrams are visual ways of **presenting data** concisely. They are often also called **figures**. In an academic article they are usually **labelled** Fig. (Figure) 1, Fig. 2, etc. A **pie chart** is a circle divided into **segments** from the middle (like slices of a cake) to show how the total is divided up. A **key** or **legend** shows what each segment **represents**. A **bar chart** is a diagram in which different amounts are represented by thin vertical or horizontal bars which have the same width but **vary** in height or length. A **histogram** is a kind of bar chart but the bar width also varies to indicate different values. A **table** is a grid with **columns** and **rows** of numbers.

A **cross-section** is something, or a model of something, cut across the middle so that you can see the inside. A cross-section of the earth's crust, for example, shows the different **layers** that make it up. A **label** gives the name of each part of the cross-section. Cross-section can also be used to mean a small group that is representative of all the different types within the total group (e.g. *the survey looked at a cross-section of society*).

A **flowchart** is a diagram which indicates the **stages** of a process.

B A graph

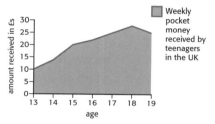

The **graph presents** data relating to teenagers and pocket money. A **random sample** of 1,000 teenagers were **surveyed** and the average pocket money received at each age has been **plotted** on the graph. The **x axis** or **horizontal axis indicates** age and the **y axis** or **vertical axis shows** the amount of money received per week. The **graph shows** that 15-year-olds receive twice as much pocket money as 13-year-olds. **From the** graph **we can see** that the amount received **reaches a peak** at the age of 18 and then starts to **decline**. This **decline** can perhaps **be explained by the fact that** many teenagers start earning and stop receiving pocket money at the age of 18.

Graphs are drawn by **plotting** points on them and then drawing a line to join **adjacent** points. If there are two lines on a graph – separate lines, for example, to indicate boys' and girls' pocket money – then the lines would probably **cross** or **intersect** at various points. Lines that **run parallel** to one another never intersect.

Graphs show how numbers **increase** or **decrease**. The nouns **increase** and **decrease** have the stress on the first syllable, but the verbs have the stress on the second syllable. Numbers can also be said to **rise** or **grow** and **fall**, **drop** or **decline**. The nouns **rise**, **growth**, **fall**, **drop** and **decline**, like **increase** and **decrease** are followed by **in** (to explain what is rising) or **of** (to explain the size of the change), e.g. *a rise of 10% in the number of cars*. Other verbs used about growth include **double**[1], **soar**[2], **multiply**[3], **appreciate**[4] and **exceed**[5].

[1] grow to twice the size; opposite = **halve** [2] (dramatic word) rapid movement upwards; opposite = **plummet** [3] grow rapidly to a very large number [4] used about the value of something, e.g. a painting or car; opposite = **depreciate** [5] go over, expresses a number in relation to another number; opposite = **fall below**

ERROR WARNING

Note that **graph** is a noun and **graphic** [relating to drawing: vivid, especially when describing something unpleasant] is usually an adjective. *The economics textbook contains a lot of fascinating **graphs**. My nephew studied **graphic** design. The book contains some very **graphic** descriptions of the massacre.* **Graphics** can be used as a plural noun to refer to pictorial material, e.g. *The **graphics** in that computer game are brilliant.*

Exercises

27.1 Look at the chart. Complete the commentary with words from the opposite page.

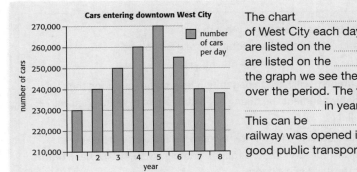

Cars entering downtown West City

The chart _____ the number of cars entering the downtown area of West City each day over an eight-year period (years 1–8). The totals are listed on the _____ axis (*give two answers*), while the years are listed on the _____ axis (*give two answers*). To the right of the graph we see the _____. The number of cars _____ over the period. The total rose in the first few years and _____ a _____ in year 5, after which the numbers started to _____. This can be _____ by the _____ that a new mass transit railway was opened in year 6, which is a _____ illustration of how good public transport can dramatically affect car use.

27.2 Answer the questions.

1 Draw examples of a pie chart and a bar chart.
2 What would be the best type of diagram to present the different layers of rock in the Grand Canyon?
3 In a table, what is the difference between columns and rows?
4 What would be the best type of diagram to present the different stages in a research project you did?
5 How many segments are there in the pie chart opposite?
6 If you look at two adjacent columns in a table, are they next to each other or separated?
7 What is another name for a legend in a diagram?
8 What type of data collection are you doing if you survey the first 50 people you come across?
9 What do two lines on a graph do if (a) they intersect and (b) they run parallel to each other?

27.3 Make the rather informal words in bold sound more precise and academic.

1 The different **bits** of the pie chart show the numbers of people in each age group.
2 She kept a record by **marking** the midday temperature on a graph for a month.
3 People's salaries usually reach their **highest point** when they are in their late 40s.
3 This flowchart shows the different **bits** of our project over the next five years.
5 The two lines on the graph **cross each other** at point A.
6 Draw a line connecting the points that are **next** to each other.
7 The government's popularity in the opinion polls is beginning to **fall**.
8 If you look along the top **line** of the table you can see the figures for the 1950s.

27.4 Change the sentences using words with the same meanings as the words in bold.

1 Populations of some bird species in South Asia have **crashed** by 97% in recent years. The **number of cases** of death by poisoning has **increased** sharply.
2 In 2007 the child mortality rate **was lower than** 60 deaths per 1,000.
3 The average family car in the UK **goes down in value** by 20% per year. This means its value has **fallen by more than half** after just three years.
4 A typical piece of land on the edge of the city will **go up in value** by 15% per year, and house prices have **gone up rapidly** in the last six months.
5 Business courses have **increased greatly in number** while science programmes have **gone down**.
6 The temperature **was higher than** 45°C in some parts of the country during the heatwave.
7 Between 1983 and 2006, the number of this species of condor* **went up** from 22 pairs to 273. Other bird populations have **gone up by two times** in the same period.
8 The numbers of old soldiers attending regimental reunions are **becoming smaller** each year.

* large birds from South America

28 Money and education

A Financing your studies in the UK

- Search for funding – **are you eligible**[1] for a **scholarship** or other **award**[2]?
- Budget planner – work out your yearly **expenditure**[3] and total cost of your course.

Tuition fees[4]: From 2006/07, no full-time student will have to pay tuition fees before or during their course. Instead, students will be able to **defer payment**[5] by taking out a student loan, which they will only start to repay once they have left college.

Grants: From September 2006, new full-time students from lower income households will be able to apply for a **non-repayable maintenance grant**[6] of up to £2,700 (approximately US $5,400) a year. Grants are payable in three **instalments**[7], one at the start of each term.

Bank accounts: Student bank accounts are similar to normal **current accounts** but they also have additional benefits such as **interest-free overdrafts**[8].

Student loans: Student loans are available to help you meet your living costs while studying. The loans are fixed at a low interest rate. 75 per cent of the maximum loan is available to all students regardless of other **income**[9]. After your **entitlement**[10] has been assessed the information will be passed to the Student Loans Company who will make any payments and maintain your account.

Managing debt: Since student grants were abolished in 1998, most students struggle to **make ends meet**[11]. Student debt has **soared**[12] and many can now expect to **accumulate**[13] debts of over £10,000.

Cost of living: London is the most expensive place to study in the UK. Although students in London receive bigger loans to compensate for the increased costs, there is no variation in the amount of **financial support** available for students in other more expensive areas.

[1] do you meet the requirements [2] money available for students to get (e.g. by doing well in an exam or by fulfilling certain requirements [3] spending (AmE: expenditures) [4] what students pay for being taught [5] arrange to pay later [6] money to live on which does not need to be paid back [7] parts [8] amount that can be borrowed from the bank without paying any interest charges [9] money you receive from work or parents, for example [10] how much you can be given [11] manage financially [12] risen dramatically [13] build up

B Conference Grants for graduate students in the US

Conference Grants cover up to 60% of an applicant's **accountable expenses**[1]. The maximum Conference Grant per applicant is $700. Amounts spent in excess of a Grant allocation, even if documented with **original**[2] **receipts**[3], cannot be **reimbursed**[4].

Transportation (by the most **economical**[5] means available), **lodging**[6] (excluding food), **registration fees**[7], and expenses related to presenting a paper (photocopying, etc.) are all accountable. Restaurant bills and costs related to personal advancement, such as copying and distribution of **résumés**[8], are not accountable expenses.

[1] spending money that can be claimed back [2] not photocopies [3] pieces of paper proving money was paid [4] paid back (after money has already been spent) [5] spending as little money as possible (cf. **economic** = relating to the economy) [6] BrE: **accommodation** [7] money paid to register for a conference [8] pronounced /ˈrezʊmeɪ/; BrE: **CV**, pronounced /ˌsiːˈviː/

Exercises

28.1 Use the words from the box to fill the gaps in the text.

a grant	compensate	the cost of living	tuition fees	debt
earning	make ends meet	repay	take out loans	considerable expenditure

Few students get _____ to help them study and so many _____ while they are at university. This is because they have to pay _____. They also cannot avoid _____ on everyday life. This is particularly hard for students in London where _____ is higher than elsewhere in the country. Students living in London are allowed to have bigger loans to help _____ for this. Students do not need to start to _____ their loan until they are _____ a reasonable salary. But starting working life with a large _____ makes it much harder for young people to _____ even once they start earning.

28.2 Rewrite these sentences using the word in brackets.

1 Answer these questions to find out whether you have the right to apply for a student grant. (ELIGIBLE)
2 I've opened a bank account that I can take money out of at any time. (CURRENT)
3 Most people seem to be finding it harder to find enough money for their everyday living costs. (MEET)
4 Increasing numbers of students leave college owing a lot of money. (ACCUMULATE)
5 Parents often help their children financially while they are at university. (SUPPORT as a noun)
6 The amount of tax that people pay depends on how much money they receive from earnings or other sources. (INCOME)
7 It is possible to pay back your loan later but you may well end up paying more than you would have done if you had repaid it sooner. (DEFER)
8 You pay for your hotel first and we pay you back later. (REIMBURSE)

28.3 Correct the two vocabulary errors in each of these sentences.

1 The cost of life is so high here that students have to live in the most economic way they can.
2 As student debts have soured over the last few years, far more students now leave university with a huge overdrawn.
3 Our Student Loans Officer will let you know if you have any entitle to a loan and, if so, will help you to organise taking one off.
4 You must have original recipes if you want to claim your expense.
5 If you run out of money before the next installation of your grant is due you can get an interest-less loan.

28.4 Answer these questions about student finance.

1 Do students have to pay tuition fees for higher education in your country?
2 Should all students get a non-repayable maintenance grant to study? Why (not)?
3 What kinds of scholarships and other awards are available in your country?
4 Do you think all students should be eligible for free loans? Why (not)?

 FOLLOW UP Find a website relating to financial arrangements for students at a university you know or are interested in. Which of the words and expressions from this unit do you see there? Make a note of any other useful vocabulary you find there.

29 Time

A Periods of time

A **century** = 100 years. A **decade** = 10 years. An **annual** conference is one that happens every year. A **quarterly** journal is one that comes out four times a year. An **era** is a particular **period of time** that is marked by special events or developments, e.g. *the post-war era, an era of rapid social change*.

A **phase** is any **stage** in a **series of events** or process of development. A phase or stage can be **initial** [beginning], **intermediate** [middle] or **final**. It may also be described as **preceding** [happening before now], **current** [happening now], **critical** [particularly important] or **transitional** [in the process of change].

B Adjectives relating to time

adjective	example	meaning
concurrent	There were **concurrent** riots in several northern towns.	occurring at the same time
contemporary	I studied all the **contemporary** accounts of the battle I could find. Jo is researching **contemporary** music.	dating from the same period existing now
eventual	The **eventual** cost of the project is likely to exceed €10 million.	happening or existing later, after effort or problems
forthcoming	My article will be published in the **forthcoming** issue of the *New Scientist*.	happening soon
ongoing	Helen has a number of **ongoing** projects.	happening now
simultaneous	There were **simultaneous** concerts in several cities.	happening at the same time
subsequent	The book examines the war and the **subsequent** changes in society.	happening after something else
successive	**Successive** governments would face similar problems.	happening immediately after something else
temporary	Georgia got a **temporary** position at the university.	not for a long period; not **permanent**

C How times change

In recent times – particularly **the last 20 years** – society has **gone through a period** of considerable change. **Prior to** the 1990s very few people had access to a home computer. **Nowadays**[1] the majority of homes have at least one computer. This expansion in home computing has **coincided with**[2] **the emergence**[3] of internet technology. **At the moment** we are **at a stage** where the situation is still **evolving**[4]. Subsequent generations will live in a very different world although we do not know exactly how things will develop **over the next few years, in the near future**[5], or, least of all, **in the distant future**[6].

[1] at the present time (used to compare with the past, particularly in spoken English or more informal writing) [2] happened at the same time as [3] appearance [4] gradually changing [5] at a time which is not far away [6] far away in the future

ERROR WARNING — Some time words, e.g. **early**, **late**, **daily** can be both adverbs and adjectives, e.g. *a(n) early/late/daily meeting, we met early/late/daily*. But **nowadays** is only an adverb. We talk about *present/present-day/current problems* NOT ~~nowadays problems~~.

Exercises

29.1 Read these emails sent out to staff and postgraduate students from their university. Complete the time expressions. You are given the first letters.

1
The i................. p................. of the construction of the new sports centre will begin on 1st March. From that date until completion of the works, the West Car Park will be closed. A t................. car park will be available during the period at Campus East, and a new, p................. car park will be opened when the f................. stage of construction of the centre is completed.

2
Due to o................. technical problems, emails with large attachments may not be accepted by the university's server. This is likely to continue during the t................. period while a new server is being installed. This will reach a c................. stage next week, when problems may be greatest. We apologise for the inconvenience.

3
Please report by 29 July 2007 all publications for the c................. academic year, including f................. papers and books (with the expected date of publication). These are needed for the University's a................. report for 2007. Include any publication from the p................. year (2006) which was not published at that time but which has since appeared.

4
The University today celebrates a c................. of research. 100 years ago this month, the Centre for Medical Research was officially opened. In the last d................. alone, five major new research centres have opened, a record for a ten-year period. We look forward to the start of a new e................. of research over the n................. f................. years.

29.2 Choose the correct words in italics to complete these sentences.

1 *In / At* the moment, I'm writing up my thesis. I hope to finish in the *near / next* future.
2 Our research is *at / in* an *intermediate / ongoing* stage – we now need to analyse our data.
3 The *emergency / emergence* of internet technology has transformed the travel industry.
4 The university has *gone / got* through a period of great change in the *latest / last* decade.
5 In the *far / distant* future, scientists may be able to cure almost all common diseases.
6 Anti-social behaviour is *a nowadays problem / a problem nowadays* in many big cities.
7 A *series / serial* of events occurred in 1986 which changed the political climate in the country. In *consequent / subsequent* years, two new parties were formed which became engaged in *concurrent / eventual* attempts to win over voters.
8 Prior *of / to* 2001, the industry was unregulated. In *recent / the last* years, however, the government has introduced new regulations.
9 In 1968, a monetary crisis coincided *with / to* a huge budget deficit, and most *contemporary / temporary* political commentators warned that the *eventual / forthcoming* cost to the nation would be enormous.

29.3 Fill in the missing forms. Do not fill the shaded boxes. Use a dictionary if necessary.

noun	verb	adjective	adverb
		eventual	
		successive	
	evolve		
emergence			
	coincide		
period			

Write five sentences relevant to your discipline using forms from the table.

30 Cause and effect

Much academic study is concerned with establishing cause and effect or the relationship that exists between events, objects, variables or states of affairs. Cause and effect is often described using conjunctions like *because*, prepositions like *due to* and *because of* and adverbs like *therefore* and *consequently*. In this unit, however, we focus on nouns and verbs relating to cause and effect. Pay particular attention to the prepositions they are used with.

A Verbs relating to cause and effect

You are probably already familiar with these verbs relating to cause and effect: *make, cause, create, do, produce, force*. Here are some other useful verbs.

Her grandmother **influenced / had a considerable influence on** Sarah's choice of career.
Parental attitude **largely determines** how well a child adapts to school. [is the main factor affecting]
The teacher **motivated** them to work hard. [made them want to do something positive]
The flow of traffic through the town is **facilitated** by the one-way system. [made easier]
The speech **provoked** an angry response. [caused, usually something negative]
The explosion was **triggered** by the heat. [started, usually something sudden and negative]
The tilting of the earth on its axis **accounts for** the change in the seasons. [explains]
Sid's determination **springs/stems from** his desire to improve the world. [is the result of]
The country's victory **gave rise to** a new mood in society.
The mobile phone **contributed to** the information revolution. [was one factor influencing]
The child was given drugs to **stimulate** growth. [cause something to develop or function]
The exhibition **generated** a lot of interest. [aroused, caused to exist]
The drugs may **induce** nausea. [cause, often used in a medical context]
The teacher's presence **inhibited** the teenagers' discussion. [prevented it from being as free as it might otherwise have been]
A number of benefits can be **derived** from this situation. [gained as a result]

B Nouns relating to cause and effect

noun	example	meaning/comment
chain reaction	The incident set off a **chain reaction** which affected us all.	set of related events in which each one causes the next one
consequence	The war had major **consequences**.	results
effect, impact	The **effect/impact** of the film **on** the audience was very powerful.	influence
end	Does the **end** justify the means?	note how end here means aim
origin/source	The accident was the **origin/source of** her later problems.	beginning or cause
outcome	We hope for a positive **outcome to** the discussions.	result or effect of an action
precedent	There are several **precedents for** taking such a decision.	something that already happened and provides a reason for doing the same
reason	What was the **reason for** his success / why he succeeded?	note how reason is often followed by for or why

ERROR WARNING

While **cause** can be both a noun and a verb, **effect** is usually a noun. The equivalent verb is **affect**. *Her father's problems **affected** her deeply. Her father's problems **had a profound effect** on her.* Note the formal and infrequent verb **effect** [= achieve], mainly used in the phrase to **effect a change**. (See also Unit 3.)

Exercises

30.1 Replace the underlined words with a more precise verb of cause or effect. Note that all the sentences below are appropriate for essays apart perhaps from 6 with its use of 'got'.

1 Researchers are investigating why chocolate <u>causes</u> headaches in certain people.
2 Wilson's most recent paper has <u>caused</u> a great deal of interest among sociologists.
3 The drug <u>caused</u> headaches and dizziness among a number of subjects in the test.
4 Having an end-of-term prize <u>helps</u> students to do well in their class tests.
5 Intensive farming has <u>been a significant factor in</u> the decline of bird populations.
6 The missile test <u>got</u> an immediate and very strong response from adjacent governments and from the United Nations.
7 Astrologists believe that people's lives are <u>largely affected</u> by the planets and stars.
8 The barrier <u>affects</u> the flow of water into the area to prevent flooding in the rainy season.
9 A leak in the tank <u>explained</u> 40% of the fuel loss, and evaporation took away another 5%.
10 The renovated college buildings have wider doors and corridors to <u>make</u> the use of wheelchairs <u>easier</u>.
11 The Minister cut taxes in an attempt to <u>affect</u> the economy, which was performing poorly.
12 Britain has <u>received</u> many economic benefits from membership of the European Union.

30.2 Match the beginning of each sentence with the most appropriate ending.

1 The article explores the origins   major consequences for larger families.
2 One small explosion set off a chain   precedents for his decision.
3 The confusion probably stemmed   rise to a widespread sense of disillusionment.
4 The proposed new tax could have   of the concept of democracy.
5 The disastrous events of 2003 gave   reaction, causing massive damage.
6 The judge explained that there were   from a lack of communication.

30.3 Choose the correct word in italics to complete these sentences.

1 De Routa's work in the 1970s influenced *on / to / –* the development of computer science.
2 The acid seemed to have no *affect / effect* whatsoever on the plastic.
3 Everyone hoped for a positive outcome *upon / off / to* the meeting between the two governments.
4 The reason *for / to / of* the failure of the project was a lack of funding.
5 The impact of global warming *for / on / to* the polar ice caps is now understood more clearly.
6 The journalist wondered what particular *ending / end* the government had in mind when it decided to build a national tennis academy.

30.4 What are the nouns from the same root as these verbs? Use a dictionary if necessary.

motivate   facilitate   influence   provoke   trigger   contribute   stimulate   induce   derive

30.5 Now rewrite these sentences using a noun instead of the verb.

1 Byron's poetry influenced Romantic poets in a number of other European countries.
2 Tree pollen can trigger hay fever attacks in vulnerable people.
3 In obstetrics the drug can be used to help induce labour.
4 The new economic measures were introduced to stimulate the faltering economy.
5 Tomoko is studying what motivates world-class athletes.

> **FOLLOW UP** Find a text describing a major event or series of events (e.g. an accident, a war, a social change) and note all the verbs and nouns in it relating to causes and effects or results. Write your own example sentences using these words.

31 Talking about ideas

A Postmodernism

Look at the useful language for talking about ideas in the description of one idea below.

Postmodernism describes a **movement**[1] of intellectual **thought**[2] which has had a major impact on a number of academic **disciplines**[3] since the late 20th century. Perhaps the best way to understand postmodernism is as a **reaction**[4] to modernism. Modernism **emphasises** purity, honesty and total truth; for example, when an artist attempts to express the **essence**[5] of a whole subject with a single line. In contrast, postmodernism asserts that experience is personal and cannot be **generalised**[6] and that meaning is only for the individual to experience, not for someone else to dictate. Thus, postmodernists maintain that the person who, for example, admires a painting or reads a poem is free to **interpret** its meaning, and that different people will come to very different, but equally **valid**[7], conclusions as to what that meaning is.

[1] group of people sharing aims or beliefs [2] thinking in general [3] subjects [4] process of change stimulated by something else, often moving in the opposite direction [5] the most important quality or characteristics [6] presented as something that is always true [7] appropriate

> **TIP**
>
> A number of words that are useful for talking about ideas have irregular plurals – **criterion/criteria, phenomenon/phenomena, hypothesis/hypotheses, analysis/analyses, thesis/theses**. They all originate from Ancient Greek. Perhaps this sentence will help you remember them. *There are several different **hypotheses** which claim to explain these **phenomena** and in his doctoral **thesis** Kohl offers an **analysis** of each **hypothesis** in accordance with a rigorous set of **criteria**.*

B Some useful nouns relating to ideas

word	meaning	example
concept	principle, idea	The **concept** of honesty is understood differently in different cultures.
framework	system of rules, beliefs or ideas used as the basis for something	Mary is working on an analytical **framework** to help people design and evaluate training courses.
model	simple description useful for discussing ideas	The writer uses a Marxist **model** as the basis for his discussion of the economy.
notion	belief, idea	She doesn't agree with the **notion** that boys and girls should be taught separately.
perception	belief, opinion, held by many people	The novel had a powerful impact on people's **perception** of the war.
stance	way of thinking, often publicly stated	The government has made their **stance** on the boycott issue clear.
viewpoint	opinion, way of looking at an issue	The article provides a different **viewpoint** on this difficult topic.

> **ERROR WARNING**
>
> In academic writing it is best to avoid *In my opinion* and to use a less personal expression like **It can be argued that ...** or **Most (people) would agree that ...**
> You **discuss** an idea or talk/write about an idea but NOT ~~discuss about an idea~~.

Exercises

31.1 Replace the words in bold with words from A with similar meanings.

1 Many educators believe that different learning styles are equally **acceptable**.
2 In the UK a university faculty is a unit where similar **subjects** are grouped together.
3 The French impressionists were a key **group with shared aims** in European art.
4 The **most important quality** of international law is the application of a single standard for strong and weak nations alike.
5 Researchers spend much of their time trying to **understand the meaning of** their data.
6 Some 19th century artistic styles were a **direct response** to the ugliness of industrialisation.
7 Harvey (2003) **stresses** that the findings of the study cannot be **said to be always true**, as only a small amount of data was used.
8 In the late 20th century, intellectual **ways of thinking** were greatly influenced by ideas of gender and race.

31.2 Change the words in bold from singular to plural or vice versa, as instructed. Make any other necessary changes to each sentence.

1 There's **an interesting PhD thesis** on water resources in the library. (make plural)
2 What were your main **criteria** in designing your survey? (make singular)
3 She was interested in strange **phenomena** connected with comets. (make singular)
4 The **hypothesis** was never proved, as the data were incomplete. (make plural)

31.3 Match the beginning of each sentence with the most appropriate ending.

1 We must never accept the notion	on the role of the United Nations in times of war.
2 The task of choosing an analytical	on gender and language use very clear.
3 The book expresses his viewpoint	of dark matter to explain certain observations.
4 Tannen has always made her stance	that intelligence is connected to race.
5 Consumers have different perceptions	of family healthcare which changed everything.
6 The report laid out a new model	of what low price and high quality mean.
7 Physicists developed the concept	framework is an important stage in any research.

31.4 Read the text and then answer the questions. Use a dictionary if necessary.

> Autonomy and creativity are two key concepts in the humanities which are often thought to be not part of scientific thinking. However, recent projects in the sciences suggest this is not true. For example, the attempt to load the components of human consciousness into a computer is a fundamentally creative activity which has profound implications for our understanding of what a human being is. Such science may make us change our way of thinking about moral and philosophical questions and may make it possible for those in the humanities to find a new grounding for their own work.

1 Which noun means 'independence / the right to think in one's own way'?
2 Which noun means the opposite of 'the sciences'?
3 Which adjective means 'felt or experienced very strongly or in an extreme way'?
4 What are the noun forms of *think* and *understand* used in this text?
5 Which adjective in the text means 'relating to standards of good or bad behaviour, what is right and wrong, etc.'?
6 Which noun in the text means the same as 'foundation/basis'?

 Choose five words that you particularly want to learn from this unit and write sentences using them in relation to your own discipline.

32 Reporting what others say

A Reporting verbs

Reporting what others say is a key aspect of academic English and you need a range of verbs to do this in an appropriate and varied way. Note the structures used with each verb.

In her latest article Morton **explains** how information technology is changing society.
Schmidt **describes** the process of language change.
Kon **suggests** that all poets are strongly influenced by their childhood. [says indirectly or tentatively]
Lee **states** that problems arose earlier than was previously thought. [says directly]
Uvarov **claims/asserts/contends/maintains/declares** that the causes of the revolution can be traced back to the 18th century. [says something is true directly and firmly, often used when others disagree]
Van Ek **implies** that other historians have misinterpreted the period. [suggests indirectly]
Patel **argues** that governments should continue to fund space research. [use of this verb suggests he gives reasons for his view]
Greenberg **emphasises/highlights/stresses** the importance of taking a liberal approach. [gives particular importance to]
Levack **observes/notes/comments/points out** that there are contradictions in Day's interpretation of the poem. [states but does not develop at length]
Kim **demonstrates/shows** how Bach's music draws considerably on earlier composers' work.
Gray **proves** there is a link between obesity and genes. [shows that something must be true]
In the book Dean **mentions** some new research in the field. [refers to briefly]
McIntosh **pinpoints** the key features of the period in question. [focuses in on]
Vaz **advances/puts forward/proposes** a new theory. [used with idea, theory, hypothesis]
Davidson **casts doubt on** previous research in the field. [suggests it is inaccurate]
Gerhard **questions** previous interpretations of the play. [expresses doubts about]

B Reporting nouns

Academic writing also frequently uses nouns rather than verbs to report others' ideas (see Unit 1). Notice the corresponding nouns for some verbs in A. Note how these nouns often head long phrases (underlined below) which can be either the subject or the object of the verb.

Morton **provides** <u>an explanation as to how information technology is changing society</u>.
Schmidt **gives** <u>a description of the process of language change</u>.
Kon's **suggestion** <u>that poets are influenced by their childhood</u> is uncontroversial.
Lee's **statement** <u>that problems arose earlier than previously thought</u> has been challenged.
Uvarov's **claim/assertion/contention** <u>that the causes of the revolution can be traced back to the 18th century</u> is worth considering in some depth.
Van Ek's **implication** <u>that other historians have misinterpreted the period</u> has caused some controversy. [suggests indirectly]
Patel's **argument** <u>that governments should continue to fund space research</u> is convincing.
Greenberg's **emphasis/stress on** <u>the importance of taking a liberal approach</u> is not new.
Levack's **observation** <u>that there are contradictions in Day's interpretation of the poem</u> has been supported by a number of other scholars.
Kim's **demonstration** <u>of the way in which Bach's music draws on the work of earlier composers</u> is fascinating.
Gray's **proof** <u>of the link between obesity and genes</u> is of considerable interest.

According to is used when reporting others' viewpoints rather than one's own. For example, *according to* Greene and Willis … but *in my opinion* … NOT ~~according to me~~.

Exercises

32.1 Fill in the missing verbs and nouns.

noun	verb	noun	verb
implication			describe
	observe	statement	
argument			emphasise
assertion			explain
	contend	demonstration	

32.2 Rewrite the sentences using nouns instead of the verbs in bold and beginning as shown.

1 Harkov **contends** that continued population growth will be a more serious problem than global warming, but this is not accepted by many scientists. (Harkov's ...)
2 'Global symmetry' **states** that the laws of physics take the same form when expressed in terms of distinct variables. ('Global symmetry' is ...)
3 The report **implies** that no individual government will ever be able to control the internet. (The report makes ...)
4 Dudas **demonstrates** how dangerous genetic modification might be. (Dudas provides ...)
5 Groot **emphasises** the role of schools in preventing teenage drug abuse. (Groot puts ...)
6 Lenard **observes** that women use expressions such as 'you know' in English more than men but this was later proved to be inaccurate. (Lenard's ...)
7 Plana **explained** the possible origins of the pyramids in Guelcoga but this has been disputed by Ruiz. (Plana's ...)
8 Wilson **describes** the ancient alphabet of the Guelcoga people. (Wilson gives ...)
9 Wu **argues** that daylight-saving time should be extended throughout the year. (Wu puts ...)
10 The President **asserts** that he cares about fighting poverty. (The President makes ...)

32.3 In each sentence two of the options in italics are possible and one is not. Which is not?

1 The author *notes / observes / pinpoints* that commodity prices change depending on the season.
2 Grey *puts forward / proves / advances* a controversial theory to explain climate change.
3 Philipson *claims / questions / challenges* the accuracy of Malwar's figures.
4 Trakov *stresses / emphasises / asserts* the importance of pilot testing before carrying out a survey.
5 Ripoll *advances / demonstrates / shows* how large-scale urban planning can go wrong.
6 Thompson's *assertion / contention / description* that no member of the committee was informed of the director's plan is incorrect.
7 Evans *declared / cast doubt / maintained* there was no causal link between the events.

32.4 There is one mistake in each of these sentences. Find and correct it.

1 According to me, courses in academic writing should be compulsory for all new students.
2 It has not yet been proof that the virus can jump from species to species.
3 Richardson emphasises on a number of weaknesses in the theory.
4 Taylor mentions to several studies which have looked at the problem in the past.
5 Pratt's suggest that the poet may have suffered from depression is an interesting one.
6 Our latest results cast doubt to our original hypothesis.

 Find some examples of reporting what others say in an academic article or textbook in your own field. Do they use language from this unit? Copy out any interesting examples.

33 Analysis of results

A Analysis in academic texts

Academic texts often include sections which deal with the analysis of data. In analysing a social or political issue, the writer may need to **come to / reach a conclusion** about the **advantages** and **disadvantages** of a particular **course of action**[1]. The writer may, for instance, conclude that the **benefits outweigh**[2] the **drawbacks**[3] or vice versa. An analysis may be a matter of **weighing up**[4] both **sides of an argument, taking into account** all the **relevant aspects**[5] of the issue and discussing all the **points**[6] **raised** by the research. When analysing the results of a scientific experiment, the writer is likely to need to **take account of** a range of **variables**[7]. In their analysis scientists try to **deduce**[8] as much as they can from their data, **drawing conclusions** that are **soundly**[9] **based** on their results.

[1] way of doing something [2] are of more importance than [3] disadvantages [4] think carefully about [5] (of a problem or situation) parts, features [6] idea, opinion or piece of information that has been presented in relation to the topic [7] number, amount or aspect of a situation which can change [8] reach an answer by thinking carefully about the known facts [9] completely, firmly

B Weighing up results

In the text in A did you notice an interesting metaphorical use of language – the image of **weighing up** ideas and of considering whether advantages **outweigh** disadvantages? Arguments are, as it were, placed on each **side** of the scales and the judge or jury then have to **come down on one side** or the other. A particularly strong argument may **tip the scales in favour of** one side.

> **TIP** Noticing how language can be used metaphorically may help you to extend the use of the words you know. Make a note of any examples that you come across and try to find other examples of language based round the same metaphor.

C Sentences relating to analyses

The survey provided some useful **insights into** the problem. [points that help us to understand more clearly]
The results **point to** an interesting trend. [show, indicate]
On the basis of our data we would **predict** continuing social unrest. [say something will happen in the future]
We found that women **constitute** 40% of the workforce. [account for]

We began with a **critical** review of the literature in the field. [giving opinions]
Most of our respondents were **critical of** the new law. [not pleased with, negative about]
We are reaching a **critical** period in terms of global climate change. [very important]
The patient is in a **critical** condition. [serious]
deeply critical = very negative   **absolutely critical** = extremely important

> **TIP** Remember how English words often have several distinct meanings. Note examples as you meet them.

Exercises

33.1 Complete the expressions with a word which can combine with the words given.

1
- moment
- review
- comments

_____

2
- come to
- draw
- reach

a _____

3
- come down on one
- be in favour of one
- see both

_____(s) of an argument

33.2 Now complete the sentences with a word from 33.1.

1 You should write a _____ review of the literature at the start of your dissertation.
2 It is difficult to reach a _____ without a lot more data.
3 A good essay presents both _____ of an argument and evaluates them properly.

33.3 Complete these extracts using words from the opposite page. You are given the first letters of the missing words to help you.

1
Which is better the night before an exam? To study longer and get less sleep or to study less and sleep longer? After w_____ up the evidence scientists have come to the c_____ that the advantages of getting more sleep o_____ the d_____. Research has provided i_____ into the link between sleep and memory development, suggesting that sleep is essential for memory. But there are many v_____ to t_____ account of in sleep and memory research, such as dreaming, phases of sleep and types of memories. Dreams c_____ about 25% of a typical eight-hour sleep, but research p_____ to a connection between memory development and non-dreaming sleep time.

2
When considering energy conservation, we have to t_____ i_____ account various r_____ factors. But how do we relate a particular c_____ of action to its outcome? For example, flying from London to Paris instead of taking the train is quicker but causes more pollution. You opt to cycle to work instead of driving in order to avoid adding to pollution. What can we d_____ from the evidence? Do our individual choices make a difference? On the b_____ of global data we can p_____ that climate change will increase, but how much do personal choices affect the big picture? Could my choice to buy a second car tip the s_____ and cause a global catastrophe?

33.4 What does *critical* – or one of its related forms – mean in each sentence?

1 The hospital announced that the President remains critically ill.
2 Dixon was asked to write a critical review (or critique) of contemporary Irish poetry.
3 The writer was imprisoned for his open criticism of the government.
4 It is absolutely critical all measurements are recorded every hour.

33.5 Look at these sentences and underline any metaphorical uses of language. Explain them in your own words. Use a dictionary if necessary.

1 A recent survey has unearthed some interesting facts about commuting habits.
2 In predicting trends in inflation, economists often look at which direction the political winds are blowing.
3 Martins published a ground-breaking study of the formation of galaxies.
4 By digging into the archives, Professor Robinson was able to shed important new light on the history of the period.

34 Talking about meaning

A The importance of meaning

Academic study in any subject inevitably requires precision with regard to the meanings of the **terms**[1] used. Many textbooks provide a **glossary**[2] of the **terminology**[3] of the subject and this should be referred to frequently, whenever the meaning of some new term is not **transparent**[4]. Often there are **subtle distinctions**[5] between the way in which a word is used in a non-academic context and the way in which it is used in a specific academic discipline and the student needs to be able to **distinguish between** these different **senses**[6] of the same word. When writing an essay or an article it is often appropriate to begin by **defining**[7] the key words relating to the topic. If this is not done then the reader may find the writing **ambiguous**[8] and may **misinterpret**[9] the text. In lectures, too, the audience will require the lecturer to **clarify** what they are saying by providing a **definition** of any unfamiliar terms. This is essential if the lecturer is to **communicate** their meaning in a clear and **coherent**[10] way.

[1] words or expressions used in relation to a specific context [2] list of words with explanations of their meanings [3] special words or expressions used in relation to a specific subject [4] clear, often used when referring to meaning [5] small differences [6] meanings [7] explaining the meaning of [8] having more than one possible meaning [9] understand in the wrong way [10] carefully organised and making sense

B The power of words

Writers may use words to **express ideas** or to **convey** a **message**[1] or to **evoke**[2] an **atmosphere**[3]. In scientific **discourse**[4], if words are not used precisely, then it is hard for the reader to **comprehend**[5] what the writer is trying to say. In literature, especially in poetry, the **connotations**[6] that words have may be at least as important if not more important than what those words **denote**[7]. The reader has to **infer**[8] the poet's meaning and this may involve a sensitivity to **nuances of meaning**[9] and the ability to see things from the poet's **perspective**[10].

[1] key idea (e.g. in a book or film) [2] make someone feel something [3] feeling or mood [4] written or spoken text [5] understand [6] associations [7] mean [8] form an opinion on the basis of indirect evidence [9] small differences in meaning [10] point of view

TIP

Use prefixes to help you work out the meaning of some words that initially look unfamiliar. For example, the prefix **mis-** carries the idea of wrongly or badly as in **misinterpret/ misinterpretation**. Other examples include **mistranslate/mistranslation** and **mispronounce/ mispronunciation**. (See Reference 5.)

Exercises

34.1 Dr Babayan is advising Tomoko, one of his students who is about to start writing up her dissertation. Complete their conversation with words from the opposite page.

Dr Babayan: In the first chapter, you need a section where you d................ your
t................ .

Tomoko: I'm sorry, what does that involve exactly?

Dr Babayan: You explain your t................ , the special technical words or phrases you're going to use and what precise meaning they have so that your text is t................ , and every reader knows exactly what you mean when you use a word or phrase.

Tomoko: Does it have to be in the first chapter?

Dr Babayan: Well, usually, yes, though an alternative way of doing it is to provide an alphabetical g................ at the back of the dissertation where readers can look up the meaning. And remember, if you're using different s................ of the same word you must explain each one.

Tomoko: That's my problem. I sometimes find it difficult to d................ between the different meanings. There are so many s................ d................ between words and between the different meanings of the same words in English.

Dr Babayan: Yes, I know, but all languages are like that; it's just that you don't notice it in your own language. Look, a dissertation is all about c................ your ideas in a clear, c................ manner. If you use words which are a................ , your readers might m................ your text. So it's always important to c................ what you intend to say.

Tomoko: Hmm. Oh well, I'll try.

34.2 Add negative prefixes to the words in bold, using a dictionary if necessary.

1 The sign had been ....**translated**, so no one could understand what it meant.
2 I .... **understood** one of the exam questions and wrote about the wrong subject.
3 The text was quite ....**ambiguous**, so there was only one way of interpreting it.
4 Some of the totals had evidently been ....**calculated**, so the results were unreliable.
5 The essay was quite ....**coherent**, so it was almost impossible to follow the argument.
6 Sandra is good at French but ....**pronounces** a lot of words.

34.3 Use the words from the box in an appropriate form to complete the text.

denote	perspective	express	comprehend	evoke	nuance	discourse	convey	infer	connotation

'And it's a hard rain's a-gonna fall'

The American songwriter Bob Dylan is often considered to be as much a poet as a musician. He .... his political ideas through folk songs in his early period. His melodies were often simple but his words .... complex messages, often with subtle .... In one of his songs, he speaks of a 'hard rain' which will fall after a nuclear war. On one level the words .... real, radioactive rain, but the .... of the words are many: life will be hard, perhaps impossible. Perhaps the consequences will fall hard on the politicians who started the war too. There are many things we can .... from these words. The song is part of the political .... of the Cold War of the 1960s. It .... an atmosphere of fear and hopelessness. Seen from the .... of the post-Cold-War era, it may seem difficult to .... such fear, but at the time, that fear very real.

35 Research and study aims

A Expressing aims

word	example	comment
deliberate	We took the **deliberate** decision to keep our study small.	= **intentional**; is often used for something negative
goal	**have something as a goal, achieve your goal**	we don't usually say 'reach your goal'
intention	**with the intention of** -ing, **have no intention of** -ing	verb = *intend* followed by the infinitive
motive	**motive for** -ing [reason]	verb = **motivate**; more general noun = **motivation**
objective	**meet**[1]**/achieve objectives**	= what you plan to do or achieve
priority	**top priority, take priority over**	implies a list of important things
purpose	Our **purpose** was to test our theory.	**on purpose** means deliberately
strategy	Their **strategy** was to proceed slowly.	detailed plan for success
target	**reach/achieve/attain a target**	= level or situation you hope to achieve

[1] we also talk about meeting criteria

B An example of a mission statement

Look at this web page for the Centre of Research into Creation in the Performing Arts. Note how the aims are expressed through the infinitive and in formal language.

MISSION STATEMENT[1]

ResCen exists **to further**[2] the understanding of how artists research and develop new processes and forms, by working with professional artists and others.

AIMS

To **establish**[3] new **understandings**[4] of creative methods and their **application** in practice-as-research, extending **knowledge bases**[5] in these areas

To explore and **challenge**[6] traditional **hypothesis-based** and critical-analytical **research methodologies** established within the university

To establish a **critical mass**[7] of artist-researchers, meeting regularly, to **instigate**[8] and **inform**[9] new creative work across **disciplines**

To provide an **infrastructure**[10] for **practice-led** and artist-informed postgraduate study within the university

To further develop **criteria**[11] for the **definition** and **evaluation** of **creative practice-as-research**, as part of the wider **national debate**

To **contribute to** the development of a national infrastructure supporting practice-as-research, at the **interface**[12] between academic and other centres of art-making and its study

[1] short written statement of the aims of an organisation [2] move forward, advance [3] encourage people to accept [4] *understanding* can be used as a countable noun in this context [5] the basic knowledge shared by everyone working in the areas [6] question [7] influential number [8] initiate, cause to start [9] provide knowledge that can influence [10] basic systems and support services [11] standards; singular = *criterion* [12] place where two things come together and affect each other

Exercises

35.1 Rewrite the sentences using words and expressions from the opposite page and beginning as shown.

1 Protecting the privacy of our subjects must take priority over absolutely everything else. (We must give ...)
2 Our intention in designing the questionnaire was to make it as simple as possible to answer. (We designed the questionnaire with ...)
3 We aimed to define and evaluate a new approach to urban planning. (We had as our goal the ...)
4 I did not intend to become a scientist when I began my studies. (I had no ...)
5 A methodology based on a hypothesis does not work in some cases. (A hypothesis- ...)
6 Our project is located in the area where sociology and psychology meet. (Our project is located at ...)

35.2 Read these descriptions of their research by academics and then answer the questions. Use a dictionary for any unknown words.

Dr Janeja (in a lecture): 'We wanted to see if we could explain the fact that the expansion of the universe is accelerating.'
Dr Finstein (in an introduction to an article): 'Our research questioned the notion that larger mammals only appeared long after the dinosaurs had died out.'
Prof. Li (in a lecture): 'We carefully restricted our sample to people born within ten kilometres of the lake.'
Prof. Simons (in a lecture): **'We wanted to build on existing research and offer new insights into the effects of stress.'**
Dr Andreas (in a conference presentation): 'We really wanted to put into practice some of the research on e-learning to improve our present system.'
Prof. Horza (in an article): 'We were hoping to instigate a new type of investigation.'
Dr Tadeus (in a conference presentation): 'We had no detailed plan at the outset; things developed as we went along.'

1 Whose team took a deliberate decision to do something?
2 Whose team wanted to further the understanding of something?
3 Whose team did not have a strategy for their research?
4 Who wanted to start something that had not existed before?
5 Whose team was interested in the application of something?
6 Whose purpose was it to establish a reason for something?
7 Whose research challenged an existing idea?

35.3 Answer the questions about the vocabulary in this unit.

1 What word can we use to refer to the basic support services and systems of a country?
2 What phrase can we use if everyone in a country seems to be discussing an issue?
3 What is another word for academic subjects?
4 What phrase means 'the basic knowledge of an academic field'?
5 How could the phrase *the place where theory meets practice* be reworded?
6 What verbs are typically used with (a) *objective* and (b) *target*?
7 What are the two noun forms connected with the verb *motivate*?
8 What is the opposite of theory-led research?

Go to the website for a course or institution that you are interested in. What does it state on its *Aims* page? Note any interesting language there.

FOLLOW UP

36 Talking about points of view

A Commenting on others' views

> No one can be completely **objective**[1] in their point of view. Inevitably, we all see things to some extent **subjectively**[2]. It is impossible to be truly **impartial**[3]. We tend to be **biased in favour of**[4] things we're familiar with and **prejudiced against**[5] things we have little experience of. Of course, everyone believes their own views are totally **rational**[6].

[1] not influenced by personal beliefs or attitudes, based only on facts [2] influenced by personal beliefs or attitudes [3] uninfluenced by personal beliefs or attitudes [4] showing an unreasonable liking for something based on personal beliefs or opinions; opposite = **biased against** [5] showing an unreasonable dislike for, based on personal beliefs or opinions (stronger and more pejorative than *biased*); opposite = **prejudiced in favour of** [6] based only on reason; opposite = **irrational**

> People's views tend to change as they grow older and begin looking at life from a different **standpoint**[7]. Young people are more likely to be **radical**[8] but then become more **reactionary**[9] or **conservative**[10] with age, considering their younger opinions **immature**[11].

[7] set of principles or beliefs on the basis of which opinions are formed [8] believing that there should be extreme political or social change [9] (disapproving) opposed to political or social change or new ideas [10] not inclined to trust change, especially if it is sudden [11] (disapproving) lacking in experience; opposite = **mature**

> An **ideology** is a theory or set of beliefs or principles, particularly one on which a political system or organisation is based. It often has slightly negative associations in English, implying something that is rigid and restricting. A **philosophy**, on the other hand, suggests a set of beliefs that is much more thoughtful and serious.

B Word combinations relating to points of view

word combination	example	meaning
to hold views	My grandfather **holds** some surprisingly progressive **views**.	has opinions
to adopt/take a stance	It is important that the university should **adopt a** principled **stance** towards research.	take a position
to change/shift your position	Luisa was initially totally opposed to the idea but she has slightly **shifted her position**.	changed her point of view a little
have ethical objections to	Increasing numbers of people **have ethical objections** to the war.	dislike for reasons relating to morality
the principles underlying	'Treat others as you would like to be treated' is a **principle underlying** much religious teaching.	basic idea lying behind
to encounter prejudice	As one of the few female students of the 1920s, my grandmother **encountered** a certain amount of **prejudice**.	experienced unreasonable negative behaviour
deep-rooted prejudice	John does not share his father's **deep-rooted prejudices** against women.	strong, unreasonably negative views

 ERROR WARNING

You can say **in my opinion** but NOT ~~in my point of view~~. You can say **from (someone's) point of view** but it means *from that person's way of looking at something* rather than *in that person's opinion*. **From the language teacher's point of view**, it's good that all children have to learn a foreign language at school.

Exercises

36.1 Change the words in bold to words which mean the *opposite*.

1 The views she expressed were totally **rational**.
2 The committee seemed to be biased **against** applications from younger people.
3 The book is an **objective** account of life in a small town in the 1920s.
4 The club rules were prejudiced **in favour of** children.
5 The President's daughter was quite **mature** for her age.
6 He has rather **radical** views about marriage.
7 Her views on education are rather **radical**. (use a different word from 6)
8 Supreme Court judges always act in a **biased** way.

36.2 Use the words in the box in an appropriate form to complete the sentences.

root	shift	adopt	encounter	underlie	philosophy	hold	ethical

1 The _____ principles of Asian and European _____ are very similar.
2 People tend _____ a more conservative stance as they get older.
3 She has always _____ the view that primary education should not start before the age of seven.
4 Many people have _____ objections to investing in companies which support corrupt regimes.
5 Some employers still have a deep-_____ prejudice against employing older people, and many older people _____ such prejudice when they apply for jobs.
6 The government seems to have _____ its position recently.

36.3 Answer the questions.

1 What verb could be used instead of *shifted* in exercise 36.2?
2 What verb could be used instead of *adopt* in exercise 36.2?
3 Which is incorrect: (a) in my point of view, (b) in my opinion, (c) from my point of view?
4 In what way does calling something an ideology make it sound slightly more negative than calling it a philosophy?
5 What single noun is formed from the noun *point* and the verb *stand*?

36.4 Vary these sentences by rewriting them using the word in brackets.

1 The people of the area have some unusual views about nature. (HOLD)
2 Most young people seem not to like the proposals on student fees. (OBJECTIONS)
3 Examiners tend to prefer candidates with clear handwriting. (BIASED)
4 Girls look at their careers in a different way from their mothers. (STANDPOINT)
5 Let us now discuss the principles behind this approach. (UNDERLYING)

36.5 Read this short text and underline any words and phrases connected with points of view, opinions and ideas. Look them up in a dictionary if necessary and note them in your vocabulary book.

> Academics have traditionally taken the view that their discipline is intellectually independent from all others. However, inter-disciplinary degrees are becoming more and more common, suggesting that preconceptions about what and how one should study may be somewhat misplaced. A more liberal view of education would advocate greater freedom to explore the links between different fields of learning, thus pushing the frontiers of knowledge in new and exciting directions. Many academics now feel that the future lies in this blending of ideas and the cross-fertilisation of thought which emerges from it.

37 Degrees of certainty

This unit looks at the ways writers express how certain they are about the facts or opinions they are presenting. This unit deals with some vocabulary which will help you to handle certainty in academic writing appropriately.

A Being tentative

It is a common mistake for students to present something as a proven fact when it is actually an opinion. In a serious piece of academic writing you should not, for example, write *Girls are better at learning languages than boys*; you could write, instead, ***There is some evidence to suggest that** girls **may be** better at learning languages than boys* or ***It can be argued that** girls are better at learning languages than boys*.

Here are some other expressions that are useful when presenting ideas that may be true but are not proven facts.

It may not be the case that girls are naturally better at foreign languages.

It would seem/appear that girls are more interested in languages than boys.

We can presume that all humans have the ability to learn a second language. [believe something to be true because it seems very likely]

There appears/seems to be some evidence linking diet with language ability.

There is some evidence that previous studies are unreliable.

We can draw the **tentative** conclusion that early language skills determine how successful a child will be at school. [possible, not yet certain]

B It is true or almost certainly true

It is **undoubtedly** true that language ability is not simply a matter of intelligence. [without doubt, certainly]

It is, **of course,** essential to check data carefully. [shows the writer sees this as obvious]

It is **evident** that girls and boys develop at slightly different rates. [obvious, clear]

The best age for language learning is, **apparently,** the teenage years.

Pronunciation of unfamiliar sounds **presumably** comes more easily to young children.

The research **is likely to** lead to some interesting results. = The research **will probably** lead to some interesting results.

Boys **tend to** have better practical skills than girls. [are likely to]

There is a tendency for boys to be more enthusiastic about team sports than girls. [it is often the case that]

There is every likelihood that the research will be completed by June. [it is probable]

The situation **is liable to** change. [may change, is likely to change]

C The writer is unsure

The research has **allegedly** come to some very significant conclusions. [it is claimed; the use of this adverb suggests that the writer does not believe the claims are true]

Boys **are considered to be** more inclined to take risks than girls. [people think that – the implication is that the writer may not agree]

The **perception** of boys as poor language learners can be shown to be false. [common view, often one which the writer feels is inappropriate in some way]

The article is **reportedly** an excellent piece of work [it is reported that; the use of the adverb makes it clear the writer has not seen the article]

In the absence of evidence to the contrary we can assume that Laing is correct. [as there is no evidence to suggest the opposite]

Exercises

37.1 Match the beginning of each sentence with the most appropriate ending.

1 We may	assume that the exchange rate will continue to fluctuate.
2 It would seem	not to be the case that all the questions were answered honestly.
3 Of course it	to appear from all the findings that the test is reliable.
4 We can certainly	well discover that the problem was caused by overheating.
5 It may well turn out	argued that conflict was inevitable after the events of recent years.
6 It could be	is true that not all factories cause huge amounts of pollution.

37.2 Insert adverbs based on the words in italics into suitable places in the sentences.

1 Russo was a member of a terrorist organisation, but it was never proved. *allege*
2 At that time, the population of tigers was widespread in the region. *report*
3 The collapse of the roof caused a sprinkler system pipe to burst. *appear*
4 To get a better job is a main motivation for going on to higher education. *presume*
5 We may conclude that water shortages are likely to increase rather than decrease. *tentative*
6 The students were guessing some of the answers instead of using their knowledge of the context. *evidence*

37.3 Complete the missing forms in the table. Use a dictionary if necessary. Do not fill the shaded boxes.

noun	verb	adjective	adverb
	tend		
evidence			
	seem		
		likely	
	perceive		

37.4 Change these sentences. Use different forms of the words in bold, as instructed.

1 There is little **likelihood** that everyone will fail the test. (use the adjective)
2 Students **tend** to leave preparation for exams till the last minute. (use the noun)
3 We saw **evidence** that some students had copied each other's answers. (use the adjective)
4 People commonly **perceive** that older people cannot learn musical instruments to a professional standard. (use the noun)
5 The melting of the polar ice caps **seems** to be inevitable. (use the adverb)

37.5 Make the sentences more formal by replacing the underlined words or phrases.

1 <u>People generally think that</u> rats are carriers of diseases.
2 There <u>isn't much</u> evidence to support the opinion that diesel cars cause more pollution than petrol cars.
3 <u>It is extremely likely</u> that rail passenger numbers will continue to decline.
4 In the absence of <u>other</u> evidence, we must conclude that right-handedness is not linked to intelligence in any way.
5 <u>Of course,</u> it is true that engineering graduates are in increasing demand.
6 The area near the river <u>often floods</u> in winter.

38 Presenting an argument

A Developing an argument: what it is about

Read these extracts from the opening paragraphs of student essays. Note the prepositions.

This essay **is based on** findings from recent research into cold fusion.
The arguments I shall **put forward** are **relevant to** our understanding of Newton's laws.
For the purposes of this essay, two opposing theories will be **scrutinised**. I shall **refer to** Ashbach's and Linn's work, **respectively**.
Many articles have been published **on the subject of** genetic modification of crops.
The political arguments concerning population control are **beyond the scope of** this essay.
The first section reviews recent literature, **with reference to** the arguments concerning economic policy.

B Adding points to an argument

Bad diet and high stress levels, **as well as** lack of exercise, are key factors in causing heart disease; **on top of which** there is smoking, which is one of the most damaging factors.
In addition to the questionnaire, we also conducted interviews with some of the subjects.
A **further** argument in support of raising the retirement age is that life expectancy is increasing. **Moreover/Furthermore**[1], many people enjoy working; **for example / for instance**[2], in a recent survey, 68% of people said they would like to work till they were at least 70.

[1] *moreover* is much more frequently used in academic style than *furthermore* [2] *for example* is much more frequently used in academic style than *for instance*

C Qualifying: limiting and specifying an argument

Dr O'Malley is leading a class discussion on human rights.

O'Malley: OK. 'Human rights are rights which you possess simply because you are human.' **To what extent** can we say that? What are **the pros and cons**[1] of this view?
Anna: Well, I think it's too simplistic, **in the sense that**[2] it ignores the rights of victims and everyone else's right to life. So, **provided that** we remember this, then we can give people basic rights, **albeit**[3] with limitations.
Kirsten: Mm, **that's all very well, but**[4] if you say human rights depend on, **say**, government decisions about national security, then they're no longer *rights*, are they? They become privileges. **Having said that**[5], it's a complex issue with no simple answer. **Even so**, I still think we must be careful not to give our rights away.
O'Malley: OK. Fine. **Apart from** victim's rights, are there other arguments for restricting rights? I mean we could look at protecting property, ending a chronically sick person's life, **and so on / and so forth**[6]. Let's talk about **the degree/extent to which** these are relevant.
Ricardo: Every sick person has the right to life, **but at the same time** we should be free to decide when we want to die.
O'Malley: Well, a lot of sick people can't make that decision for themselves, **despite the fact that** we may respect their right to a dignified death.
Ricardo: Hmm. **Nevertheless/Nonetheless**[7], I think it's a key issue.

[1] (slightly informal) advantages and disadvantages [2] used to explain precisely what has just been said [3] (formal) although [4] (informal, typical of spoken contexts) indicates a partial agreement, followed by a disagreement [5] (typical of spoken contexts) said when you wish to add a point which contrasts with what has just been said [6] (typical of spoken contexts) can be used separately or together (*and so on and so forth*); can also be *et cetera* (more common in writing – *etc.*) [7] however; *nevertheless* is more frequent in academic style than *nonetheless*

Exercises

38.1 Fill in the prepositions in this text about the first wife of Henry VIII of England (1491–1547).

This essay examines the early life of Catherine of Aragon (1485–1536), focusing particularly .... the period of her brief marriage to Prince Arthur, his death at the age of 15 and her subsequent marriage .... his brother Prince Henry, later to become King Henry VIII of England. .... the purposes .... this essay, I shall pay little attention .... either the earlier or the later periods of her life. Her eventual divorce from King Henry is, thus, ... the scope .... this essay. Much more has already been written .... the subject .... this later period of her life. The literature .... reference .... the period is extensive but my essay is largely based .... a couple of key sources, which are particularly relevant .... any discussion of this period, and I shall refer .... these throughout.

38.2 Which word comes next in these phrases?

1 the pros and ....
2 at the same ....
3 and so on and so ....
4 having said ....

5 that's all very well ....
6 the extent to ....
7 in addition ....
8 as well ....

38.3 Use phrases from the box to replace phrases from the paragraph with the same meaning.

nevertheless	the degree	as well as	provided that
advantages and disadvantages	for instance	furthermore	

There are a number of pros and cons to take into account when considering the purchase of a hybrid (gasoline-electric) car. Such cars are, for example, undoubtedly better for the environment in the sense that they cause less air pollution. Moreover, the extent to which they rely on oil, a natural resource which is rapidly becoming depleted, is much less than is the case with conventional cars. Nonetheless, hybrid cars are not without their problems. Cost may be an issue and also the technical complexity of this relatively new type of engine. As long as you take these factors into account, there is no reason not to buy a hybrid car.

38.4 Choose the correct word or phrase to complete each sentence.

1 She wrote an excellent essay .... with a certain amount of help.
   A even so   B albeit   C despite the fact
2 A .... point must also now be made against a change in the law.
   A furthermore   B respective   C further
3 He is a great poet .... his work has had a great influence on other writers.
   A in the sense that B on top of which   C provided that
4 Let us now discuss the influence of the revolution on the rich and the poor ....
   A say   B respectively   C moreover
5 The riots resulted in much damage. .... , we should not ignore the fact that the disorder brought benefits to some.
   A As well as   B With reference to   C Having said that
6 But there is a negative side to new technology. .... the advantages we also need to consider a number of disadvantages.
   A Be that as it may B Apart from   C That's all very well but

39 Organising your writing

A Openings

Look at these openings from students' written work, and note the items in bold.

This assignment will **address** the problem of socio-economic data in health studies.
This dissertation **is concerned with** individual differences in the ability to connect thoughts and emotions.
The **aim of** this paper is to explore constant acceleration formulae, **with a focus on** motion along a slope.
The **purpose of** this essay is to investigate the use of focus group interviews.
This thesis **consists of** four parts. Each part describes a different set of experiments which contribute to the final results.
This assignment is **divided into** three sections, with each section **devoted to** a different aspect of world trade.

B Organising the main points

useful when ...	items	examples
working through a list of different things	• first(ly), secondly, thirdly • next • lastly/finally	**First(ly)**, let us look at the history of the problem. [*firstly* is more formal than *first*] **Next**, there is the issue of air resistance. **Finally**, let us consider increased taxation as a possible solution.
changing topics / bringing in new points	• we now / let us turn to • at this point	**We now turn to** the question of which model provides a better explanation of the phenomenon. **At this point** it is important to look again at the data.
referring forward in the text	• below • in the next section • later • the following	We shall see **below** that depopulation has been a major factor. [lower on the page or later in the essay/article] **Later**, I shall look at other possible reasons for this. The **following** example comes from Hillson (1998).
referring back to something	• above • in the preceding section • earlier • (as) we saw / have seen that/in	The **above** figures indicate a significant decrease. Three hypotheses were listed in the **preceding** section. [the section immediately before this one] I noted **earlier** that lack of fresh water was a serious problem. **As we saw in** section 2, this is a complex topic.
referring to examples, diagrams, pages, etc.	• see • consider • take, for example, • as can be seen in	For the complete results, **see** Appendix A, page 94. **Consider** Figure 1, which shows changes from 1976–8. **Take, for example**, Sweden, where industrialisation was rapid, **as can be seen in** Figure 2.
referring separately to different people or things	• respectively • the former • the latter	Groups A and B consisted of 14-year-olds and 16-year-olds, **respectively**. [i.e. group A was 14-year-olds and group B was 16-year-olds] Rostov and Krow both studied the problem. The **former** wrote a book; the **latter** published two papers. [the first and then the second person or thing mentioned]

ERROR WARNING Don't confuse *first(ly)* with *at first*. At first means 'at the beginning', and refers to situations which change: *At first* there was no increase in temperature, but later, the temperature rose by 0.5°C. See Unit 50 for the difference between *lastly* and *at last*.
Say *as can be seen* in Figure 1, NOT *as it can be seen in Figure 1*.

See Units 16 and 50 for more useful expressions for organising your writing.

Exercises

39.1 Choose a word from A to fill in the missing words in this introduction to a paper.

> The (1) .... of this paper is to consider the nature of moral education in Soviet children's literature. It is particularly (2) .... with the moral values presented in books published with the (3) .... of teaching reading at primary school. The thesis (4) .... of four parts. The first part attempts to (5) .... a number of general questions relating to children's literature from any historical period. Parts 2, 3 and 4 are (6) .... specifically to the Soviet example. Part 2 is (7) .... into three main sections, the first of which discusses the nature of the Soviet value system with a particular (8) .... on the work ethic.

39.2 Read the sentences and answer the questions about them.

1 Tolstoy's most famous novels are *War and Peace* and *Anna Karenina*, the former being first published between 1865 and 1869 and the latter between 1875 and 1877.
   Which of Tolstoy's novels was published in the 1860s?
2 More precise data can be found in Table 3 below.
   Does Table 3 appear before or after this sentence?
3 Let us now turn to the question of the country's economic situation.
   Has the writer already begun discussing the country's economic situation or not?
4 The brothers, Olaf and Erik, would go on to become professors of archaeology and Greek, respectively.
   Which brother taught archaeology?
5 The preceding example is taken from Atakano (1991).
   Does the example come before or after this sentence?

39.3 Choose the correct word in italics to complete each sentence.

1 *Take / Put / Look*, for example, the case of Megginson which was described in Chapter 2.
2 *At first / Firstly* I would like to discuss the nature of 16th century English and then the impact that this had on the works of Shakespeare.
3 The article *concerns / devotes / addresses* the issue of the relationship between religion and politics in the modern world.
4 Look at Figure 3 *under / below / beneath* for more detailed information.
5 In the *following / preceding* section we shall deal with this issue in more detail.
6 For more detailed information *see / go / turn* Appendix B.
7 Let us now *deal / see / consider* Figure 2.1.
8 This aspect of the problem will be discussed *latter / later / lastly* in this article.

39.4 Rewrite the parts in bold using a phrase which includes the word in brackets.

1 **As Table V shows** there has been an increase in the numbers of students in higher education. (SEEN)
2 In Section 3 we take up again some of the arguments from **Section 2**. (PRECEDING)
3 **Now** let us turn our attention to developments in Constantinople. (POINT)
4 The country **consists of** six provinces. (DIVIDED)
5 Let us now **consider** the issue of the reunification of Germany. (TURN)

40 Making a presentation

The language of presentations often contains less formal vocabulary than that of academic writing, so take care not to use the less formal expressions in your written work.

A Introducing the presenter

Let's welcome Carmen Gregori, who's going to talk to us today **on the subject of** 'Healthcare in Paraguay'.

Now I'd like to **call on** Mieko to **make/give** her **presentation**. Mieko, thank you.

OK, thank you everybody. Now, Dr Ulla Fensel is going to **present** her research to us.

I'd like to introduce Dr Li Meiju, who's going to **address**[1] the **topic of** 'Preventive medicine'.

[1] rather formal; we can also say formally *speak to the topic of* X, or, less formally *talk about* X

B Getting started

'In this presentation I'd like to **focus on** recent developments in biomass fuels. I'll speak for about 45 minutes, to **allow time for** questions and comments. **Feel free to**[1] interrupt if you have any questions or want to **make a comment**.'

'First I'll **give a brief overview of** the current situation **with regard to** intellectual property rights, then I'd like to **raise** a few **issues** concerning the internet. I'll try to **leave**[2] **time for questions** at the end.'

'**I'd like to begin by** looking at some previous studies of ocean temperatures. There's **a handout going round**[3], and there are some **spare**[4] **copies** here if you want them.'

'In this talk I'll **present the results of** a study I **did**[5] for my dissertation. I'll try not **to go over time** and **keep to** 20 minutes.'

[1] an informal way of giving permission [2] less formal than *allow* – see 1 [3] a more formal version would be *which is being distributed* [4] extra [5] or, more formal, *carried out / conducted*

C During the presentation – and closing it

Now let's **turn to** the problem of workplace stress.	begin to examine or talk about
Moving on, I'd like to look at the questionnaire results **in more detail**.	going on to the next point; less formal than *in greater detail*
I also want to talk about the supply of clean water, but I'll **come back to** that later.	or, more formal, *return to*
I'd just like to **go back to** the graph on the previous slide.	or, more formal, *return to*
Anyway, getting back to / to return to the question of inflation, let's look at the Thai economy.	*getting back to* is less formal than *to return to*
The results were not very clear. **Having said that**, I feel the experiment was worthwhile.	a less formal way of saying *nevertheless*
I'll **skip** the next slide **as time is (running) short**.	*skip* (informal) = leave out / omit
To sum up, then, urban traffic has reached a crisis. **That's all I have to say***. **Thank you for listening**.	have no more time left * informal – not used in writing
Well, I'll stop there as I've **run out of time**. Thank you.	have no time left
Dr Woichek will now **take questions***. Are there **any questions or comments**?	* rather formal = accept and answer questions

Exercises

40.1 Fill in the missing words in these introductions to presentations.

1 Dr Anwar Musat will now _____ his research on soil erosion in Malaysian forests.
2 I'd now like to _____ on our next speaker, Eva Karlsson, to _____ (*give two answers*) her presentation.
3 Ladies and gentlemen, let's _____ our next speaker, Professor Prodromou from the University of Athens.
4 Thanks, everybody. So, Masanori is going to talk to us now _____ subject _____ 'Mental health issues in Japan'.
5 I'd like to _____ today's speaker, Dr Krishnan Guptar, who is going to _____ the topic of metal fatigue in rail tracks.

40.2 Rewrite these sentences by changing the words in bold so they are less formal. Remember that both formal and informal styles may be correct, but that it may not always be appropriate to be informal.

1 We need to consider family income too, but I'll **return** to that later.
2 So, **to proceed to the next point**, I'll **omit** item 4 on the handout and instead talk about number 5 in **greater** detail.
3 I'll try to finish by 3.30, but **don't feel you need to ask permission** to leave if you have a class or other appointment to go to.
4 There is a handout **being distributed** and I have some **further** copies too if anyone wants them.
5 I'll finish there as my time has **come to an end**.
6 We didn't want to make people uncomfortable by having a camera in the room. **Nevertheless**, we did want to video as many of the sessions as possible.
7 I'd like to **return** to a point I made earlier about river management.
8 So, I believe our experiments have been successful. **I shall end there**. Thank you.
9 **To return to** the problem of large class sizes, I'd like to look at a study **carried out** in Australia in 2002.
10 I'll try not to **exceed my time**, so I'll speak for 30 minutes, to **allow** time for questions at the end.

40.3 Fill in the missing prepositions.

1 I'd like to focus _____ waterborne diseases in this presentation.
2 The situation _____ regard _____ exports has been very good in recent years.
3 I'd now like to turn _____ a different problem.
4 I always find it difficult to keep _____ just 30 minutes, so please tell me when I have five minutes left.
5 I'd like to begin _____ asking you all to do a small task.

40.4 Write six sentences you might hear during a presentation using appropriate combinations of the words in boxes A and B. You may use words in box A more than once.

Box A	present	take	raise	make	give	

Box B	issue	presentation	results	overview	comment	questions

FOLLOW UP College and university libraries and departments often have audio or video recordings of talks, guest lectures and other presentations which can be borrowed. If you are able to do this, make a note of any useful words or expressions the speaker uses.

41 Describing research methods

A Useful word combinations

We may **carry out a procedure** or **an experiment** or a **pilot study**. [preliminary study]
We **use** or, more formally, **employ a method** or a **technique** or an **approach** or an **instrument**
or a **device**. [an object or method used for a special purpose] You can also **use** or **employ** any
particular type of **research methodology**.
Apparatus [equipment for a lab experiment] is **assembled** and **checked**. *Apparatus* is an
uncountable noun but you can talk about **a piece of apparatus**.

B Types of research method

research method	what the researcher does	limitation of method
experimental study	**manipulates**[1] a variable [anything that can vary] under highly **controlled conditions** to see if this produces [causes] any changes in a second [dependent] variable	done in the highly controlled **setting** of the **laboratory** – these conditions are **artificial**[2] and may not **reflect what happens** in the infinitely more complex real world; other researchers often try to **replicate**[3] successful experiments
correlational study	attempts to **determine** the **relationship between two or more variables**, using **mathematical techniques** for summarising data	only shows that two variables are **related in a systematic way**, but does not **prove** or **disprove**[4] that the relationship is a **cause-and-effect relationship**
naturalistic (empirical) observation (also known as **field study**)	**observes** and **records** some behaviour or **phenomenon**[5], often over a prolonged period, in its **natural setting** without **interfering with**[6] the **subjects** or **phenomena** in any way	can be very **time-consuming** as researcher may have to wait for some time to observe the behaviour or phenomenon of interest; difficult to observe behaviour without **disrupting**[7] it
survey	**makes inferences from**[8] **data collected** via interviews or questionnaires	intentional deception, poor memory, or misunderstanding of the question can all contribute to **inaccuracies in the data**
case study	keeps **in-depth**[9] descriptive records, as an **outside observer**, of an individual or group	often involves only a single individual as the **subject** of the study and this person may not **be representative**[10] of the general group or **population**

[1] makes changes to [2] not natural [3] do in exactly the same way [4] show something is not true [5] something that exists and can be seen, felt, tasted, etc. [6] altering [7] making it change [8] comes to conclusions on the basis of [9] detailed [10] typical

ERROR WARNING Remember that **phenomenon** is the singular and **phenomena** is the plural. The same applies
to **criterion/criteria**. [a standard by which you judge, decide about or deal with something]
See also Unit 31.

Exercises

41.1 Complete the sentences in these two texts with words from the opposite page.

> Scientists disagree as to whether cold fusion, the controlled power of the hydrogen bomb in the laboratory, is possible. In the past, some believed that e_____ s_____ under la_____ c_____ using palladium and platinum electrodes could in fact cause heavy hydrogen atoms to fuse into helium and release energy, as the sun does. In carefully controlled experiments, researchers believed they could ma_____ the v_____ arising from the complexity of the electrodes and other equipment used. In such co_____ co_____, they argued, cold fusion was possible. However, attempts to r_____ some of the experiments which claimed to be successful failed, and many now believe that cold fusion is in fact theoretically impossible.

> Some linguists believe that we can best d_____ how language is processed by laboratory experiments. However, laboratory experiments are by definition ar_____ and may not r_____ what happens in the real world. Other linguists believe, therefore, that em_____ o_____ is better, and prefer to carry out f_____ studies and c_____ studies of individuals in na_____ se_____. In this way, i_____ -d_____ data can be c_____ by observers without i_____ with the process in any way, even though this may be a more t_____ -c_____ method. However, individual studies in real situations may not be r_____ of the general p_____ of second language learners. In short, both approaches have their advantages and disadvantages.

41.2 Use the words in the box to complete the diagrams. Add *a/an* and anything else needed to complete the phrase.

| check methodology pilot study procedure assemble technique experiment device piece |

carry out ⊢ _____ / _____   employ/use ⊢ _____ / _____   _____ / _____ ⊣ apparatus

41.3 Now complete the sentences using phrases from 41.2.

1 It was a new _____ of apparatus so we _____ it first and then _____ it before using it.
2 The team carried out a _____ _____ before conducting the main _____ to see if the _____ they were using was reliable.
3 The team needed to employ a different _____ for measuring the pressure, so they used a new _____ which they manufactured in their own laboratory.

41.4 Correct the eight spelling and other vocabulary mistakes in these sentences.

1 It was very difficult to make reliable interferences from the data as we had so little.
2 A correlational study is a good way of seeing if one phenomena is related to another in a system way.
3 The experiment neither proved nor deproved Jessop's theory.
4 We had to explain the unusual scores of five of the subjects in the sample, who all had totals well below the norm. It was possible there were unaccuracies in the data.
5 An exterior observer can often unintentionally erupt the behaviour of the subjects they are observing.

42 Classifying

Classifying means dividing things into groups according to their type.

A Useful nouns when classifying

word	example	meaning
category	Each of our students falls into one of three **categories**.	a group that shares some significant characteristics
component	Milk is an essential **component** of any young child's diet.	a part which combines with other parts to create something bigger
existence	The **existence** of 'dark matter' in the universe was first proposed in 1933.	the fact that something or someone is or exists
feature	Effective use of metaphor is a **feature** of the poet's style.	typical part or quality
hierarchy	Humans can be described as being at the top of a **hierarchy** with amoebas on the bottom level.	system in which people or things are arranged according to their importance or power
nature	The **nature** of her work means that she is under a lot of stress.	type or main characteristic of something
structure	In this unit we shall be looking at the **structure** of the heart.	the way in which the parts of a system are arranged
type	The lion is one **type** of large cat.	group with similar characteristics, a smaller division of a larger set

B One example of a classification system

There is an enormous **variety/diversity** of living things (or organisms). To help study them, biologists have **devised**[1] ways of naming and classifying them **according to** their **similarities** and **differences**. The system most scientists use puts each living thing into seven groups organised from most **general** to most **specific**. Therefore, each species **belongs to**[2] a genus, each genus belongs to a family, each family belongs to an order, etc. Species are the smallest groups. A species **consists of**[3] all the animals **of the same type** who are able to breed and produce young of the same kind; each species is **distinct from**[4] all other species. Biologists **allocate**[5] all organisms to a position in this system.

[1] thought of, invented [2] is part of [3] includes, **is made up of** [4] significantly different from [5] place (also **assign**)

C Categorising people

When categorising people, it is often necessary to take **age, gender**[1], **social class, occupation, marital status** and **ethnic background**[2] into account. It may also be appropriate to consider the **urban-rural**[3] **dimension**[4]. Age, for example, is important in that different **generations** tend to have different attitudes and other **characteristics**. Social class **can be described** in different ways; the term **blue collar** may be used to mean working class while **white collar** **denotes**[5] middle class. The categories of student, **homemaker** (i.e. **housewife/househusband**), and **senior citizen**, as well as types of **employment**[6] are **subsumed**[7] under the **heading**[8] of occupation or **occupational background/status**.

[1] sex, male or female [2] racial background [3] city versus countryside [4] aspect, way of considering something [5] means [6] paid work [7] included as part of a larger group [8] title summing up a group

Exercises

42.1 Choose the words to complete these extracts from (1) a lecture and (2) a class.

1

> belong   categories   components   consist   distinct   diversity   fall   feature   structure   type

> 'Computer programming languages usually _____ into one of four _____:
> imperative, functional, object-oriented and logic. These languages are _____ from one
> another in how they operate. The _____ of imperative languages is based on commands,
> you know, "do this, do that thing". Languages such as Fortran and COBOL _____
> to this _____ . Functional languages _____ of mathematical functions. The
> _____ of object-oriented languages are commands which are combined with the data to
> create "objects". The main _____ of logic languages is that they state facts or relations
> between things. Now, in the case of human languages, _____ is considered a good
> thing. In the case of programming languages, it suggests we still haven't found the best one!'

2

> blue collar   class   devise   employment   ethnic   gender   generations   homemakers   occupational
> senior citizens

> 'For your end-of-year project, you must carry out a survey of consumer preferences for one
> product or a type of product. You'll need to _____ a questionnaire, and you'll need to
> take a lot of factors into account. These include _____ , that is how many males and/or
> females are in your sample, social _____ , and so on. And also different _____ ;
> will it just be adults, or young people too? And what about _____ ? They may be
> retired, but they still buy a lot of things. Also, what about _____ status? Are you going
> to separate _____ and white collar workers? Or are you also interested in people who
> are not in _____ , such as _____ , but who are often the ones who buy the
> goods? And in our multicultural society, don't forget _____ background.'

42.2 Complete the table. Use a dictionary if necessary.

noun	verb	adjective	adverb
		similar	
		different	
	allocate		
	describe		

42.3 Now choose a word from 42.2 to complete these sentences.

1 It is hard to _____ between these two _____ plants. They hardly _____ at all.
2 The professor persuaded the university to _____ more resources to his department.
3 There are some magnificent _____ passages in the writer's later novels.
4 In your essay comment on the _____ and the _____ between the two poems.

42.4 Vary the sentences by using words of similar meaning instead of the words in bold.

1 It is difficult to **categorise** human emotions as we know little about their **basic characteristics**.
2 Sensation and action can both be **included** under the term *behaviour*.
3 Linguists **allocate** all languages to a place in the system of language families, based on
   their grammars and other key **aspects**.
4 The atmosphere of the planet **consists** of different gases.
5 **City** and **country** people often differ in their political attitudes. **Whether one is married or
   single** is also a relevant factor.

43 Making connections

A Connecting data and evidence

Read how a scientist used 14 cameras to study his baby son learning language.

> In a child's life the progression from just making noises to using words meaningfully is still not completely understood. So an American scientist has collected 24,000 hours of video, **complemented**[1] by 33,000 hours of audio, of his baby son. The scientist hopes computers will **reveal links**[2] between the child's activities and his learning of language. He has divided each room into sections such as sink, table, fridge and stove. The computer picks out **combinations** of movements between these sections which are repeated. Researchers then **piece together**[3] how these fragments **correlate with**[4] specific activities, such as making coffee or doing the dishes. Eventually the computer will **bring** all the information **together** and provide statistics on how often the child observed an activity before finally producing a **related** word.

[1] which has made the video better or more useful [2] show connections not seen before [3] try to discover the truth about something by collecting different pieces of information and considering them at the same time [4] are connected with, often in a way in which one of them influences the other

B Expressing links and connections between people and things

Nowadays, the term 'hacker' is **synonymous with**[1] a criminal who attacks computer systems. Originally, the word **referred to**[2] a skilled programmer, and only later did it become **associated with**[3] malicious attacks.

In humans and in chimpanzees, hand movements **accompanied by** speech or vocal sounds are made more often with the right hand than the left hand. **Taken together**, the data **suggest**[4] that this phenomenon may date back as far as 5 million years ago.

In the 1980s, the wages of less-skilled US workers fell **relative to**[5] those of more-skilled workers. The **mutual**[6] influence of the inflow of less-skilled immigrants and the growth in US imports is also important.

Scientists have found **evidence of** an animal that can shrink and then grow again. Galapagos marine iguanas seem to change size, growing smaller or larger, possibly **reflecting** changes in the food supply.

The book examines the development of the **bond**[7] between children and their parents. **The relationship between** individual development and the strength of the bond varies between sons and daughters.

In questionnaire A, zero **corresponds to** 'disagree strongly' and 5 indicates 'agree strongly'. In questionnaire B, the **reverse**[8] is true, **in that**[9] 5 is **equivalent to** 'disagree strongly'.

[1] the two are so closely connected that one suggests the other [2] related to [3] connected in people's minds [4] show an idea without stating it directly or giving proof [5] if something is relative to something else, it varies according to the speed or level of the other thing [6] influencing each other [7] close connection [8] opposite [9] used before giving an explanation for something

The prefix *inter-* indicates a link or relationship between things (see Reference 5).

Interaction[10] between learner and learning material is a defining characteristic of education. He studied the **interrelated**[11] effects of families and peers on African-American youths. The article is concerned with the **interplay**[12] between emotions and logical thinking.

[10] communication with or reaction to [11] connected in such a way that each thing has an effect on or depends on the other [12] the effect two or more things have on each other

Exercises

43.1 Match the beginning of each sentence with the most appropriate ending, and add the missing prepositions.

1 The study found links .... gentle curves and sharp angles.
2 Jill's thoroughness is complemented .... scholars from all over the world.
3 Musical talent correlates .... information from a range of sources.
4 The sculpture is an unusual combination .... his previous research.
5 The conference has brought .... a computer programmer.
6 The researcher is trying to piece .... use of the drug and heart problems.
7 Peter's study is closely related .... her co-researcher's originality.
8 The term 'hacker' used to refer .... mathematical ability.

43.2 Correct the errors in these sentences.

1 There is usually a very strong bind between a mother and her child.
2 Salaries have fallen over the last few years not in real terms but relating to inflation.
3 In the UK black cats are associating with good luck.
4 In the experiment, group A performed best on the manual dexterity test and least well on the memory test whereas for group B the reversal was the case.
5 'Malicious' is more or less synonym with 'nasty'.
6 The problems discussed above are all closely interrelationship.
7 Took together, the studies by Johnson and Mahesh provide very strong evidence that previous theories on the nature of this disease were flawed.
8 The research is original in this it approaches the topic from a completely fresh angle.
9 The painter loved to explore the interplaying between light and shade.

43.3 Choose words from the box to fill in the missing words in this text.

associated	corresponds	equivalent	evidence	suggest
interaction	mutual	reflects	relationships	reveals

.... within a chimpanzee community is the theme of Gavros's fascinating new book. It describes the various different .... between the animals, and .... how an individual's behaviour .... his or her position in the community, showing how the older females in particular offer each other .... support. The book also provides .... to .... that chimpanzees use sounds in systematic ways to communicate with each other. One particular sound, for example, clearly .... to the human cry of 'Watch out!' while another would seem to be the .... of 'Help!' Certain gestures also seem to be .... with specific meanings.

43.4 Here are some more examples of words beginning with *inter-*. Use your knowledge of what this prefix means to help you explain what the words mean.

1 Alf won a prize in an **inter-university** chess competition.
2 **Interstate** highways in the USA are usually wide and well-maintained.
3 Our economic **interdependence** means that recession in the US also affects us.
4 **Intermarriage** throughout the centuries had meant that most European monarchs at the beginning of the twentieth century were quite closely related.
5 The internet has enormously facilitated the **interchange** of information between scholars worldwide.
6 The design was a complicated construction of **interconnecting** parts.

44 Comparing and contrasting

A Prepositional expressions

Note the items in bold in these titles of journal articles and also note the prepositions.

expression	notes
Problems in pain measurement: **a comparison between** verbal **and** visual rating scales	*Between* is used when two different things are being compared. *Of* is used when different examples of the same thing are being compared.
A **comparison of** different methods and approaches to homeschooling	
Mobility in the EU **in comparison with** the US	*With* and *to* are both used nowadays with similar meanings in these expressions. American English generally prefers *compared with*.
The effects of risk on private investment: Africa **compared with** other developing areas	
An exploration of the average driver's speed **compared to** driver safety and driving skill	
Reduced rate of disease development after HIV-2 infection **as compared to** HIV-1	This expression indicates that there is indeed a difference between the things which are compared.
Some psycho-physical **analogies between** speech and music	Comparisons between things which have similar features; often used to help explain a principle or idea.
Differences and **similarities between** mothers and teachers as informants on child behaviour	*Between* is used with *difference* when different groups of people or things are compared. *In* is used when different aspects of one thing are compared (here 'ethical perceptions').
Differences in ethical standards between male and female managers: myth or reality?	
Children's understanding of **the distinction between** real and apparent emotion	A distinction is a difference between two similar things.
Is globalisation today really **different from** globalisation a hundred years ago?	*Different to* is also used in UK academic usage, but *different from* is much more frequent. *Different than* is often found in US English.

B Useful linking expressions for comparison and contrast

44% of the male subjects responded negatively. **Similarly,** 44% of the female subjects said they had never voted in any election. [*likewise* could also be used here]
There is a **contrast between** fiction and reality.
Older teenagers were found to be more likely than younger teenagers to purchase music CDs. **Conversely,** younger teenagers purchased more video games. [in an opposite way]
Unlike Scotland, Irish mortality rates were relatively low for such a poor country.
Verb endings in some languages can show present, past or future tense, **whereas** in English, verb endings can only show present or past. [*while* could also be used here; note the comma]
A recent study suggested that building a network of good friends, **rather than** maintaining close family ties, helps people live longer into old age.
On the one hand, critics accuse the police of not protecting the public from crime. **On the other hand,** people also complained that the police were too oppressive. [used to compare two different facts or two opposite ways of thinking about a situation]
In the north, the rains are plentiful. In the south **the reverse is true** and drought is common.

ERROR WARNING

Remember to say **the same as**, NOT ~~the same that~~ or ~~the same than~~. Say **similar to**, NOT ~~similar as~~.
Don't confuse **on the other hand** (see above) with **in contrast**. *In contrast* expresses a marked opposition between two ideas: *Chan sharply condemned the diplomatic moves; **in contrast**, his deputy, Tiong, saw them as an attempt to create political stability.*

Exercises

44.1 Complete these sentences about comparing and contrasting.

1 The study looked at the different life chances of working-class children .... to those of middle-class children.
2 The results showed a marked .... (*three possible answers*) between the two groups of plants being tested.
3 The title of her paper was: 'Retail price differences in large supermarkets: organic foods .... to non-organic foods'.
4 My project was a .... of different styles of industrial architecture in the late 20th century.
5 The result of the second experiment was very different .... that of the first.
6 It would be interesting to do a .... between the musical skills of teenage girls and those of teenage boys.
7 The physicist drew an .... between the big bang and throwing a stone into a pond.
8 Gronsky believes cold fusion will soon be achieved in the laboratory. ...., his colleague Ladrass believes cold fusion is simply theoretically impossible.

44.2 Rewrite the sentences using an expression which includes the word in brackets instead of the underlined words.

1 The two groups were <u>not the same as</u> each other. (DIFFERENT)
2 The two groups of children <u>were different</u>. (CONTRAST noun)
3 The three liquids <u>had many things in common with</u> one another. (SIMILAR)
4 The data revealed <u>that the informants' responses were different</u>. (DIFFERENCES)
5 The title of her paper was: '<u>A comparison of</u> male attitudes towards prison sentencing <u>and</u> female attitudes'. (COMPARED)
6 <u>In a similar way to the manner in which</u> the economy of the north is booming, the south is also enjoying an economic upturn. (SIMILARLY)

44.3 Use linking expressions based on the word(s) in brackets to rewrite these pairs of sentences as one sentence. Make any other changes necessary.

1 The south of the country has little in the way of forests. The north of the country is covered with thick forests. (UNLIKE)
2 A questionnaire is good. In this case, face-to-face interviews are better. (RATHER)
3 Asian languages such as Vietnamese are quite difficult for learners whose first language is a European one. The opposite is also true. (CONVERSELY)
4 Oil is plentiful at the present time. It will run out one day. (HAND)
5 Boys tend to prefer aggressive solutions to problems. Girls, on the other hand, prefer more indirect approaches. (WHEREAS)
6 In the post-war period, public transportation enjoyed a boom. Nowadays, it is little used. (REVERSE)

44.4 Are these statements true or false? Circle T or F. Use a dictionary if necessary. If the statement is false, explain why.

1 If two things are mutually exclusive, one makes the other impossible.   T F
2 If two methods of doing something are compatible, they cannot both be used.   T F
3 If two things are equated, they are said to be similar or the same.   T F
4 If there are parallels between two phenomena, they are very different from each other.   T F
5 If there is an overlap between two things, they share some properties.   T F

45 Describing problems

A Introducing a problem

Note the way words are combined in these extracts from academic articles.

As the mining operations became deeper and deeper, **the problem of** flooding **arose**[1].
In a recent survey, 34% of customers **experienced difficulties with** online buying.
Walsh's paper discusses the **controversy**[2] **surrounding** privatisation of health services.
Conservation driven by market forces seems to be **a contradiction in terms**[3].
The topic is inadequately treated, and several **errors are apparent**[4] in the analysis.
Integrating the new member states **poses**[5] **a challenge** to the European Union.
The research **raises**[6] **the issue of** rainforests and the people who live in them.
The patient **had difficulty in** remembering very recent events.
Most theories of the origin of the universe **contain inconsistencies**[7].
The results **revealed shortcomings**[8] **in** the design of the questionnaire.

[1] *question/issue/difficulty/controversy* also often combine with *arise* [2] a lot of disagreement or argument about something [3] a combination of words which is nonsense because some of the words suggest the opposite of some of the others [4] can be seen [5] *threat/problem/danger* also are often used with *pose*; the verb *present* can also be used with these nouns [6] *question/problem* also are often used with *raise* [7] if a reason, idea, opinion, etc. has inconsistencies, different parts of it do not agree [8] faults or a failure to reach a particular standard

B Responding to a problem

verb	noun	example	meaning
react	react/ reaction	It was a study of how small firms **react to** the problem of over-regulation.	act in a particular way as a direct result of
respond	response	The Minister's **response to** the problem of inflation was to impose a price freeze.	his/her reaction to what has happened or been said or done
deal with		How should training courses **deal with** the issue of violence in the healthcare setting?	take action in order to solve a problem
tackle		Governments do not seem to be able to **tackle** the problem of urban congestion.	try to deal with
address		Governments need to **address** the problem of waste from nuclear power plants.	(formal) give attention to or deal with
mediate	mediation	The community leaders attempted to **mediate between** the police and the people.	talk to the two groups involved to try to help them find a solution to their problems

C Solving a problem

The researchers **solved** the problem by increasing the temperature.
The team **came up with / found a solution to** the problem of water damage.
By using video, the researchers **overcame** the problem of interpreting audio-only data.
The two governments finally **resolved**[1] the problem of sharing water resources. A successful **resolution**[2] **to** the crisis came in 1998.
The **answer to** the problem **lay in** changing the design of the experiment.
The book was entitled: '**Conflict Resolution**: the Management of International Disputes'.

[1] (more formal) solved or ended [2] noun form of the verb

Exercises

45.1 Match the beginning of each sentence with the most appropriate ending.

1 Students always seem to have difficulty	surrounding the President.
2 Ford pointed out that the methodology had	apparent.
3 The need to find replacement fuels poses	some important questions for the Party.
4 The media continue to focus on the controversy	many difficulties.
5 In the figures he presented several errors were	arose fairly recently.
6 On their way across Antarctica they experienced	in remembering this formula.
7 The results of the opinion poll raise	a number of inconsistencies.
8 Problems caused by pollution in this area	considerable challenges for scientists.

45.2 There is a preposition missing in each of these sentences. Add it in the right place.

1 It is no easy task mediating unions and management.
2 In this lecture I plan to deal the later novels of Charles Dickens.
3 The answer to most problems in agriculture lies the soil.
4 He thought for a long time but was unable to come with a solution.
5 Green tourism may initially feel like a contradiction terms.
6 I wonder what the professor's reaction the article will be.
7 The company has experienced a number of difficulties the computer operating system.
8 Have you found a solution the problem yet?

45.3 Complete these tables. Use a dictionary to help you if necessary.

noun	verb
	solve
reaction	
	contain
error	

noun	verb
resolution	
	respond
contradiction	
	mediate

45.4 Choose one of the words from the tables in 45.3 to complete each sentence. You may need to change the form of the verbs.

1 The professor was very angry when the student .... him so rudely and so publicly.
2 As the saying goes, to .... is human – we all make mistakes.
3 I hope someone will eventually come up with a .... to the problem of global warming.
4 The diplomats are hoping to .... between the two sides and so prevent a conflict.
5 The library .... many rare and beautiful books.
6 I am still waiting for the committee's .... to my request for an extension for my dissertation.
7 At the beginning of the new academic year Marie .... to make much more effort with her assignments.
8 The lecturer .... very angrily when I questioned one of her conclusions.

 Much academic work is based on asking questions or raising problems and finding solutions to them. Find an article relating to your own discipline which discusses a problem. Note down any interesting vocabulary that you find there.

46 Describing situations

A Existence and location

Look at these extracts from history lectures. Note the words in bold.

> The **existence** of a large population of migrant workers put pressure on the country's **infrastructure**[1].

> Historians noted the **absence**[3] of a clear political ideology in the actions of the workers.

> We need to look at all the **circumstances**[2] surrounding the events of 1926.

> Looking at events in their social **context** means taking *all* the factors of a person's social **environment** into account.

> The **conditions** in which the poorest sector of the population lived were bad.

> The **status**[4] of women was not a serious subject of debate until the 1960s.

[1] basic systems and services, such as transport and power supplies [2] facts or events that make the situation the way it is [3] opposite = *presence* [4] official position, especially in a social group

B Factors affecting situations

(n) = noun   (v) = verb   (adj) = adjective   (opp) = opposite

word	examples	notes
constrain (v) constraint (n)	Scientists are **constrained** by the amount of funding they can obtain / are **subject to the constraints of** funding.	being controlled and limited in what they can do
restrain (v) restraint (n)	Growth in car ownership could be **restrained** by higher taxes. High land prices are a **restraint on** the expansion of private housing in the city.	limiting the growth or force of something
minimum (n/adj) (opp) maximum minimal (adj)	The **minimum/maximum** temperature was recorded at each stage. Damage to buildings was **minimal**.	smallest/largest amount allowed or possible very small in amount
confine (v)	Major industrial pollution is **confined to** the big cities in the north of the region.	limited to
restrict (v) restriction (n)	The government took measures to **restrict** the sale of tobacco products to young people. To fight traffic congestion, the city **imposed a restriction of** one car per household.	limiting something and reducing its size or preventing it from increasing
intrinsic (adj) (opp) extrinsic	English language is an **intrinsic** part of the college curriculum.	extremely important and basic characteristic of it
integral (adj)	Users' experiences are **integral to** the way libraries measure their performance.	necessary and important as a part of a whole
finite (adj) (opp) infinite	Oil is a **finite** resource; it will run out one day. There is evidence to suggest the universe is **infinite**.	having a limit or end /ˈfaɪnaɪt/ having no limit or end /ˈɪnfɪnət/
stable (adj) (opp) unstable stability (n) (opp) instability	It takes decades to create a **stable** democracy. Political **instability** is a threat to the whole region.	if something is stable, it is firmly fixed or not likely to move or change

Exercises

46.1 Choose one of the words in bold in A to complete each sentence.

1 To understand the problem, we need to look at all the many factors which may influence development in the child's social and physical _____ .

2 It has been claimed that the _____ of teaching as a profession is not as high as it used to be or as it should be.

3 The infrared aerial photograph seems to show the _____ of a large village around 1,000 years ago.

4 The company's president died in rather suspicious _____ and his son took over.

5 In the _____ of any clear instructions from above, I think we should decide ourselves how to proceed.

6 The country can never become a major economic player unless it improves its _____ .

7 I can't tell you what the word means unless you tell me it in _____ .

8 Students today live in very luxurious _____ compared with students in the past.

46.2 Change the words in bold to the *opposite* meaning.

1 The economy has been **stable** for several years.

2 **Stability** has been a feature of government in the country for the last decade.

3 The northern region possesses an apparently **finite** supply of uranium.

4 The **presence** of cholera in the area was noted by scientists in 1978.

5 A **minimum** temperature of 20 degrees must be maintained at all times.

46.3 Rewrite the sentences without changing the meaning, using the word in brackets.

1 In the 1960s the government restricted the amount of money you could take out of the country. (RESTRICTION)

2 The problem exists only in the capital city. (CONFINED)

3 All fossil fuels will run out one day. (RESOURCES)

4 In the accident there was very little damage to the car. (MINIMAL)

5 All research is constrained by funding decisions. (SUBJECT)

6 The fact that the country is socially unstable deters investors. (SOCIAL)

7 Normally we would not behave in this way. (CIRCUMSTANCES)

8 Most small children believe that fairies exist. (OF FAIRIES)

46.4 Choose the best word in italics to complete each sentence.

1 The government has introduced legislation to *restrict / constrain* smoking in public places.

2 Learning from your mistakes is an *infinite / intrinsic* part of making progress.

3 Her attempt to *confine / restrain* the children from making a noise in the library met with little success.

4 The professor always insists that even the most junior research associate is an *unstable / integral* part of the team.

5 What are the *minimum / minimal* requirements for getting a place on the course?

6 During the exam period restrictions are *posed / imposed* on visitors to the college.

7 There were some rather curious *circumstances / contexts* surrounding the case.

8 The level of taxation in the country is a major *constraint / restraint* on foreign investment there.

FOLLOW UP Find a news article about a scientific development and read the description of the situation which led to it (often to be found in the introduction). Note any useful general nouns used there.

47 Processes and procedures

A General nouns and verbs

Note the prepositions which follow the nouns in bold.

The next **stage/step in** the process of data collection was to send out 100 questionnaires.
The **procedure**[1] **for** Experiment B was different from that of Experiment A.
The **application**[2] **of** Thoren's method produced some interesting results.
They studied the **behaviour of** large corporations during periods of economic crisis.
The team carried out a computer **simulation**[3] **of** climate change over the next 30 years.
Twenty-five subjects were **selected from** the first group to take part in the second analysis.
She **designed** a course to train students to **utilise**[4] self-motivation strategies.
The article sets out to **unify**[5] some concepts in the theory of economic growth.
Personal interviews were conducted to **supplement**[6] the statistical data.
The experiments were repeated, in order to **verify**[7] the results observed in the original data.

[1] carefully controlled set of actions [2] using it for a practical purpose [3] a model of a problem or course of events [4] (formal) use something in an effective way [5] bring together/combine [6] add something to something to make it larger or better [7] make certain that they are correct

B Social/political/economic processes

example with noun	equivalent verb	meaning
The **emergence of** nation states changed Europe in the 19th century.	Nation states **emerged** in the 19th century.	process of appearing or starting to exist
The paper is a study of water **consumption** in Brazil during 2001.	Millions of litres of bottled water are now **consumed**.	process of using fuel, energy, food, etc.
Ratification of the trade agreement took place in 2004.	The agreement was **ratified** in 2004.	process of making an agreement official
Security of supply is the most important priority in the gas industry.	The new pipeline will **secure** gas supplies for the region.	(formal) process of getting something
Before the **advent of** computers, scientific analysis was a slow process.	Before computers were **developed/invented**, analysis took a long time.	arrival of an invention (the noun has no verb form)

C Technological processes and procedures

Look at these questions on a college website dealing with computer problems.

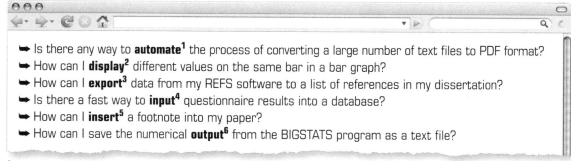

➡ Is there any way to **automate**[1] the process of converting a large number of text files to PDF format?
➡ How can I **display**[2] different values on the same bar in a bar graph?
➡ How can I **export**[3] data from my REFS software to a list of references in my dissertation?
➡ Is there a fast way to **input**[4] questionnaire results into a database?
➡ How can I **insert**[5] a footnote into my paper?
➡ How can I save the numerical **output**[6] from the BIGSTATS program as a text file?

[1] make a process be operated by machines or computers, instead of by humans [2] arrange something or a collection of things so that they can be seen [3] copy a large amount of it either to a different part of the computer's storage space or to another form of storage [4] put them into the computer's system [5] add [6] results produced by the programme

Exercises

47.1 Choose the best word in italics to complete each sentence.

1 It is sensible to *unify / select / verify* your results before publishing them.
2 Hip replacement is usually a simple medical *application / procedure / behaviour*.
3 Many students *supplement / utilise / verify* their scholarships by doing some part-time work.
4 A computer *stage / procedure / simulation* shows what will happen if the ocean current does indeed change direction and start flowing from the Arctic to the West Indies.
5 As the next *step / behaviour / application* in our study we plan to carry out interviews.
6 Her aim is to *form / design / function* a radically different type of electric engine.

47.2 Rewrite each sentence, replacing the underlined word with a word from B or C opposite. Both the underlined words and the replacement words are correct in academic English; the difference is that the replacement words are more formal.

1 It is hardly surprising that people <u>use</u> far more electricity than they did ten years ago.
2 The <u>arrival</u> of the mobile phone has transformed the way young people manage their social lives.
3 The software allows you to <u>present</u> your data in a range of different types of chart.
4 A number of talented new designers have <u>appeared</u> this year.
5 You've missed out a letter here – you need to <u>add</u> a *p* between the *a* and the *t*.
6 He spent many years trying to <u>create</u> a machine that would automatically sort large numbers of coins.
7 The research assistants had to <u>put in</u> a huge amount of data to run the experiment.
8 The political party managed to <u>gain</u> more support than was anticipated.

47.3 Complete these tables and add the preposition which usually follows the verb or noun where you see (+). Use a dictionary for prepositions not given on the opposite page.

verb		noun	
apply	(+)		(+)
behave			(+)
simulate			(+)
	(+)	selection	(+)
		design	(+)
ratify			(+)
	(+)	insertion	

verb		noun	
		verification	(+)
		utilisation	(+)
emerge	(+)		(+)
consume			(+)
secure			(+)
	(+)	input	
		display	(+)

47.4 Choose a word from the tables in 47.3 to complete each sentence.

1 The article traces the _____ of Korea as a major economic force.
2 Because of the drought everyone has been asked to reduce their water _____ .
3 I think it would be a good idea to _____ some tables into the first part of your article.
4 It took considerable negotiations before all parties were prepared to _____ the treaty.
5 This course will focus on the _____ of theory to practice.
6 It took me a long time to _____ into the computer all the data from the survey.
7 Most psychology students choose to do a course on animal _____ .
8 My instructor gave some useful advice on how to _____ a new group of experiments.

> **FOLLOW UP** Use a dictionary to find some typical word combinations for these words – *process, procedure* and *stage*. Then write five sentences about aspects of your own subject using five of the word combinations.

48 Describing change

A Historical changes and their effects

The **transition**[1] **from** agriculture **to** industry challenged the economic and political **status quo**[2] in many countries. Millions of people **abandoned**[3] villages and rural areas and moved into cities. The **shift**[4] **away from** self-sufficiency meant most people became dependent on large corporations in one way or another, and had to **adapt**[5] **to** new social environments and **adjust**[6] **to** new ways of doing things. The **move**[7] **towards** smaller, nuclear families brought about **fundamental**[8] changes in family patterns in many parts of the world. **Maintaining**[9] the old ways became **increasingly**[10] difficult. On the other hand, the **elimination**[11] **of** diseases such as smallpox **transformed**[12] millions of people's lives, and the **expansion**[13] **of** healthcare in many countries saved countless lives. Technology **enhanced**[14] most people's lives in some way. For many people, nonetheless, the negative **impact**[15] **of** technology on the environment **altered**[16] the way we think of our relationship with nature, and **sustainable**[17] **development**, rather than development for its own sake, became an important goal for a number of countries.

[1] change from one form to another [2] the situation as it was at that time [3] left for ever [4] change in position or direction [5] change to suit different conditions [6] become more familiar with a new situation [7] action taken to achieve something [8] in a very basic way [9] not allowing them to change [10] more and more [11] removal of [12] changed completely so that they are better [13] increase in size or extent [14] improved the quality of [15] powerful effect that something, especially something new, has on a situation [16] changed (usually slightly) [17] causing little or no damage to the environment and therefore able to continue for a long time

B More verbs for describing change

The exchange rate between the euro and the dollar has **fluctuated** recently. [changed or varied, especially continuously and between one level and another]
The technicians **modified** the flow of oil through the engine. [changed it slightly to improve it]
The company's lawyers **amended** the contract to take account of the new situation. [changed the words of a text, typically a law or a legal document]
Seven power plants were **converted from** oil **to** gas. [caused to change in form or character]
After 20 years of trading in the US, the firm **transferred** their operations **to** Brazil. [moved]
The economy **recovered** after three years of depression. [returned to a satisfactory condition]
Oil supplies are **diminishing** rapidly. **Acquiring** new supplies is vital for many countries. [becoming less; (formal) obtaining, getting]
We need to **refine** our analysis to obtain more accurate results. [improve it, especially by removing unwanted material]
The government **relaxed** controls on imports in 1997. [make less strict or severe]
Plans have been drawn up to **restore** 50,000 acres of wetland to their former state. [return something or someone to an earlier good condition or position]

C Adjectives which often describe change

There was a **gradual change** in attitudes in the 1980s. [slow, over a long period of time]
A **sudden change** in the temperature of the liquid occurred after some minutes.
There is a **marked change** in how people perceive antisocial behaviour. [very noticeable]
There was no **perceptible change** in the learning outcomes between Time 1 and Time 2. [which could be perceived, i.e. noticed or seen]

 A change **in** and a change **of** are different. A change **in** temperature/behaviour/attitudes/composition/policy, etc. suggests a process where something has become different (e.g. smaller, more radical). A change **of** clothing/government/approach, etc. means the complete substitution of one thing for another.

Exercises

48.1 Fill in the missing words in each sentence with a word formed from the same root as the word in brackets. You may need a dictionary to help you with items 7 to 10.

1 There has been an enormous .... in aviation in recent years. (EXPAND)
2 Economists are increasingly concerned that development should be .... (SUSTAIN)
3 There has been no .... change in the patient's condition. (PERCEIVE)
4 The survey found that most people feel that modern life is becoming .... difficult. (INCREASE)
5 Industrial .... has, of course, transformed people's working lives. (DEVELOP)
6 The group's aims include the .... of famine and poverty. (ELIMINATE)
7 The apparatus worked well after we had made some .... to it. (MODIFY)
8 With increasing unemployment many people have had to make .... to their lives. (ADJUST)
9 Many linguists have studied first language .... , or how people learn their mother tongue. (ACQUIRE)
10 There is unlikely to be any .... of controls in the near future. (RELAX)

48.2 Answer these questions about the language in this unit.

1 If prices *fluctuate* what do they do?
2 If a disease is *eliminated* how much of it remains?
3 If interest in something is *diminishing* is it becoming less or more?
4 If there is a *marked* change in someone's behaviour is it a big or a small change?
5 If most people feel that mobile phones *enhance* their lives, do they feel that their lives have become better or worse?
6 If controls on imports are *relaxed* do they become more or less strict?

48.3 Choose the best word in italics to complete each sentence.

1 The economy now seems to be *recovering / amending*.
2 Many people now are *converting / transforming* to using solar power.
3 Our survey did not succeed in getting all the information we need and so we shall have to *diminish / refine* our questions a little.
4 Why do some people *abandon / shift* their families and disappear without a word?
5 It takes most people some time to *alter / adjust* to living in a new country.
6 In recent years most societies have seen a major change in the *transition / status quo*.
7 It is increasingly hard to *adapt / maintain* traditions in the face of progress.
8 There have been some attempts to *restore / alter* the environment to its original state.

48.4 Which preposition is needed to complete each phrase?

1 a change .... the climate
2 to transfer money .... a Swiss bank account
3 a shift .... the countryside towards the towns
4 to have an impact .... the cost of living
5 to relax controls .... immigration
6 to adjust .... changes
7 the transition .... one period to the next
8 to adapt .... a new way of life

49 Evaluation and emphasis

A Adjectives for evaluating: opening sentences from science articles

The first **comprehensive**[1] survey of coral reefs is being carried out in the Indian Ocean.
Fundamental[2] problems exist in current theories of the universe, a physicist claims.
A **ground-breaking**[3] discovery has been made in research into ageing and death.
Important new information about the planets has been gained from the *Orbis* space probe.
Working hours have increased and pressures at work have become more **intense** in the UK.
A **crucial** stage in global warming could be reached within ten years, scientists say.
The search for a unified theory of the human mind is **misguided**[4], says a psychologist.
The discovery of a dinosaur-like bone fossil in Africa is **unique**, according to scientists.
In 1997, Irkan published a **significant** piece of research on open structures in bridges.
Current responses to the global energy crisis are **inadequate**, a scientist has warned.

[1] complete, including everything that is necessary [2] basic, from which everything else originates
[3] very new and a big change [4] based on bad judgement or on wrong information or beliefs

B Teachers' evaluations of student assignments

- Good! The only **criticism** I have is that there is a **notable**[1] lack of **key** references to work before 1990. You should have **given credit to**[2] earlier work by Wilson and Healey.
- I am concerned about the **validity**[3] of some of your analysis, and as a result, some of your conclusions may be **invalid**. **Significantly**, you had problems in Section C.
- I don't think the two different analyses you did are **compatible**[4]. **It is not surprising that** you had problems matching the two results, which **could be viewed as** almost **contradictory**.
- There are some **solid**[5] arguments in Section A, but I think your conclusion in B is **mistaken** and lacks **hard**[6] **evidence**. Your data are* rather **limited**. [*may also sometimes be *is*]

[1] important and deserving attention [2] stated the importance of [3] basis in truth or reason [4] able to exist successfully together [5] of a good standard; giving confidence or support [6] clear, able to be proven

C Other evaluative expressions

It is noteworthy that Holikov (1996) also had difficulty explaining the phenomenon.
It is worth recalling that three previous studies failed to find a link between the two events.
We should **recognise/acknowledge** how difficult it is to interpret these data.
These results **are borne out by**[1] two other studies: Hermann (1998) and Wilson (2001).
In his **seminal**[2] work, Abaka **challenges**[3] current techniques, revealing **flaws**[4] in data interpretation.

[1] confirmed, shown to be true [2] containing important new ideas, very influential [3] questions whether they are correct [4] faults, mistakes or weaknesses; we can say a method is *flawed* (adj)

D Emphasising

The research **underlined/highlighted** the need for a new social policy for childcare.
- When used at the beginning of a sentence for extra emphasis, negative expressions are followed by inversion of the subject and verb. A form of *do* is used when there is no other auxiliary or modal verb.

Under/In no circumstances / On no account <u>is it</u> right to video people without consent.
Seldom/Never (before)/Rarely in the history of Europe <u>has there</u> been such a crisis.
In no way / By no means <u>does this new study</u> invalidate existing studies.
Only in 1985 <u>did the government accept</u> that something needed to be done urgently.

Exercises

49.1 Look at A and answer the following questions about the adjectives there.

1 Which two adjectives have negative associations?
2 Which adjective sounds most positive and exciting?
3 Which two words can be quite close synonyms and could be used, for example, in the phrase *to play a(n)* _____ *role in the development of?*
4 Which word has a similar meaning to the adjectives in 3 but is stronger or more extreme?
5 Which word means *the only one of its type?*

49.2 Choose the best words from the box to complete each of these sentences.

acknowledged	borne	challenged	credit	crucial
evidence	flawed	flaws	ground-breaking	
limited	mistaken	seminal	validity	viewed

1 Nierinck gave _____ to the input of her research associates and _____ that they had played a _____ role in the project.
2 Unfortunately, these results are not _____ out by other work in the field and you are _____ to claim that there is hard _____ to support your theory. There are _____ in some of your calculations, and they need redoing.
3 Herbert _____ Evensson on the _____ of his conclusions claiming that his data were _____ and were too _____ to be reliable.
4 This superb article can be _____ as a _____ piece of work which has made _____ discoveries about the nature of cancerous cells.

49.3 Rewrite these sentences beginning in the way indicated.

1 It is by no means certain that all the students will pass their final exams.
  By no means _____
2 Never before had he taught such an outstanding student.
  He _____
3 The country has rarely witnessed such a display of public feeling.
  Rarely _____
4 In no way will we be able to halt the process of global warming.
  We _____
5 Students will not be allowed to defer the completion of their thesis longer than one month under any circumstances.
  Under no circumstances _____
6 We will only know the answer when we gather a lot more data.
  Only when we _____

49.4 Rearrange the letters to make the word that fits the sentence.

1 The study _ _ _ _ _ _ _ _ _ _ the need for more research. SHHHLTIIGG
2 I don't find your arguments either _ _ _ _ _ or convincing. DOILS
3 Unfortunately, the two studies came up with results which were not
  _ _ _ _ _ _ _ _ _ _ . ABCELIMOPT
4 She wrote the first _ _ _ _ _ _ _ _ _ _ _ _ study of this _ _ _ period of Athenian history. OIRCPMEENHVES / YEK
5 It is _ _ _ _ _ _ _ _ _ _ _ _ _ _ that his work was initially criticised for being too _ _ _ _ _ _ _ _ . TROWH / LLARIGNEC / IMITLDE
6 The article _ _ _ _ _ _ _ _ _ _ the importance of literacy and numeracy skills in early education. DLSIUENREN

50 Summary and conclusion

A Conclusions and summaries: typical paragraph starters

Summarising is concerned with expressing the most important facts or ideas about something or someone in a short and clear form.
Concluding is concerned with (a) stating your position or opinion after considering all the information about something, or (b) stating that you have come to the end of something.
Recapitulating is concerned with briefly repeating your main points.

Read these openings of the final paragraphs of academic articles. Note the useful expressions.

As we have seen, the data are consistent across the three separate tests.

To conclude / In conclusion, it seems that women's greater risk of depression is a consequence of gender differences in social roles.

To recapitulate[1] the findings of the present experiments: mothers' speech to young children was simpler than their normal speech.

From these comparisons we may **draw the following conclusions.** As was expected, there are large differences between Russia and the two Nordic countries (Finland and Sweden).

To sum up / To summarise / In summary[2], in the case of high achievers in all professions, emotional competence is twice as important as purely mental abilities. **In short**[3], emotional competence is the key.

To bring the paper **to a close**[4], I **summarise the main points**[5] here: siblings influence the development of behaviour, and problems among siblings are linked to other problems.

[1] a less formal alternative is the short form *to recap* [2] (more formal) can also be *in sum* [3] used before describing something in as few words and as directly as possible [4] or *bring to an end* [5] or *summarise the key points*

B Other useful words and expressions for summarising and concluding

We may summarise the findings **in a few words**: conserving wetlands is an urgent priority.
The **final** point to stress is that pay is rarely the only factor in industrial disputes. **To put it briefly / Stated briefly,** complex motives contribute to strikes. [*final* is more formal than *last*]
Praditsuk (1996) **provides/gives a (brief) summary of** Asian economic cooperation.
In the **abstract** of the article, the authors claim to have made a breakthrough in cancer research. [shortened form of an article, book, etc., giving only the most important facts or arguments, usually printed at the beginning of the book or article]
The government only published a **précis** of the report, not the full report. [/'preɪsi/ a short form of a text which briefly summarises the important parts]
In this essay, I have **attempted** to review **concisely** the arguments in favour of intellectual property rights in relation to the internet. [in academic style it is common to say that you have attempted/tried to argue or demonstrate something instead of directly saying you did it; *concisely* means in a short and clear way, without unnecessary words]
On balance, the **overall** picture seems to be that the political climate influences corporate strategy. [after thinking about the different facts or opinions; general rather than in particular]
In the final/last analysis, the only safe prediction is that the future is likely to be very different from the present. [said when talking about what is most important or true in a situation]

Don't confuse *lastly* and *at last*. *Lastly* refers to the final point or item in a list or a series of points being discussed, and is similar to *finally*. *At last* refers to something which happens after people have been waiting for it for a long time.
Remember, *eventually* does NOT mean 'perhaps'. It means 'in the end, especially after a long time or a lot of effort, problems, etc.'

Exercises

50.1 Look at A. Rewrite each sentence, using the word in brackets.

1 To conclude, the tests suggest the drug has no dangerous side effects. (CONCLUSION)
2 In short, losing the war was a humiliating defeat for the country on a number of different levels. (SUMMARISE)
3 To sum up, it is impossible to blame the disaster on one person alone. (SUMMARY)
4 From the survey we can conclude that advertising has a stronger effect on teenage girls than on other groups of the population. (DRAW / COME *give two answers*)
5 To recap, there were a number of different reasons why the experiment was less successful than had been hoped. (RECAPITULATE)

50.2 Choose a word from the box to complete each sentence.

abstract	analysis	balance	close	eventually	points	provide	put	words

1 On _____ it would seem that more people are against the proposed law than for it.
2 Authors submitting an article for the journal are requested to provide a brief _____ outlining the contents of their article.
3 To _____ it briefly, General Pachai's attempts to manipulate the situation to his own advantage _____ led to his own downfall.
4 Most theses _____ a summary of the literature in the field in their opening chapter.
5 In the final _____ no one can be completely certain as to what caused the crash.
6 To summarise the problem in a few _____ : manufacturing in the country has declined drastically in the last ten years.
7 Let us now recap the main _____ in the argument.
8 Before bringing this paper to a _____ , I should like to suggest some areas requiring further research.

50.3 Choose either *lastly* or *at last* to complete each of these sentences.

1 After several months of negotiations, the two sides have _____ reached agreement.
2 First, we shall consider the causes of the war, then we shall look at the events of the war and, _____ , we shall discuss the consequences of the war.
3 She decided not to apply to Melbourne University. First and foremost, her marks were not likely to be good enough but also her parents did not want her to apply there. _____ , none of her friends were considering going there.
4 My brother was very relieved when, _____ , he finished writing his dissertation.
5 Many congratulations on having reached the final unit of this book _____ .

50.4 What can you learn about the difference between the expressions *in the end* and *at the end* from these two sentences? Use a dictionary if necessary.

1 In the end, the government realised that the tax law had been a mistake and abolished it.
2 At the end of the book, Tao states that privatisation of public services is the solution.

50.5 Correct the six errors in this paragraph.

> This paragraph is a précise of *Academic Vocabulary in Use*. To sum, the book provides 50 units covering key aspects of academic vocabulary. Stated brief, each unit has tempted to present and practise the words that all students need. The overalls aim of the book is to help students not only to understand but also to use academic vocabulary. In bringing the book to a closure, we hope we have helped you and wish you success in your future academic studies.

Reading and vocabulary 1

This section will give you further practice in the kinds of vocabulary you have studied in this book and will help you to become more aware of academic vocabulary as you read. The texts will be useful for you whatever discipline you are studying.

Read the text. Use a dictionary if necessary but note that it is not essential to understand every word. Then answer the questions.

Good friends

Psychologists have long known that having a set of cherished companions is crucial to mental well-being. In addition, a recent study by Australian investigators concluded that our friends even help to prolong our lives. The scientists analyzed data from a decade-long survey called the Australian Longitudinal Study of Aging, which was initiated in 1992. It concentrated on the social environment, general health, lifestyle and age of death of 1,477 persons older than 70 years. Study participants were asked how much personal and telephone contact they had with friends, children, relatives and acquaintances.

Researchers were surprised to learn that friendships increased life expectancy to a far greater extent than, say, frequent contact with children and other relatives. This benefit held true even after these friends had moved away to another city and was independent of factors such as socioeconomic status, health and way of life.

What exactly underlies this effect on longevity? Apparently, the scientists posit, it is not merely the mutual buoying of spirits that occurs among associates. What is more important is that the support given and received by friends is voluntary and pleasurable and not just the result of a sense of duty or convention. In contrast to our own families, we are able to choose our friends.

According to the Australian scientists, the ability to have relationships with people to whom one is important has a positive effect on physical and mental health. Stress and the tendency toward depression are reduced, and behaviors that are damaging to health, such as smoking and drinking, occur less frequently. The investigators speculate that in times of calamity in particular, our support networks can raise our moods and feelings of self-worth and offer helpful strategies for dealing with difficult personal challenges.

1 **Which words and expressions in the first paragraph could the following substitute for?**

   1 friends one loves and cares for   3 extend   5 focused
   2 extremely important   4 begun   6 subjects

2 **Find in the text a word which:**

   1 means 'people' (more formal)   3 would be spelt differently in British English. How?
   2 means 'is the hidden cause of'   4 means a 'serious accident or very bad event'

3 **Use words from the text to complete this table.**

noun	verb	adjective
		conventional
help	help	
	expect	expectant
pleasure	please	

> **TIP** Once you have read the content of a text, look over it again and check that you know the different forms of important words in it, as in the table above.

Reading and vocabulary 2

Read the text. Use a dictionary if necessary but note that it is not essential to understand every word. Then answer the questions.

Australia

Of the seven continents, Australia is the flattest, smallest, and except for Antarctica, the most arid. Including the southeastern island of Tasmania, the island continent is roughly equal in area to the United States, excluding Alaska and Hawaii. Millions of years of geographic isolation from other landmasses accounts for Australia's unique animal species, notably marsupial mammals like the kangaroo, egg laying mammals like the platypus, and the flightless emu bird. Excluding folded structures (areas warped by geologic forces) along Australia's east coast, patches of the northern coastline and the relatively lush island of Tasmania, the continent is mostly dry, bleak and inhospitable.

Topography and origin of Australia

Australia has been less affected by seismic and orogenic (mountain building) forces than other continents during the past 400 million years. Although seismic (earthquake) activity persists in the eastern and western highlands, Australia is the most stable of all continents. In the recent geological past, it has experienced none of the massive upheavals responsible for uplifting the Andes in South America, the Himalayas in south Asia or the European Alps. Instead Australia's topography is the end result of gradual changes over millions of years. Australia is not the oldest continent, a common misconception arising from the continent's flat, seemingly unchanged expanse. Geologically it is the same age as the Americas, Asia, Africa, Europe and Antarctica. But Australia's crust has escaped strong earth forces in recent geological history, accounting for its relatively uniform appearance. As a result, the continent serves as a window to early geological ages.

Splitting of Australia from Antarctica

About 95 million years ago, tectonic forces (movements and pressures of the earth's crust) split Australia from Antarctica and the southern supercontinent of Gondwanaland. Geologists estimate that the continent is drifting northward at a rate of approximately 18 inches (28 cm) per year. They theorize that south Australia was joined to Antarctica at the Antarctic regions of Wilkes Land, including Commonwealth Bay. Over a period of 65 million years, beginning 160 million years ago, Australia's crust was stretched hundreds of miles by tectonics before it finally cleaved from Antarctica.

1 **True or false? Write T or F after these statements. If they are false, say why.**

1 Australia is the driest continent in the world.
2 Australia has some animals which no other continent has.
3 These animals came to Australia when it was still joined to other landmasses.
4 There is no seismic activity nowadays in Australia.
5 The general geological appearance of Australia is very different in its different regions.

2 **Underline in the text word combinations which mean:**

1 approximately the same
2 huge changes
3 result of a series of events or a long process
4 a wrong idea which many people believe is true
5 which apparently has remained the same

3 **Which word in the text means:**

1 having a lot of green, healthy plants, grass and trees
2 not suitable for humans to live in
3 a metaphor that means 'something that enables you to see and learn about a situation'
4 develop a set of ideas to explain something

 FOLLOW UP Find a general geography text about your own country or region written in English and make a note of any useful word combinations you find there.

Reading and vocabulary 3

Read the text. Use a dictionary if necessary but note that it is not essential to understand every word. Then answer the questions.

The World Wide Web

Until the appearance of the World Wide Web (WWW), the Internet was mainly used by people who had some computer expertise. File transfer protocol (FTP) was the standard method by which data could be stored on or removed from a server, and if a document that had been transmitted had references to other documents then it was not straightforward to access them. In other words, FTP does not link separate documents together.

In 1992, Tim Berners-Lee, working at Europe's high-energy physics research centre in Switzerland, wrote the first browser program which used a protocol called **hypertext transfer protocol** (HTTP). This operates as follows:

When a client requests a Web server to send a document, the request is sent using HTTP (rather than FTP). The Web server finds the document in its memory and transmits it along with extra information. It is this extra information that distinguishes a Web server from an Internet server. The extra information transmitted is composed of two main parts:

* **control codes, using hypertext markup language** (HTML), by which the client computer screen can display the document, i.e. the layout, headings, bordering, etc. Images can be transmitted as separate files and incorporated on the visible page by HTML code.
* **links** to other documents. These links are specific words or phrases in the text of the transmitted document that will allow related documents to be accessed.

When the mouse pointer of the client computer is moved over the document on the screen, the arrow changes to a hand with a pointing finger whenever it falls on any hypertext. If the user clicks on this link, the browser will automatically set up the link address and request the appropriate Web server to transmit the new document to the client. When this new document arrives, it is displayed on the screen.

A browser, therefore, is a program, stored in the client's computer, that is able to read hypertext. While the Internet is the huge collection of computer networks and databases connected by backbone cable and optic fibre, the WWW is essentially a browsing and searching system. It allows users with virtually no expertise to access the information stored at certain sites on the Internet.

1 **From memory if you can, fill in the missing prepositions.**

   1 until the appearance .... the World Wide Web
   2 the method .... which data could be stored
   3 the data could be stored on or removed .... a server
   4 references .... other documents
   5 the server transmits the document .... extra information
   6 the information is composed .... two parts
   7 the extra information provides links .... other documents

2 **Use words and phrases from the text to rewrite the words in bold.**

   1 Accessing web pages is **easy and simple,** and people with **almost** no expertise use the web.
   2 The browser contacts the **right** server to transmit the document.
   3 The WWW is **in its basic character** a search system.
   4 The information added to documents **makes** web servers **different** from Internet servers.
   5 Years ago, the Internet was **mostly** used by experts.

 Search an online encyclopedia for a text on either how the mobile/cell phone system works, or on how the satellite global positioning system (GPS) works. Read the text and make a note of any useful noun + preposition or verb + preposition combinations.

Reading and vocabulary 4

Read the text. Use a dictionary if necessary but note that it is not essential to understand every word. Then answer the questions.

The human brain

1   The brain is the most complex organ in the human body. It produces our every thought, action, memory, feeling and experience of the world. This jelly-like mass of tissue, weighing around 1.4 kilograms, contains a staggering one hundred billion nerve cells, or neurons. Each neuron can make contact with tens of thousands of others, via tiny structures called synapses. Our brains form a million new connections for every second of our lives. The pattern and strength of the connections is constantly changing and no two brains are alike. It is in these changing connections that memories are stored, habits learned and personalities shaped, by reinforcing certain patterns of brain activity, and losing others.

2   While people often speak of their 'grey matter', the brain also contains white matter. The grey matter is the cell bodies of the neurons, while the white matter is the branching network of thread-like tendrils – called dendrites and axons – that spread out from the cell bodies to connect to other neurons. The brain also has another, more numerous type of cell, called glial cells. These outnumber neurons ten times over. Once thought to be support cells, they are now known to amplify neural signals and to be as important as neurons in mental calculations. There are many different types of neuron, only one of which is unique to humans and the other great apes, the so-called spindle cells.

3   Brain structure is formed partially by genes, but largely by experience. Only relatively recently it was discovered that new brain cells are being born throughout our lives – a process called neurogenesis. The brain has bursts of growth and then periods of consolidation, when excess connections are pruned. The most notable bursts are in the first two or three years of life, during puberty, and also a final burst in young adulthood. How a brain ages also depends on genes and lifestyle too. Exercising the brain and giving it the right diet can be just as important as it is for the rest of the body.

4   The neurons in our brains communicate in a variety of ways. Signals pass between them by the release and capture of neurotransmitter and neuromodulator chemicals. Some neurochemicals work in the synapse, passing specific messages from release sites to collection sites, called receptors. Others also spread their influence more widely, like a radio signal, making whole brain regions more or less sensitive.

1   **Choose the correct word to complete each sentence. Look for words that the underlined words combine with in the article.**

   1   The skin is the largest organ in <u>the</u> .... <u>body</u>.
   2   Psychologists disagree as to how exactly <u>memories are</u> .... in the brain.
   3   Humans share almost all of their genes with the other .... <u>apes</u> such as gorillas.
   4   As children become young adults they have .... <u>of growth</u>.
   5   It is important that animals in captivity are given <u>the</u> .... <u>diet</u>.
   6   People have approached the problem <u>in a variety of</u> ....

2   **Find words in the text which have an *opposite* meaning:**

1 simple (para 1)	4 are fewer than (para 2)	7 initial (para 3)
2 converge (para 2)	5 diminish (para 2)	8 general (para 4)
3 scarce (para 2)	6 wholly (para 3)	9 restrict (para 4)

3   **These words from the text can be used in a number of different ways. Write sentences exemplifying three different uses for each of them.**

     matter   pass   formed   cells

4   **Highlight six words or phrases that might be used in your discipline. Write sentences using them.**

Reading and vocabulary 5

Read the text. Use a dictionary if necessary but note that it is not essential to understand every word. Then answer the questions.

Nanotechnology

1 Nanotechnology is science and engineering at the scale of atoms and molecules. It is the manipulation and use of materials and devices so tiny that nothing can be built any smaller. Nanomaterials are typically between 0.1 and 100 nanometres (nm) in size – with 1 nm being equivalent to one billionth of a metre (10^9 m).

2 This is the scale at which the basic functions of the biological world operate – and materials of this size display unusual physical and chemical properties. These profoundly different properties are due to an increase in surface area compared to volume as particles get smaller – and also the grip of weird quantum effects at the atomic scale.

3 Unwittingly, people have made use of some unusual properties of materials at the nanoscale for centuries. Tiny particles of gold for example, can appear red or green – a property that has been used to colour stained glass windows for over 1,000 years.

4 Experimental nanotechnology did not come into its own until 1981, when IBM scientists in Zurich, Switzerland, built the first scanning tunnelling microscope (STM). This allows us to see single atoms by scanning a tiny probe over the surface of a silicon crystal. In 1990, IBM scientists discovered how to use an STM to move single xenon atoms around on a nickel surface.

5 Engineering at the nanoscale is no simple feat, and scientists are having to come up with completely different solutions to build from the 'bottom-up' rather than using traditional 'top-down' manufacturing techniques. Some nanomaterials, such as nanowires and other simple devices have been shown to assemble themselves given the right conditions, and other experiments at larger scales are striving to demonstrate the principles of self-assembly. Micro-electronic devices might be persuaded to grow from the ground up, rather like trees.

6 In the short term, the greatest advances through nanotechnology will come in the form of novel medical devices and processes, new catalysts for industry and smaller components for computers. In medicine, for example, we are already seeing research on: new ways to deliver drugs with contact lenses; the directing of drugs to tumours with tiny 'smart bombs'; gold 'nano-bullets' that seek and destroy tumours; starving cancer with nanoparticles; diagnosing diseases such as Alzheimer's, monitoring health and fighting sickness with tiny probes; and growing new organs from scratch.

1 **Answer these questions about the word combinations used in the text.**

1 In the first paragraph which adjective is used with *device*?
2 In the second paragraph which verb is used with *properties*?
3 In the third paragraph which noun is used with *make*?
4 In the fourth paragraph which adjective is used with *nanotechnology*?
5 In the fifth paragraph which adverb is used with *different*?
6 In the sixth paragraph which adjective is used with *advances*?

2 **What other words of the same part of speech as in exercise 1 could be used with** *device, properties, make, nanotechnology, different* **and** *advances*? **Suggest at least two others.**

3 **What do these adverbial expressions used in the text mean?**

1 unwittingly (para 3)   2 in the short term (para 6)   3 from scratch (para 6)

 Use a search engine on the web to find a recent article relating to nanotechnology + medicine or computing or industry, depending on which interests you most. Make a note of any new interesting new facts and vocabulary that you find there.

Reading and vocabulary 6

Read the text. Use a dictionary if necessary but note that it is not essential to understand every word. Then answer the questions.

International law: an overview

International law consists of rules and principles which govern the relations and dealings of nations with each other. Public International Law concerns itself only with questions of rights between several nations or nations and the citizens or subjects of other nations. In contrast, Private International Law deals with controversies between private persons, natural or juridical, arising out of situations having significant relationship to more than one nation. In recent years the lines between public and private international law have became increasingly uncertain. Issues of private international law may also implicate issues of public international law, and many matters of private international law have substantial significance for the international community of nations.

International Law includes the basic, classic concepts of law in national legal systems – status, property, obligation, and tort (or delict). It also includes substantive law, procedure, process and remedies. International Law is rooted in acceptance by the nation states which constitute the system. Customary law and conventional law are primary sources of international law. Customary international law results when states follow certain practices generally and consistently out of a sense of legal obligation. Recently the customary law was codified in the Vienna Convention on the Law of Treaties. Conventional international law derives from international agreements and may take any form that the contracting parties agree upon. Agreements may be made in respect to any matter except to the extent that the agreement conflicts with the rules of international law incorporating basic standards of international conduct or the obligations of a member state under the Charter of the United Nations. International agreements create law for the parties of the agreement. They may also lead to the creation of customary international law when they are intended for adherence generally and are in fact widely accepted. Customary law and law made by international agreement have equal authority as international law. Parties may assign higher priority to one of the sources by agreement. However, some rules of international law are recognized by international community as peremptory, permitting no derogation. Such rules can be changed or modified only by a subsequent peremptory norm of international law.

1 **Find words or phrases in the first paragraph which could be substituted by the following:**

1 is made up of	4 contrastingly	7 distinctions
2 regulate	5 disagreements	8 more and more
3 focuses on	6 stemming from	9 bring in

2 **Paraphrase these words or phrases from the second paragraph:**

1 basic	4 derives from	7 conduct
2 classic	5 in respect to	8 parties
3 is rooted in	6 conflicts with	9 assign

 3 **Use a dictionary if necessary. Find at least five other words with the same root as each of the following:**

1 nation	3 acceptance	5 creator
2 significant	4 extent	

FOLLOW UP Find a definition of your own subject area or one specific aspect of it. Write it out. Does it include any of the more general vocabulary from this text? What other interesting words and expressions does it use?

Reference 1

Formal and informal academic words and expressions

There are many differences between formal, neutral and informal vocabulary in English. Here we list a number of words and expressions that are frequent in academic contexts and which may present problems in terms of choosing between formal, neutral and less formal alternatives.

You may often hear some of the informal words and expressions during classes, seminars, etc., but be careful not to use them where they are not appropriate, for example in formal essays or dissertations. Use a good dictionary which gives information about formality if you are in doubt. Where words are informal, we make a special note here. Space is provided at the end for you to add further examples of your own.

(n) = noun   (v) = verb   (adj) = adjective

formal	neutral (or informal where indicated)	example or comment
accord	agreement	an accord/agreement between two countries
acquire	obtain, get (less formal)	See Unit 48
address (v)	give attention to	address / give attention to a topic / an issue
address, speak to	speak/talk about	See Unit 40
adjudicate	judge	adjudicate/judge a contest/dispute
administer	give	administer/give a drug/medicine to a patient
advantages and disadvantages	pros and cons (informal)	See Unit 38
advocate (v)	support, encourage	We do not advocate/support/ encourage the use of questionnaires with young children.
aim	set out (to do X)	In this paper, we aim/set out to challenge some current assumptions.
albeit	although	See Unit 38
appeal for	ask for	The police are appealing/asking for any information the public can offer.
attempt	try, have a shot at (informal)	See Unit 1
attire	clothes	She always wore rather old-fashioned attire/clothes.
be accepted / be offered a place	get in (informal)	(for entry into a university or college) I hope to get in / be accepted / be offered a place to study engineering.
call on	ask (somebody to do something)	See Unit 40
catalogue (v)	list	See Unit 23
characteristic (adj)	typical	See Unit 4
check	go through	See Unit 6
compose	write	e.g. a poem/letter/symphony
conduct	carry out, do (less formal)	(an experiment / research / a study) See Unit 6
conduct (n)	behaviour	(in the social sense) Such conduct/behaviour is unacceptable.
consist of	be made up of	See Unit 6

formal	neutral (or informal where indicated)	example or comment
constitute	make up	See Unit 6
consult (v)	read, look at	e.g. a document/archive See Unit 23
contest (v)	argue against, disagree with	contest / argue against / disagree with a judgement
convention	agreement	No written convention/agreement existed until 1984.
cordial	friendly	cordial/friendly relations between governments
correct	right	It took hours of calculations to arrive at the correct/ right answer.
deliver	give	deliver/give a talk/lecture
demonstrate	show	See Units 3 and 12
describe	set out	See Unit 6
diminish	decrease, grow smaller	The population has diminished/decreased / grown smaller.
discuss	go into	See Unit 6
dispose of	get rid of	dispose of / get rid of nuclear waste
document (v)	record, write about	See Unit 23
dormitory	dorm	BrE = hall of residence See Unit 19
dwelling	house, flat, apartment	There were originally 50 dwellings/houses/flats/ apartments on the site.
endure	last	The dynasty endured/lasted for eight centuries.
examination	exam (slightly informal)	(formal test) degree examinations/exams
examine	take, have a look at (informal)	See Unit 12
exceed	be more, higher, greater than	See Unit 7
exchange	swap (informal)	The tube was exchanged/swapped for one of a larger calibre.
final	last	See Unit 50
hierarchy	pecking order	e.g. in an institution
highlight	point up	See Unit 6
improper	wrong	improper/wrong procedure
in excess of	over, higher than	See Unit 7
in greater detail	in more detail	See Unit 40
in respect of, with respect to	with regard to, as far as X is concerned, as far as X goes (informal)	See Unit 16
in sum, in summary	in short, to sum up, summing up	See Units 1, 40 and 50
inappropriate	unsuitable	inappropriate/unsuitable form of words
incorrect	wrong (rather more direct than incorrect)	The totals in column 3 are incorrect/wrong.
incur	result in, experience	See Unit 21
instigate	initiate, start something	See Unit 35
instruct	direct, order	instruct/direct/order somebody to carry out a task

formal	neutral (or informal where indicated)	example or comment
investigate	look into (slightly informal)	investigate / look into a problem
laboratory	lab	See Unit 41
maintain	keep	See Unit 48
make reference to	refer to	See Unit 23
negotiations	talks	negotiations/talks between governments
nevertheless	having said that	See Unit 40
observe	point out	See Unit 6
occasion	time	It happened three times / on three occasions.
occupation	job, profession	(on a questionnaire) Question 3: What is your occupation/profession?
omit, not attend something	skip (informal)	skip a lecture, skip/omit a chapter
pledge	promise	as a noun or as a verb
pose	ask	pose/ask a question See Unit 12
postgraduate	postgrad (informal)	See Unit 18
present	put forward	an idea/view/theory, etc. See Unit 6
primarily	mainly	See Unit 5
recapitulate	recap	See Unit 50
recently	lately	These animals have not been seen recently/lately.
representative	rep (informal)	She's the student representative/rep on the Departmental Committee.
resign	quit (informal)	The President resigned/quit in 1986.
resolve	solve, end	resolve/solve a problem, resolve/end a conflict
rest on	be based on	See Unit 14
return	come back, go back, get back	See Unit 40
revise	look back over, go over	See Unit 6
sanction (v)	permit	The government cannot sanction law breaking.
secure (v)	obtain, get (informal)	e.g. secure oil supplies See Unit 47
sole(ly)	only	See Unit 1
somewhat	slightly, a little, a bit (informal)	See Unit 5
speak of	talk of, talk about (less formal)	See Unit 14
spouse	husband, wife	The President's spouse/husband/wife attended the ceremony.
substantial	large, big	a substantial number/amount See Unit 7
treat	deal with	This issue was not treated / dealt with fully in Holstedt's earlier work.
undergraduate	undergrad (informal)	The undergrads/undergraduates mostly live in halls of residence.

formal	neutral (or informal where indicated)	example or comment
undertaking (n)	promise	an official undertaking/promise to do something
utilise	use something effectively	utilise a resource/method
virtually	almost, more or less	See Unit 1
write of	write about	See Unit 14
X is not possible / not correct	There's no way X ... (rather informal)	See Unit 1
Yours faithfully	Yours sincerely, best wishes (less formal), best (informal)	way of ending a letter or email

Reference 2

Numbers, units of measurement and common symbols

You know how to say all the numbers in English. Here we look at how combinations of numbers are said aloud.

BrE = British English   AmE = North American English

For spelling differences between BrE and AmE, see Reference 4.

A   Fractions

Fractions are normally spoken as in these examples:

$\frac{1}{2}$	*a (one) half*
$\frac{1}{4}$	*a (one) quarter*
$\frac{3}{4}$	*three quarters*
$\frac{1}{5}$	*a (one) fifth*
$\frac{2}{3}$	*two thirds*
$\frac{1}{4}$ kilometre	*a quarter of a kilometre*
$\frac{1}{2}$ centimetre	*half a centimetre*

Complex fractions and expressions of division are usually said with *over*.

$\frac{27}{200}$	*twenty-seven over two hundred*
	twenty-seven divided by two hundred

B   Decimals

Decimals are normally spoken as in these examples:

0.36	*nought point three six* (BrE) *zero point three six* (AmE)
5.2	*five point two*

C   Percentages

Percentages are spoken as *per cent*.

16.3%	*sixteen point three per cent*

D   Calculations

Calculations are normally said in the following ways:

7 + 3 = 10	*seven and three is/are ten* (informal)
	seven plus three equals ten (more formal)
28 – 6 = 22	*six from twenty-eight is/leaves twenty-two* (informal)
	twenty-eight minus six equals twenty-two (more formal)
8 × 2 = 16	*eight twos are sixteen* (informal BrE)
	eight times two is sixteen (informal) (the most common form in AmE)
	eight by two is/equals sixteen (informal)
	eight multiplied by two equals/is sixteen (more formal)
27 ÷ 9 = 3	*twenty-seven divided by nine equals three*
500 ± 5	*five hundred plus or minus five*
>300	*greater than three hundred*
<200	*less than two hundred*

$3^2 = 9$ *three squared is/equals nine*

$\sqrt{16} = 4$ *the (square) root of sixteen is four*

$3^3 = 27$ *three cubed is/equals twenty-seven*

$\sqrt[3]{8} = 2$ *the cube root of eight is two*

$2^4 = 16$ *two to the power of 4 is/equals sixteen* (AmE = *two to the fourth power ...*)

E   Units of measurement

Although the metric system is now common in the UK and other English-speaking countries, non-metric units are still used in many contexts, especially in the USA.

Units of length and distance are normally spoken as follows:

3 in, 3"	*three inches*
2 ft 7 in, 2' 7"	*two feet seven inches* (or, very informally, *two foot seven inches*)
500 yds	*five hundred yards*
3 m (AmE = 3 mi.)	*three miles*
500 mm	*five hundred millimetres* (or, more informally, *five hundred m-m*)
1.5 cm	*one point five centimetres*

Units of area are normally spoken as follows:

11 sq ft	*eleven square feet*
5 sq m, 5m²	*five square metres*
7.25 cm²	*seven point two five square centimetres*

Units of weight are normally spoken as follows:

3 oz	*three ounces*
5 lb	*five pounds*
300 g	*three hundred grams*
18.75 kg	*eighteen point seven five kilograms*

Units of volume, capacity and temperature are normally spoken as follows:

300 cc	*three hundred cubic centimetres* (or, less formally, *three hundred c-c*)
5 pt	*five pints*
3.2 gal	*three point two gallons*
75 cl	*seventy-five centilitres*
200 l	*two hundred litres*
20°	*twenty degrees*

F   Common symbols

&	'ampersand' – this symbol is read as 'and'
*	asterisk
©	copyright symbol
™	trademark symbol
®	registered trademark
•	bullet point
✓	BrE = tick; AmE = check
✗	BrE = cross; AmE = an 'X'
#	BrE = hash symbol (Note: in American English, this symbol is used for numbers, e.g. #28 AmE; no. 28 BrE)
@	this symbol is read as 'at' – used in email addresses
∞	infinity symbol
"	this symbol is read as 'ditto' – used in lists to avoid writing a word if the same word is written immediately above it

Reference 3

British and North American academic vocabulary

There are numerous differences in vocabulary between the English of the UK and Ireland, and the English of the USA and Canada, the two dominant areas which have historically influenced English in many other parts of the world. **However, there is also a great amount of mixing, and Americans and Canadians are often familiar with British and Irish usages, and vice versa. So the table below is for general guidance only.** Also, nowadays, thanks to the media and the internet, American vocabulary is influencing and being imported into British, Irish and international English more and more. In the case of Ireland, this is more noticeable than in Great Britain. Other important varieties of English, such as Indian, Australian, African, Caribbean, etc., also have their own words and phrases, but have probably, for historical reasons, had less influence overall on international usage or academic usage in particular.

The first column of the table shows words and phrases that are commonly used in North American English, but which are not used, or used to a far lesser extent, in British and Irish English, and which are likely to occur in academic texts or in general college and university contexts and student life. Be prepared to meet others in everyday life in English-speaking countries.

See also Units 18 and 19 of this book. Space is provided at the end for you to add further examples of your own.

For differences between British and American grammar, see the special chapter in the *Cambridge Grammar of English* (published by Cambridge University Press).

AmE = North American English   BrE = British/Irish English

North American	British/Irish	comment
airplane	aeroplane	
antenna	aerial	
apartment	flat	Both forms are heard increasingly in BrE.
apartment building	block of flats	
attorney	lawyer	
ATM (automated teller machine)	cashpoint	bank machine from which one can get money Both forms are used in Irish English.
bill	note	e.g. a 100 dollar bill, a 50 euro note
cafeteria	canteen	Both are common in BrE.
candy	sweet(s)	
cart	trolley	used in a supermarket to carry one's shopping
cell phone	mobile phone	
checking account	current account	bank account for day-to-day use
chips	crisps	
coach class	economy class	cheapest class of air travel
condominium, condo (informal)	block of flats	
cookie	biscuit	small, flat cake
cord	lead	electrical cable joining an appliance to a power connection

North American	British/Irish	comment
co-worker	workmate	
crosswalk	pedestrian crossing	
dirt road	unpaved road, track	
district attorney	public prosecutor	
divided highway	dual carriageway	
doctor's office	surgery	
downtown	town centre, city centre	
(the) draft	conscription	compulsory military service
drug store	chemist's, pharmacy	
eggplant	aubergine	vegetable
elementary school	primary school	
elevator	lift	
eraser	rubber	
fall	autumn	
faucet	tap	for water
field	pitch	a sports area, e.g. football pitch/field
flashlight	torch	a light powered by batteries
freeway	motorway	
(French) fries	chips	long, thin pieces of fried potato, eaten hot (see *chips* vs *crisps*)
furnace	central heating boiler	
garbage, trash	rubbish, refuse (more formal)	
gas	petrol	fuel for motor vehicles
grounded	earthed	electrical
high school	secondary school	
highway	main road	*Highway* in BrE is normally only used in technical and legal/official contexts.
intersection	crossroads	
intermission	interval	e.g. break in a cinema/theatre performance Both forms are common in Irish English.
interstate (highway)	main/major road, motorway	
jack	socket	connection for a telephone landline
kindergarten	nursery	In AmE, *kindergarten* refers to school for five-year-old children; that is, it is the year before entering first grade. In BrE, *nursery* refers to a special room for babies, while *nursery school* refers to a school for children aged 2–5 (also called *pre-school*).
legal holiday	bank holiday	
license plate, license tag	number plate	on a vehicle
line	queue	
locker room	changing room	for sports
mail	post	
mall	shopping centre	*Mall* is used more and more in BrE.
mass transit	public transport	

North American	British/Irish	comment
movie	film	
movie theater	cinema	
normalcy	normality	
operating room	operating theatre	hospital
outlet	socket	place to connect for electrical power – BrE also uses *power point*
overpass	flyover	in a road system
parentheses	brackets	In AmE, the word *brackets* refers to [ ]. In AmE, *parentheses* are ( ).
parking garage	multi-storey car park	
parking lot	car park	
penitentiary	prison	
period	full stop	referring to punctuation
petroleum	crude oil	oil when it comes out of the ground
prenatal	ante-natal	'before birth' – concerning mothers to be
private school	private school, public school	A *public school* in the UK is a private secondary school; schools run by the government are called *state schools*. In the US, *private school* only refers to schools that are privately owned, never to public institutions.
railroad	railway	
recess, break	break	e.g. gap between activities, for lunch, etc.
restroom, bathroom, washroom (Canada)	toilet, loo (informal)	*Restroom* is used for public facilities, whereas *bathroom* refers to facilities in a home.
resumé	curriculum vitae (or CV)	
round trip	return	e.g. a round trip / return ticket
running shoes, sneakers	trainers	
sales clerk	shop assistant	
sales tax	VAT (value added tax)	tax added to goods and services at the point of purchase
schedule	timetable	
scotch tape	sellotape	adhesive tape
server	waiter, waitress	
senior	pensioner, senior citizen	
sidewalk	pavement, footpath	
social security number	national insurance number	individual personal number used by officials in connection with tax, social benefits, etc.
stop lights	traffic lights	
store	shop	
subway	underground (railway)	A *subway* in BrE is an underground tunnel or passageway for pedestrians to cross a road.
takeout	takeaway	meals, food
teller	cashier	person who serves customers in a bank
thumbtack	drawing pin	e.g. used to fix a notice to a noticeboard
tractor-trailer	articulated lorry, juggernaut	

North American	British/Irish	comment
trash	rubbish, refuse (more formal)	
trashcan	(dust)bin	
truck	lorry, truck	
two weeks	fortnight	
vacation	holiday	*Vacation* is used in BrE universities to mean the periods when no teaching takes place. In AmE, *holiday* refers to a national day of observance, for example New Year's Day.
zee	zed	last letter of the English alphabet
zucchini	courgette	vegetable
zip code (USA), postal code (Canada)	postcode	

Reference 4

Spelling variations

Some words are spelt differently in different varieties of English. The main contrasts are between UK/Irish and US English. Other varieties of English tend to opt for either predominantly UK/Irish or predominantly US spellings. The US spelling tends to be simpler and a clearer reflection of the way the word is pronounced. You can, of course, use whichever spelling you prefer but it is sensible to be consistent. The main patterns of spelling variation are shown below.

Space is provided in the middle columns for you to add further examples of your own.

Word-processing and other computer programs often have spellcheck features that check the spelling of what you write for you. You can usually set these to either UK, US or Australian spelling. However, remember that it is not sensible to rely on the computer to check and correct your spelling for you. A spellcheck program will not pick up the spelling errors in this sentence, for example: *I don't no weather their are two many mistakes inn yore righting or knot.*

pattern of variation	examples of UK + Irish spelling	examples of US spelling	comment
words with -*our/or*	labour, honour, behaviour, endeavour, favourable, rumour	labor, honor, behavior, endeavor, favorable, rumor	In some words UK spelling prefers the -*or* form, e.g. humorous, honorary, glamorous.
words ending with -*er/re*	centre, theatre, centimetre, litre, lustre	center, theater, centimeter, liter, luster	UK spelling distinguishes between metre (100 cms) and meter (measuring device).
verbs ending in single *l* when they add a suffix	cancelling, labelled, counsellor, marvellous, modelled	canceling, labeled, counselor, marvelous, modeled	Sometimes the double *l* spelling will also be found in US texts.
other words with single or double *l*	fulfil, enrol, enrolment, instalment, skilful, wilful	fulfill, enroll, enrollment, installment, skillful, willful	The verb *to install* can be written with either *l* or *ll* in both UK and US English, although *ll* is more common.
words ending with -*ogue/og*	analogue, catalogue, dialogue	analog, catalog, dialog	The -*gue* ending can also be found in US texts.

pattern of variation	examples of UK + Irish spelling	examples of US spelling	comment
verbs ending with -ise/ize and nouns ending with -isation/ization	emphasise, minimise, globalise, colonise, organise, standardise, globalisation, colonisation, organisation, standardisation	emphasize, minimize, globalize, colonize, organize, standardize, globalization, colonization, organization, standardization	Some verbs always end in -ise, e.g. advertise, advise, apprise, arise, comprise, compromise, despise, devise, disguise, enfranchise, enterprise, excise, exercise, improvise, incise, premise, revise, supervise, surmise, surprise. With other words the -ize/ization endings will also sometimes be found in UK texts.
verbs ending with -yse/yze	analyse, catalyse, paralyse	analyze, catalyze, paralyze	The nouns analysis, catalysis and paralysis are spelt the same in both UK and US texts.
some words ending with -ce/se	defence, offence, pretence, practise (verb), licence (noun)	defense, offense, pretense, practice (verb and noun), license (verb and noun)	UK spelling distinguishes between practice and licence (nouns) and practise and license (verbs).
some words with -ae or -oe in UK English	anaesthetic, gynaecology, haemorrhage, orthopaedic, manoeuvre, oesophagus	anesthetic, gynecology, hemorrhage, orthopedic, maneuvre, esophagus	Words in this category are all of Greek origin and most occur in medical contexts.
miscellaneous	aluminium, cheque, grey, kerb, mould, plough, (TV, research) programme, pyjamas, storey (of building), (car) tyre	aluminum, check, gray, curb, mold, plow, program, pajamas, story, tire	In UK spelling note the spelling of computer program. In UK spelling check, curb, story and tire have distinct meanings from cheque, kerb, storey and tyre.

Reference 5

Word formation

One advantage of English vocabulary is that many words are formed from the same root. As a result, if you know the word *friend*, it is easy to understand other words from the same root such as *friendly, friendship, **unfriendly*** and *befriend*. Learning what prefixes (for example, un-, mis-, extra-) and suffixes (-ify, -ship, -less) signify can help you to extend your vocabulary in a relatively effortless way. When you meet a new word, it is a good idea to write it down with other words using the same root + different prefixes and suffixes. Thus, you might write down together, for example, *amoral, morality, immoral, morally, moralise, moralist, moralistic*.

Variations occur in the use of hyphens, especially in newspapers and popular magazines. For example, the prefix *de-* may or may not be followed by a hyphen (decontaminate, de-centralise), but some prefixes are almost always used with a hyphen (e.g. ex-, semi-). Train yourself to be aware of any prefixes which regularly occur in your academic area and make a note of how they are usually written. Note that North American English makes much less use of hyphens after prefixes than British English.

The following table includes some of the major prefixes and suffixes that are useful as far as academic vocabulary is concerned. Familiarising yourself with these will not only help you to work out what unfamiliar words mean but will also help you to remember those words. Space is provided for you to add further examples of your own.

prefix	meaning	examples	further examples of your own
a-	without	amoral /ˌeɪˈmɒrəl/, apolitical /ˌeɪpəˈlɪtɪkəl/, atypical /ˌeɪˈtɪpɪkəl/	
ante-	before	antecedent, antedate	
anti-	against, opposing	anti-establishment, anti-bacterial, anti-pollution	
arch-	more extreme	arch-capitalist, arch-rebel	
auto-	self	auto-dial, auto-rotate	
bi-	two, twice	bilingual, bisect, bi-monthly	
circum-	round	circumnavigate, circumvent	
co-	with	co-author, co-edit	
col-, com-, con-	with	collaborate, combine, connect	
contra-, counter-	against, opposing	contra-revolutionary, contraception, counter-measure, counter-claim	
de-	opposite action	decentralise, declassify	
dia-	across	diagonal, diameter	
dis-	opposite action or state	disagree, disprove, distrust, disbelief, disproportionate	

prefix	meaning	examples	further examples of your own
dys-	abnormal	dyslexia, dysfunctional	
e-	electronic	e-literate, e-book	
eco-	relating to the environment	eco-tourism, eco-disaster	
equi-	equal	equidistant, equilateral	
ex-	previously	ex-president, ex-student	
extra-	very	extra-bright, extra-strong	
extra-	outside	extra-curricular, extra-sensory	
hyper-	having too much	hyperactive, hypersensitive	
-il, -im, -in, -ir-	not	illogical, impossible, indistinct, irrational	
in-	movement to or towards the inside of something	input, inset, intake, import	
inter-	between, connected	interrelated, interact	
intra-	within	intra-generational, intramuscular	
kilo-	thousand	kilogram, kilowatt	
macro-	large in size or scope	macro-economics, macro-scale	
mal-	badly	malfunction, malpractice	
micro-	small in size or scope	micro-economics, micro-scale	
mis-	wrongly	mistranslate, misunderstanding	
mono-	one	mono-centric, monoculture	
multi-	many	multicultural, multi-level	
neo-	based on something older but in a new form	neo-classical, neo-conservative	
non-	not	non-believer, non-competitive	
out-	more, to a greater extent	outnumber, outlive	
over-	too much	over-abundance, overload, overworked	

prefix	meaning	examples	further examples of your own
post-	after	post-examination, post-modern	
pre-	before	pre-industrial, pre-war	
pro-	in favour of	pro-liberal, pro-feminist	
pseudo-	false	pseudo-intellectual, pseudo-science	
quasi-	almost, not quite	quasi-academic, quasi-legal	
re-	again	rediscover, redefine, rename	
retro-	backwards	retrogressive, retrospective	
semi-	partly	semi-organic, semi-precious	
sub-	under, lesser	sub-heading, sub-section	
super-	above, bigger	superpower, supersonic	
trans-	across	transcontinental, transcribe	
ultra-	extreme	ultra-sensitive, ultrasound	
un-	not	uncertain, unusual, unscrew, unplug	
under-	insufficient	underemployed, undernourished	
well-	useful, successful	well-designed, well-written, well-established	

suffix	meaning	examples	further examples of your own
-able	can be	identifiable, predictable	
-ant	having an effect	coolant, accelerant	
-based	forming major part of	computer-based, oil-based	
-cy	state or quality	accuracy, literacy, urgency	
-ee	person affected by something	interviewee, trainee, addressee	
-free	without	debt-free, pain-free	
-hood	state, condition, period	adulthood, motherhood	
-ic	connected with	photographic, electric	
-ics	study of	genetics, electronics	
-ify	give something a quality	clarify, purify, solidify	
-ism	belief, behaviour	modernism, heroism	
-ist	person with specific beliefs or behaviour	anarchist, optimist	
-ize, -ise	bring about a state or condition	modernize/modernise, colonize/colonise	
-less	without	childless, meaningless	
-like	resembling	bird-like, hook-like	
-ness	quality or state	effectiveness, openness	
-ocracy	type of ruling body	meritocracy, bureaucracy	
-ocrat	person ruling	technocrat, aristocrat	
-ology, -ological	study of	biology, biological, geology, physiological	
-proof	protected against, safe from	waterproof, dustproof	
-ship	state or experience of having a specific position	professorship, leadership	

Reference 6

Abbreviations

Abbreviations are frequently found in an academic context. Here are some which are common in academic writing.

abbreviation	stands for	example or comment
e.g.	for example (from Latin, *exempli gratia*)	Many large mammals, e.g. the African elephant, the black rhino and the white rhino …
i.e.	that is (from Latin, *id est*)	Higher earners, i.e. those with a monthly salary in excess of £3,000 …
etc.	and so on (from Latin, *et cetera*)	Smaller European countries – Slovenia, Slovakia, Estonia, etc. – had different interests.
NB	note carefully (from Latin, *nota bene*)	NB You must answer all the questions on this page.
et al	and others (from Latin, *et alii*)	used when giving bibliographical reference, e.g. as mentioned in T. Potts et al (1995)
ibid.	in the same place as the preceding footnote (from Latin, *ibidem*)	1 Lee (1987) *History of Tea-Drinking in Europe* 2 *ibid.*
cf	compare (from Latin, *confer*)	cf Löfstedt (2005) for a different approach to this topic
q.v.	which you can see (from Latin, *quod vide*)	used to refer the reader to another part of a book or article for further information
op. cit.	see previously quoted work by author (from Latin, *opus citatum*)	Potts op. cit. 33–54
ed.	editor	used when giving bibliographical reference
vol.	volume	used when giving bibliographical reference
p.	page	in the article referred to above (p. 43), Smith claims …
pp.	pages	See McKinley 1990 pp.11–19

There are also many abbreviations relating to academic degrees, departments, movements and organisations. We give just a few of these as examples below but most of those that you will need will be specific to your own field of study and so space is left for you to add these as you come across them.

abbreviation	stands for	used about
BA	Bachelor of Arts	a first degree in the humanities
MA	Master of Arts	a postgraduate degree in the humanities
BSc	Bachelor of Science	a first degree in a science subject
MSc	Master of Science	a postgraduate degree in a science subject
MBA	Master of Business Administration	a postgraduate business qualification
PhD	Doctor of Philosophy	a postgraduate degree, one which entitles the holder to the title Dr
BEng	Bachelor of Engineering	a first degree in engineering
LLB	Bachelor of Laws	a first degree in law
FRS	Fellow of the Royal Society	member of a high level scientific organisation in the UK
BMJ	British Medical Journal	well-known British medical publication

abbreviation	stands for	used about
WHO	World Health Organisation	United Nations organisation to promote health
UNESCO	United Nations Educational, Scientific and Cultural Organisation	United Nations organisation promoting education, science and culture
UCL	University College London	one of London's main university colleges
SOAS	School of Oriental and African Studies	well-known academic institution, part of London University
CUNY	City University of New York	one of New York's higher education institutions
MIT	Massachusetts Institute of Technology	important US research university based in Cambridge Massachusetts
UCLA	University of California Los Angeles	one of California's higher education institutions
FAAFP	Fellow of the American Academy of Family Practitioners	member of American doctors' association
MRCS	Fellow of the Royal College of Surgeons	member of British association for qualified surgeons
AMA	Australian Medical Association	professional association for Australian medical staff
ACA	Association of Consulting Actuaries	British association for legal finance specialists who work as advisors to insurance companies
FASB	Financial Accounting Standards Board	private sector organisation in the US that establishes financial accounting and reporting standards
AICPA	American Institute of Certified Public Accountants	professional organisation for accountants in the USA
AFANZ	Accounting and Finance Association of Australia and New Zealand	organisation for financial professionals in Australia and New Zealand
IFA*	Institute of Financial Advisors	professional body representing financial advisors in New Zealand

* Note that IFA – like many abbreviations – has different associations for different groups of people. It can also mean, for example, Irish Football Association, Institute of Field Archaeologists, Independent Financial Advisor, Institute of Financial Accountants, International Fertiliser Industry Association, and the Institute for Astronomy as well as, undoubtedly, a number of other things.

Key

1.1 Unit 1

1 A pose	B pose	6 A nature	B nature
2 A focus	B focus	7 A character	B character
3 A confirmed	B confirmed	8 A turn	B turn
4 A generates	B generates	9 A underlines	B underlines
5 A identified	B identified	10 A solid	B solid

1.2
1 primarily
2 Virtually
3 solely
4 In sum / To sum up (*or* In summary) (See also Unit 40.)
5 attempted
6 prime
7 characteristic
8 **In no way/respect can London** be compared to Sydney as a place to live and work. (Note the inversion of the subject (*London*) and verb (*can*) when a negative expression is used at the beginning of the sentence.)

1.3
1 depends heavily, converted easily, produced cheaply
2 relatively easily
3 production, reliance, discovery, claim

Unit 2

2.1
1 issues	3 theory	5 model
2 topics	4 theme	6 Principle

2.2 The study showed that local police can play an important role in crime prevention. It makes <u>a strong case **for**</u> boosting the numbers of community police officers although it warns against increasing police presence on the streets <u>to an alarming degree</u>. Its **methodology*** was based on a range of interviews asking members of the public for <u>their views **on**</u> how best to prevent crime. Unfortunately, how to implement this recommendation was <u>**beyond** the scope of</u> the study but at least it serves a useful purpose in <u>raising awareness of</u> the issue.
* *methodological* is the adjective form of the noun *methodology*

2.3 1 G   2 D   3 E   4 H   5 C   6 B   7 A   8 F

2.4
1 The study revealed a regular pattern of changes in temperature.
2 The research focuses on one particular aspect of modern society.
3 The writer makes a powerful case for restructuring parliament.
4 The writers take an original approach to their theme.
5 Until recently there was little awareness of the problem.
6 I think you should broaden the scope of your research.
7 To date there has been little research into the environmental effects of nanoparticles.
8 There are many important issues facing the world today.

Unit 3

3.1
affect – influence	identify – distinguish
attempt – try	include – involve
calculate – compute	investigate – study
challenge – question	provide – give
demonstrate – show	

3.2 1 be seen   3 classifying   5 show/shows   7 to establish
      2 accounted   4 to present   6 to develop   8 to explain

3.3 1 Greig's article supports Park's theory: this means that Greig's work backs up that of Park; in other words, it comes to the same conclusions.
        Greig's article challenges Park's theory: this means that Greig's work questions Park's conclusions.

      2 Describe the new tax regulations: this requests someone simply to say what the new tax regulations are.
        Discuss the new tax regulations: this requires someone to give their opinion with regard to the new tax regulations.

      3 Lodhi provides new data: this means that Lodhi's work is the source of some new data.
        Lodhi considers new data: this means that Lodhi discusses new data, giving his opinion as to their implications and significance.

      4 Titova conducted four sets of experiments: this means that Titova did the experiments herself.
        Titova examined four sets of experiments: this means that Titova considered some experiments which others had carried out.

      5 Lee established why such changes occur: this means that Lee was able to prove why such changes occur.
        Lee investigated why such changes occur: this means that Lee tried to find out why such changes occur but we do not know how successful she was in this.

      6 Okaz assumed that the data were reliable: this means Okaz accepted this without proof or questioning.
        Okaz proved that the data were reliable: this means that Okaz did something to show that it was true.

      7 Illustrate the magnitude of the deceleration: this means show how it works in some way, e.g. by drawing a graph or an illustration of some kind.
        Find the magnitude of the deceleration: this means discover it by doing calculations.

      8 The events effected economic development: this means the events made economic development happen or brought it about.
        The events affected economic development: this means the events had an influence (perhaps positive or negative) on economic development.

3.4 1 Erikson's theory provides an explanation for the fluctuations in the figures for this period.
      2 Bevan carried out an exploration of/into the relationship between family background and political ambition.
      3 The book gives/provides a description of the life and times of Abraham Lincoln.
      4 Cheng's theory puts/places emphasis on the importance of extensive reading in language acquisition.

3.5 1 investigation   4 have an **effect** on (NB keep change in first letter)
      2 illustration   5 make an **attempt** to (+ verb) / at (+ noun)
      3 analysis   6 classification

Unit 4

4.1 1 relevant **to**   3 appropriate **to** (*or* **for**)   5 Relative **to**
      2 typical **of**   4 characteristic **of**   6 common **to**

4.2 1 inaccurate   3 precise   5 concrete
      2 complex   4 an insignificant

4.3 These are the most likely combinations although some combinations such as 'apparent/principal problem' or 'apparent cause' are also possible.

      1 apparent discrepancy   3 principal cause
      2 rigorous methodology   4 potential problem

4.4 1 apparent discrepancy   3 rigorous methodology
         2 principal cause   4 potential problem

4.5 1 specific   3 potential   5 complex
         2 rigorous   4 qualitative

Unit 5

5.1 1 Heinrich's experiments were mostly successful: this means that Heinrich's experiments were largely successful or successful on the whole. In other words they were not totally successful. Heinrich's experiments were most successful: this means that Heinrich's experiments were extremely/very successful.

2 The results were somewhat surprising given the circumstances: this means that the results were rather or fairly surprising in view of the circumstances.
The results were especially surprising given the circumstances: this means that the results were particularly surprising in view of the circumstances; in other words, the results in the second sentence surprised the writer more than those in the first sentence.

3 First year students are directly affected by the new rules relating to tuition fees: this means that the new rules have a direct impact on first year students as opposed to students from other years, who may either be indirectly affected or not affected at all. First year students are particularly affected by the new rules relating to tuition fees: this means that the new rules affect first year students more than students from other years.

4 The study is primarily concerned with urban alienation: this means that urban alienation is the explicit focus of the study.
The study is ultimately concerned with urban alienation: this means that urban alienation was probably not the initial focus of the study but it turned out in the end to be its most significant theme.

5 The team eventually obtained unpredicted results: this means that the team finally, after a long time spent trying, obtained some results which they had not predicted.
The team frequently obtained unpredicted results: this means that the team often obtained results which they had not predicted.

5.2 What you are saying is *essentially* true. To put it *simply*, there is *basically* no significant difference between the two writers' theories. However, one of them writes in a *simply* dreadful style while the other has *possibly* a more impressive style than any other contemporary scientist.

5.3 1 precisely/exactly   5 implicitly
         2 frequently/often/regularly   6 generally/typically
         3 eventually/finally   7 hardly ever
         4 approximately/roughly/about/around   8 indirectly

5.4 *Suggested underlinings*

Marine conservationists are **currently** attempting to save the world's coral reefs. One plan is to **literally** glue the damaged reefs back together, using coral **artificially** raised in underwater labs. Reefs are **increasingly** under attack from human activity as well as from events occurring **naturally**, such as hurricanes and tsunamis. A recent UN report warns that 30% of the world's coral reefs have been **completely** destroyed or are **severely** damaged.	Scientists have **recently** discovered that ants can remember how many steps they have taken. By **carefully** shortening or lengthening the legs of ants, the team observed that short-legged ants **apparently** became lost and could not **easily** find their way home to the nest. **Similarly**, ants with longer legs **typically** travelled 50% further than they needed to and were also **temporarily** unable to find the nest. It seems ants can **definitely** count their steps.

Answers to questions

1 similarly
2 artificially – naturally, apparently – definitely
3 currently / recently

4 increasingly
5 severely
6 temporarily

Unit 6

6.1
1 carried out
2 go/look back over
3 goes into
4 puts forward
5 pointed out
6 go through
7 sets out
8 make up

6.2
1 on (Although *out* is not impossible it is less likely here as it suggests that the writer is coming to a definitive conclusion or solution to a problem, which is not appropriate for such a complex issue as the way children learn language.)

2 out
3 up
4 out
5 up
6 forward
7 on
8 out

6.3
1 Feudal society was made up of clearly defined classes of people.
2 Carlson was the first to put forward a convincing theory with regard to this question.
3 Her results appear to go against what she had found in her earlier studies.
4 The investigation pointed up the flaws in the school's testing methods.
5 It took him a long time to work out the solution to the algebra problem.
6 The geography book sets out a lot of basic information about all the world's countries.

6.4 *Suggested answers*
1 A scientist might carry out research or experiments or a study or an investigation.
2 If you want to study something in more depth, you might go on to do a postgraduate degree after getting your first degree.
3 Postgraduate students typically have to write up a dissertation or thesis at the end of their studies.
4 Good students regularly look back over their lecture notes.
5 In their lectures or articles scholars typically put forward ideas, views, opinions, theories, hypotheses or plans.
6 It is sensible to go through any maths calculations that you had to make as part of a research study in case you made any careless mistakes.

Unit 7

7.1
1 surprising
2 excessive
3 Considerable
4 reasonable
5 substantial
6 excess
7 total
8 exceeding
9 fewer
10 significant

7.2 *Possible answers*
(You may be able to suggest other possibilities that are equally good.)
1 Most / The majority / The larger part of our work is concerned with carbon emissions.
2 We have noticed that a steadily declining number of students are joining the course.
3 Our team spent a significant/substantial amount of time getting funding for the research.
4 In occasional / two or three / a few cases, we could not find any reason for the outbreak.
5 We spent a considerable amount of time on the project.
6 As you repeat the experiment, use increasingly small amounts of water each time.

7.3
1 For some years (now) – in other words, we are not told how many but it must be at least three
2 a massive number of, i.e. an enormous number of
3 the first few microseconds of the beginning of the universe, i.e. the very starting point of time
4 no more than ten microseconds, i.e. ten microseconds or less
5 more or less

7.4 There have been a <u>large</u> number of studies investigating the impact of email on interpersonal communications. <u>All</u> of the studies <u>have</u> been <u>small-scale</u> but they suggest some interesting trends in patterns of email use. From one of the <u>more recent</u> studies it seems that <u>fewer and fewer</u> people send <u>less than</u> 50 emails daily. Moreover, it appears that a <u>small</u> number of senior citizens use email <u>a little less frequently/often</u> than younger people do.

Unit 8

8.1 1 f – start work
2 a – get something ready so it can be operated
3 d – arrange
4 e – become solid
5 c – caused to be in a stated condition
6 b – established
7 h – that must be studied
8 g – group

8.2 1 references   4 accommodate
2 occur   5 structure
3 revolutions, revolution 6 contracted

8.3 1 points   2 set   3 issue   4 channel

8.4 *Possible answers*

word	meaning in text	other meaning(s)
contain	control	hold
maintain	say, claim	keep at a specific level; preserve; provide for
monitor	watch, observe	screen
record	store information	store sounds or pictures electronically; best or most extreme (noun)
occur	happen	exist
measures	methods for dealing with a situation	sizes; amounts; ways of judging something

8.5 The joke is based on a couple of meanings of the word *charge*. The first meaning, familiar from general English, is that of cost, as in 'There is a small charge for using the car park.' However, in physics, *charge*, also known as electrical charge and symbolised as 'q', is a characteristic of a unit of matter that expresses the extent to which it has more or fewer electrons than protons. In atoms, the electron carries a negative elementary or unit charge; the proton carries a positive charge. A neutron is said to have no charge.

Unit 9

9.1 1 shine   3 light   5 highlights   7 elucidate
2 remained, shed 4 shadow   6 illuminate   8 glaring

9.2 1 (who are) opposed to   4 retreated
2 maintain a united front   5 battle/struggle/fight/war, will be lost
3 are bombarded with   6 onslaught

9.3 *Suggested underlinings*
The human brain is a remarkably complex organic computer, taking in a wide variety of sensory experiences, **processing and storing this information**, and recalling and integrating selected **bits*** at the right moments. The destruction caused by Alzheimer's disease has been likened to the **erasure of a hard drive**, beginning with the **most recent files** and working backward. As the illness progresses, old as well as new memories gradually disappear until even loved ones are no longer recognized. Unfortunately, the computer analogy breaks down:

one cannot simply **reboot** the human brain and **reload the files and programs**. The problem is that Alzheimer's does not only **erase information**; it destroys the very **hardware** of the brain, which is composed of more than 100 billion nerve cells (neurons), with 100 trillion connections among them.

* *bit* here means a unit of information on a computer that must be either 0 or 1

Unit 10

10.1
1 *constant, frequent, intermittent* (going from most frequent to least frequent)
2 A sample chosen by chance is a *random sample* whereas a sample chosen as typical of the population as a whole is a *representative sample*.
3 an *isolated* phenomenon
4 You might prefer your results to be *conclusive*, but *inconclusive results* can also be valuable.
5 A role can also be *pivotal* or *decisive*.
6 *Excess energy* – this suggests that there is extra, whereas *sufficient* just suggests that there is enough.
7 Mother, father and brothers/sisters play an *influential role* in a child's development.
8 listening and writing

10.2
1 came
2 consumes, generate
3 played
4 investigated
5 invalidate
6 combines/combined

10.3
1 It took the team a long time to devise a way to solve their problem.
2 During the war we had to break off contact with colleagues abroad.
3 There has been a lot of heated debate surrounding the issue of global warming.
4 Ian Hartmann was invited to take on the role of project leader.
5 Part of my role was to collate the results of our experiments.
6 The doctor wanted me to provide a blood sample for analysis.
7 Scientists all over the world contributed to the debate on cloning.
8 A new and unexpected phenomenon seems to be emerging.
9 Using shading helps to differentiate the key elements in a graph.

10.4
1 taking, random
2 define
3 proper, practical
4 maintaining
5 crucial
6 engaging, heated
7 publish, interim
8 discern, conflicting

Unit 11

11.1
1 amount
2 particular (*or* special)
3 impact (*or* influence/effect)
4 major/considerable/large/significant
5 minor/small
6 important/significant/interesting

11.2
1 There is **widespread** opposition among students to the idea of longer semesters.
2 The destruction of the riverbank will cause **an inevitable** decline in the numbers of small mammals.
3 School standards are a **common** (*or* frequent) concern among parents nowadays.
4 Nowhere in the article does the author make **explicit** mention of the 20 cases which were never resolved.
5 There is very little **common** ground between the two ways of addressing the problem.
6 The paper is too general and lacks **specific/relevant** examples.

11.3

adjective	noun	adjective	noun
significant	significance	important	importance
relevant	relevance	valuable	value
interesting	interest	useful	use
frequent	frequency	broad	breadth

11.4   *Possible answers*
1 of great/considerable relevance
2 of great/considerable value
3 of huge/enormous importance
4 a work of great breadth
5 a work of great/huge/enormous/considerable significance
6 of considerable use
7 of great/considerable interest
8 of high frequency

Unit 12

12.1   1 convincingly demonstrated / demonstrated convincingly
2 observed earlier / earlier observed
3 specifically refers / refers specifically
4 is closely identified
5 briefly discusses
6 firmly establishes
7 loosely based
8 critically examine

12.2   *Suggested answers*
1 hypotheses	3 causes/origins/nature	5 need
2 trends/changes	4 issue/question	

12.3   *Possible answers*
1 interpretation, approach, solution, methodology, theory, etc.
2 threat, challenge, problem, question, dilemma, danger, menace, risk, etc.
3 facts, evidence, causes, issues, reasons, etc.

12.4   *Suggested answers*
The world is facing a looming water crisis. Disputes over allocation have <u>steadily increased</u> in the last decade, and demand has <u>grown rapidly</u>. Water is likely to generate the same degree of controversy in the 21st century as oil did in the 20th. If we take no action now, new conflicts are likely to <u>occur periodically</u> around the world. At the moment, instead of seeking solutions which <u>directly address</u> multiple needs, countries <u>focus</u> a little too <u>narrowly on</u> local issues and <u>typically opt for</u> expensive and inferior solutions. What is needed are decisions which can be <u>quickly implemented</u> and a debate which will <u>seriously consider</u> more than the short term needs of individual states.

12.5   1 directly address
2 consider seriously / seriously consider
3 steadily increasing (Although *growing rapidly* might also be possible here, it is less likely given the time period in the sentence.)
4 focuses/focused narrowly / narrowly focuses/focused
5 quickly implemented / implemented quickly

Unit 13

13.1
1 in line with	5 With the exception of
2 at this stage	6 on the basis of
3 on the one hand, on the other hand	7 on the whole, in terms of
4 In addition to	8 on behalf of

13.2   1 The conclusions are fair in most respects, though some are questionable.
2 Dr Carr's team got the grant, in spite of being the smallest team to apply.
3 We had little money to spare; in other words, we were underfunded.

4 We need people's personal data, in particular their parents' history of illnesses.
5 We made an important discovery; in some ways it was sheer luck.
6 This latest paper is quite short in comparison with other articles in the series.
7 The Indian study was carried out in conjunction with an American project.

13.3 A bone discovered <u>by chance</u> in the 17th century was the beginning of the search for dinosaurs. <u>From then on</u>, scientists and the public have been fascinated by these creatures. <u>In accordance with</u> beliefs at that time, the initial discovery was thought to be the bone of a human giant. However, in 1824, a scientist, William Buckland, calculated that the bone belonged to a 12-metre, flesh-eating reptile and named it *Megalosaurus*, <u>in the process</u> giving us the first of the wonderful list of exotic names for dinosaurs. The 17th century discovery had, <u>in turn</u>, led to a series of further finds around that time. All these <u>to a greater or lesser extent</u> confirmed Buckland's theories. <u>By far</u> the biggest dinosaur discovered to date was probably over 40 metres long. <u>For the most part</u>, dinosaurs ranged from the size of a chicken to that of a giraffe. <u>In most respects</u>, what we know about their habits is still very limited. What we do know is at least <u>to some extent</u> based on pure speculation.

Follow up

Possible sentences (from *Cambridge Advanced Learner's Dictionary*)
On the one hand I'd like a job which pays more, but on the other hand I enjoy the work I'm doing at the moment.
On behalf of the entire company, I would like to thank you for all your work.
I like all kinds of films with the exception of horror films.
The government has few options except to keep interest rates high.
There is nothing to indicate the building's past, except (for) the fireplace.

Possible sentences relating to economics
On the one hand, the country gained a certain prestige from its actions; on the other hand, it suffered quite seriously from the economic point of view.
The economics professor accepted the research award on behalf of her whole department.
With the exception of France, most European countries suffered quite serious effects as a result of the new trade regulations.
The Chancellor succeeded in all his aims except in keeping inflation below 5%.

Unit 14

14.1
1 The article focuses on the changes in the US economy in the post-war period.
2 The professor commented on a number of inconsistencies in the student's essay.
3 The theory is based on a series of experiments conducted over the last five years.
4 The professor's work relies on experiments conducted by his research assistants.
5 It is very important to concentrate on your studies until your exams are over.
6 The writer was able to draw on some primary sources which have only recently become available.

14.2

for	from	of	to	with
account	benefit	convince	assign	associate
argue	depart	dispose	attribute	equip
call	exclude	write	consent	provide
search			react	
			refer	

14.3
1 referred us to
2 account for
3 associated with
4 dispose carefully of
5 benefit enormously from
6 convince me of
7 searching for
8 provided us with
9 consented to
10 writes/wrote very movingly of

14.4 1 The course leader divided her students **into** five groups.
2 They had to trace everyone who had been exposed **to** the infection.
3 At the moment we have too few nurses attending **to** too many patients.
4 Excellent teaching coupled **with** first-class research have made this a successful college.
5 The country emerged **from** the crisis as a much stronger power.
6 Joe got an interest in politics from his uncle who often spoke **of** his days as a senator.
7 The government called **for** an investigation into the explosion at the nuclear reactor.
8 In your speech don't forget to emphasise the advantages of studying here. [No preposition after *emphasise*]

Unit 15

15.1 1 with
2 on (*or possibly* about)
3 of (*exploration* may also, occasionally, be used with *into*)
4 for/behind
5 into/on
6 into
7 about
8 of, of

15.2 1 Her dissertation produced some interesting insights **into** how young children develop a visual sense of the world and the age **at** which development is most noticeable.
2 The reason **for** the unwillingness of the people involved in the demonstration to be interviewed was fear of being arrested later.
3 Hierstat's approach **to** the analysis of solar phenomena is different from that of Donewski. He questioned the assumptions **behind** much of the previous research.
4 Changes **in** the rate of growth of the cells were observed over time.
5 A lack **of** funding led to the cancellation of the project, and social scientists blamed the negative attitude of the government **towards** (to can also be used) social science research.
6 Jawil's article puts great emphasis **on** the need **for** more research and argues the case **for** greater attention **to** the causes of poverty rather than the symptoms.

15.3

nouns	preposition
principle, rationale	behind
difference, relationship	between
preference, reason	for
insight	into
effect, emphasis	on
attitude, tendency	to/towards

15.4 *Suggested answers*
The possible ecological **effects of** climate change are often in the news, as is the **matter of** whether the potential impact can be predicted. New **work on** a migratory bird, the pied flycatcher, takes things a stage further by showing how a climate-related population decline was actually caused. Timing is key. Over the past 17 years flycatchers declined strongly in areas where caterpillar numbers (food for the nestlings) peak early, but in **areas with** a late food peak there was no decline. The young birds arrive too late in places where caterpillars have already responded to early warmth. Mistiming like this is probably a common **consequence of** climate change, and may be a major **factor in** the **decline of** many long-distance migratory bird species.

Unit 16

16.1 1 in a variety of ways 3 a wide range of 5 in excess of
2 a great deal of 4 to some extent

16.2 as a rule for this reason
at the same time in general
be that as it may in terms of
for the most part on the whole

16.3 1 by means of which – The others all mean *generally* or *for the most part* while *by means of which* means using this method.
2 with the exception of X – The others all focus on how X is affected by something whereas *with the exception of X* is focusing on other things rather than X.
3 in addition to – The others are all concerned with trying to be more specific in what they are talking about while *in addition to* is adding something extra to what is being said.

16.4 1 A For the purposes of
2 C be that as it may
3 B from the point of view of
4 B to what extent
5 C in more detail

16.5 *Possible answers*
1 I enjoy watching most sports with the exception of baseball.
2 A poor relationship between parents and children is often due to the fact that they do not spend enough time together.
3 I love reading English novels as opposed to reading English textbooks / writing English essays / reading novels in my own language.
4 In your first year of graduate school you have to take an end-of-year exam in addition to writing a 4,000-word essay.
5 It was a very useful course in the sense that I learnt an enormous amount from it.

Unit 17

17.1 1 No, it isn't. You have to have a first degree.
2 From other pages on the website or by asking the relevant department.
3 Yes, they need a transcript, translated, of your university courses and grades.
4 If the applicant has spent at least one year in English-medium education, then it is not necessary.
5 At least 6.5.

17.2 personal statement
financial guarantee
seek clarification
student loan
equal opportunities
mature student
application form
first degree
minimum score
tough competition

17.3 *Author's answers*
1 The university wants the names of two referees to make sure that the student is making accurate claims about him/herself on the application form.
2 The university wants financial guarantees to make sure that the student will be able to pay the tuition fees.

3 The university wants a personal statement to gain an impression of what kind of person the student is and how motivated he/she is with respect to the course being applied for.

4 The university wants a transcript of courses taken, with grades, to make sure that the student has an appropriate academic background for the course applied for.

5 The university wants an IELTS score of 6.5 or a TOEFL score of at least 580 to make sure that the student's level of English is good enough to cope with English-medium instruction.

17.4 This is probably the most logical order:
1 decide on what career they would like to do
2 find an appropriate course
3 check that they fulfil the necessary entry requirements
4 ask referees if it is all right to put their names on the application form
5 fill in an application form
6 attach a personal statement to the form
7 wait for the application to be processed
8 be called for an interview
9 attend an interview
10 be offered a place

17.5 Hi Miles,
I'd love a **career** as an international lawyer and am really hoping I can **get** in to Wanstow University to do a **postgraduate** course in law there. I've **filled** in all the necessary forms and just hope that my academic **profile** will be good enough for them. I think I fulfil all their **entry requirements** but who knows! It took me ages to get the **transcript** of my college **grades**, etc. translated but I managed to get everything in by the **deadline**. So now I just have to wait to see if they **call** me for an interview or not. Fingers crossed!
Lucia

Unit 18

18.1
1 the Arts Faculty Building
2 the Student Union
3 the halls of residence
4 the Administration Building
5 the Great Hall
6 the Arts Lecture Theatre
7 the University Health Centre
8 the University Library

18.2 *Possible answers*
1 More people in a seminar
2 Supervisor
3 Vacation
4 A personal tutor deals with academic matters and a student counsellor deals with more personal problems.
5 A postgrad rep is someone from the postgraduate student body (usually elected) who represents the students' point of view and a student counsellor is a member of staff whose job it is to support the students through any difficult personal situations.

18.3 Hi Mum,
I've settled in well here at Wanstow. I like my room in this hall of **residence**. I went to my first **lecture** this morning – it was on research methodology – and there were hundreds of students there. The **lecturer** was very good – it was Professor Jones, our head of **department**. Tomorrow I'll have my first **tutorial** – that'll be just me and one other student. We'll be discussing what we have to get done by the end of the **semester** (*or* **term**). I need to try to think some more about the topic for my **dissertation**. When that is finalised I'll be assigned a **supervisor**. I'll be expected to see him or her at least once a week during their office **hours**. I hope I'll like him or her. You hear some awful stories!
Daisy

people	place	event
counsellor	cafeteria	lecture
lecturer	library	seminar
librarian	sports centre	tutorial
postgrad rep	sports grounds	
professor	lecture theatre	
research assistant		
research student		
tutor		

Unit 19

19.1
1 An American – *faculty* obviously refers to people rather than academic departments.
2 An American – the use of *rubric* makes this clear. Also a British person would be more likely to talk about marking assignments than grading term papers.
3 An American – 'Going to school' in the UK means going to primary or secondary school, not college or university.
4 A British person – a *faculty* here means a group of departments concerned with similar academic disciplines.
5 A British person – a *rubric* is a set of instructions as to how a task must be done.

19.2
freshman – first-year student
sophomore – second-year student
junior student – third-year student
senior student – fourth-year student
graduate student – student who has already completed an undergraduate degree and is studying for a master's degree

19.3
None of the statements are true.
1 An *advisor* is someone who helps American students with their academic studies.
2 Women join a *sorority*; a fraternity is for men.
3 *Finals* refers to final exams at the end of a semester at a university or college.
4 A PhD committee is a group of university teachers who coach a doctoral student.

19.4

			6s						7f		
1s	c	h	o	o	l				a		
			p						c		
			h					2q	u	i	z
		3c	o	m	p	s			l		
			m						t		
		4s	o	r	o	r	i	t	y		
			r								
		5s	e	n	i	o	r				

Unit 20

20.1
1 One year
2 60
3 All students on the course have to take them
4 MA students write a dissertation as well as doing the taught courses
5 At least ten
6 3,000 words

7 Lectures, seminars, workshops and tutorials
8 A 3,000 word assignment for each module and essays, project and portfolio work for each elective module, plus the dissertation for MA students.
9 The word limit is 12–15,000 words.
10 They have to get an average mark of over 70% for all modules.

20.2
1 project	3 dissertation	5 MA	7 PhD
2 module	4 Diploma	6 sign	8 in-sessional

20.3
1 upgrade	3 enrolled	5 obligatory	7 defer
2 pre-sessional	4 proceed	6 supervisions	8 Assessment

20.4

verb	noun	adjective
opt	option	optional
oblige	obligation	obligatory
supervise	supervision, supervisor	supervisory
assess	assessment, assessor	–
–	eligibility	eligible

Unit 21

21.1

meet deadlines	lecture notes
to-do list	note-taking
extra-curricular activities	request an extension
study plan	first draft
time management	rote learning
long-term loan	draw mind maps

21.2
1 meet deadlines, request an extension, study plan
2 first draft
3 lecture notes
4 draw mind maps
5 long-term loan
6 time management
7 extra-curricular activities
8 to-do list
9 Rote learning
10 Note-taking

21.3 *Author's answers*
1 I always remember the order of the colours of the rainbow by saying a mnemonic about English medieval history – 'Richard Of York Gained Battles In Vain' – red, orange, yellow, green, blue, indigo, violet.
2 I might write down such things as:
  • revise regularly
  • organise files systematically
  • read round the subject
  • ask if I don't understand.
  In other words, any random ideas that come into my head that might be relevant.
3 Vocabulary in a foreign language, poetry, maths tables, formulae, etc.
4 It depends on the subject – a week before perhaps.
5 Sometimes it wanders, of course. I probably think of holidays or of all the other things I'd like to be doing.
6 No, I don't think I have. Or if I have, I have successfully wiped the memory from my mind.
7 When I was a student I would always prioritise essays that had a deadline.
8 If you have rough notes in front of you, you can plan your answer better and there is less chance your mind will go blank.

21.4 on loan: which have been borrowed
returned: brought back
overdue: not returned on time
incur: a rather formal word meaning 'result in'
borrowing rights: permission to take books out of the library
inter-library loans: books borrowed from other libraries through a special arrangement with them
librarian: person who works in a library (in this case the head of the library)

Unit 22

22.1

1 virtual	4 resources	7 feedback
2 means	5 links	8 quiz
3 community	6 tasks	9 submit

22.2
construct knowledge
enrol on a hybrid course
enter your username
hit the send button
moderate discussions
post messages
start a new thread
subscribe to a mailing list
take part in a discussion group
unsubscribe from a mailing list

22.3 1 enter your username
2 subscribed to a mailing list, unsubscribe from it / the (mailing) list
3 taking part in a discussion group, started a new thread
4 enrol on a hybrid course
5 hitting the send button / you hit the send button, post(ing) a/your message(s)
6 moderating discussions, construct knowledge

22.4 *Author's answers*
1 I'd feel angry and upset because it's embarrassing if someone is rude about you in a public forum.
2 Yes, they are. It's important that I write some letters in upper case and others in lower case.
3 The KISS principle is important for online posts because for many people it is harder to read online and they may just give up if what you write looks too long or dense.
4 It can be a good thing if a person is lurking before they make a contribution themselves – so they see what the conventions of the particular online group are. Lurking online generally does not have the negative associations that the word lurking has in its primary meaning of waiting or moving secretly with the intention of attacking someone or doing something else that is wrong.
5 The subject header should make it clear if the message is relevant to the recipient or not because people sometimes discard messages before reading them. Also it makes it easier to find messages later if you want to reread them.
6 Yes, I have, as both instructor and student. I really enjoyed it and found it a surprisingly positive experience.

Unit 23

23.1 1 The letters proved to be a valuable resource for the study of the poet's life.
2 An extensive body of literature exists on human to animal communication.
3 Newspapers are a good primary source for the period 1980–1985.
4 The data are not given in the main body of the book; they are in the appendix.
5 Plastics are not dealt with in the present study, which focuses on metals only.
6 The thesis begins with a review of the literature on intellectual property rights.

23.2
1 The article makes reference to the work of Hindler and Swartz (1988).
2 Schunker's book was a useful secondary source for understanding the pre-war period. I also consulted original government papers.
3 Tanaka's book draws on data from several Japanese articles on galaxy formation.
4 Elsewhere, Kallen reports on his research into cancer rates among farm workers.
5 Han consulted the archives in the Vienna Museum.

23.3

noun	verb	adjective	adverb
attribute*, attribution	attribute*		
document	document		
consultation, consultant (person)	consult	consultative	
		primary	primarily
catalogue	catalogue		
foundation	found		
note	note	notable	notably
suggestion	suggest	suggestive	suggestively
extension	extend	extensive	extensively
citation	cite		

* The noun is pronounced /'ætrɪbjuːt/; the verb is to /ə'trɪbjʊt/.

23.4
1 Expressing the same message in different words: paraphrase
2 Things known by everyone: common knowledge
3 Stating that one has obtained one's information from that source: acknowledging
4 Direct repetition of what someone has written or said: quotations
5 Stating that you have benefited from someone's work: give credit

Unit 24

24.1
Aidan: established, undeniable, offer, flimsy, convincing, collect, conflicting
Sandra: hard, demonstrates
Petra: draws, distorting, little-known, growing
Dr Li: interpret

24.2
1 The data **indicate/suggest/demonstrate** that the drug education project has been successful.
2 The data in the latest study are more **comprehensive** than in the earlier one.
3 This is the most interesting **item** of data in the whole thesis.
4 What a/an **striking/illuminating** example this is of the power of the human mind!
5 Unfortunately, the facts do not **support** the hypothesis.
6 We cannot **account for** the fact that attitudes are more negative now than five years ago.
7 The problem **stems** from the fact that the software was poorly designed.
8 The article **provides** examples of different methods which have been used over the years.
9 New evidence has **come to light** that the cabinet was not informed of the Minister's decision.
10 We need to **consider** the evidence before we can reach a conclusion.
11 The evidence suggesting that sanctions do not work is **abundant** and **powerful**.
12 A considerable **body** of evidence now exists, but we always try to **obtain** more.
13 We have a lot of **empirical** data which suggest the problem is on the increase.
14 This is a clear **instance** of how conservation can benefit local people.

24.3 The words that do not fit the sentences are:
1 bear out
2 emerges
3 reflected
4 growing
5 vivid

Unit 25

25.1
1 25
2 23
3 Each number is multiplied by 3 to produce the next number.
4 41
5 7
6 $\frac{7}{9}$ is a fraction (a vulgar fraction whereas 2.4 is a decimal fraction) and 4 is a whole number.
7 In my country (the UK) it depends – in most salaried jobs tax is automatically deducted, but for other work, such as freelance or self-employed work, the worker has to declare his/her earnings and pay tax later on.
8 He/She is pleased because it suggests that the figures are accurate. If the figures don't tally then there must be an error or an omission somewhere.

25.2
Dr Syal: calculate, approximate
Melissa: precise
Dr Syal: estimate, tally, constant
Dr Syal: continuous
Melissa: discrete
Dr Syal: round, down

25.3
1 The **incidence** of car accidents **declined/fell/dropped** last year.
2 We **estimated** the final figure.
3 The graph shows the results **in order of magnitude**.
4 A computer program helped us **calculate** the significance of the different variables.
5 **Subtracting** x from y will help you arrive at the correct answer. (Do not include 'away'.)
6 The results from the first experiment **did not tally with** those from the repeat experiment.

25.4
1 workings	3 calculations	5 figures	7 variables
2 arrived	4 area	6 values	

Unit 26

26.1
1 mode, median, average   2 sum, halfway   3 range, extremes

26.2
Life insurance companies base their calculations on the laws of **probability**, that is they assess the likely **outcome(s)**, given the different **variables** such as age, sex, lifestyle and medical history of their clients. The premiums are therefore not chosen at **random** but are carefully calculated. The **distribution** of ages at which death occurs and causes of death are studied to see if they **correlate** with other factors to be taken into account in setting the premiums. Naturally, the companies also monitor social **trends** and react to any changes which might **significantly** affect mortality rates.

26.3
1 2:1 (two to one), two thirds
2 Find more second-year undergraduates to take part in my study
3 Often
4 No. To be reliable, my results must be similar each time I use the same method.
5 10% (*or* ten per cent)
6 18
7 The total number of cases
8 c
9 Probably not. To be valid it must measure what it claims to measure. Breakfast and lunch alone will not tell us everything about eating habits.
10 The scores are normally distributed and the graph is a bell curve.

Unit 27

27.1 The chart **shows/indicates/plots** the number of cars entering the downtown area of West City each day over an eight-year period (years 1–8). The totals are listed on the **y/vertical** axis, while the years are listed on the **x/horizontal** axis. To the right of the graph we see the **key/legend**. The number of cars **varied** over the period. The total rose in the first few years and **reached** a **peak** in year 5, after which the numbers started to **decline/fall/drop**. This can be **explained** by the **fact** that a new mass transit railway was opened in year 6, which is a **graphic** illustration of how good public transport can dramatically affect car use.

27.2 1

pie chart

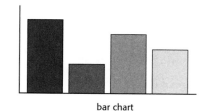
bar chart

 2 A cross-section
 3 Columns run vertically, rows run horizontally
 4 A flowchart
 5 Four
 6 Next to each other
 7 A key
 8 A random sample
 9 a) they cross each other; b) they run alongside each other with an equal interval between them

27.3 1 segments
 2 plotting
 3 peak
 4 stages
 5 intersect
 6 adjacent (With 'adjacent' this sentence does not really need 'to each other' and would be best worded as 'Draw a line connecting the adjacent points'.)
 7 decline
 8 row

27.4
 1 plummeted, incidence, risen
 2 fell below
 3 depreciates, more than halved
 4 appreciate, soared
 5 multiplied, fallen/decreased
 6 exceeded
 7 grew/rose, doubled
 8 declining/falling

Unit 28

28.1 Few students get **a grant** to help them study and so many **take out loans** while they are at university. This is because they have to pay **tuition fees**. They also cannot avoid **considerable expenditure** on everyday life. This is particularly hard for students in London where **the cost of living** is higher than elsewhere in the country. Students living in London are allowed to have bigger loans to help **compensate** for this. Students do not need to start to **repay** their loan until they are **earning** a reasonable salary. But starting working life with a large **debt** makes it much harder for young people to **make ends meet** even once they start earning.

28.2 1 Answer these questions to find out whether you **are eligible (to apply)** for a student grant.
2 I've opened a **current** account.
3 Most people seem to be finding it harder to **make ends meet.**
4 Increasing numbers of students leave college **having accumulated large debts.**
5 Parents often give their children **financial support** while they are at university. / Parents often **provide** their children **with financial support** while they are at university.
6 The amount of tax that people pay depends on **their income.**
7 It is possible to **defer (re)payment** of your loan but you may well end up paying more than you would have done if you had repaid it sooner.
8 You pay for your hotel first and we **reimburse** you later.

28.3 1 The cost of **living** is so high here that students have to live in the most **economical** way they can.
2 As student debts have **soared** over the last few years, far more students now leave university with a huge **overdraft** (or leave university **hugely overdrawn**).
3 Our Student Loans Officer will let you know if you have any **entitlement** to a loan and, if so, will help you to organise taking one **out.**
4 You must have original **receipts** if you want to claim your **expenses.**
5 If you run out of money before the next **instalment** of your grant is due you can get an **interest-free** loan.

28.4 *Possible answers (for the UK)*
1 Yes, they almost always do these days.
2 Yes, I think they should. Because otherwise it is only possible for children from well-off families to go to university.
3 There are lots of scholarships and other financial awards for students. Some are for people with special academic, musical or athletic talents. Others are for people from special places or with special family circumstances.
4 Yes, I think they should but I think that the loans should really be free and should not attract any interest even if they are not paid off for a long time. I think this because otherwise it becomes much harder for young people from poorer families to go to university. I also believe that society as well as the individual benefits from a higher general level of education.

Unit 29

29.1 1 initial phase, temporary, permanent, final
2 ongoing, transitional, critical
3 current, forthcoming, annual, preceding (*or* previous)
4 century, decade, era, next few

29.2 1 **At** the moment, I'm writing up my thesis. I hope to finish in the **near** future.
2 Our research is **at** an **intermediate** stage – we now need to analyse our data.
3 The **emergence** of internet technology has transformed the travel industry.
4 The university has **gone** through a period of great change in the **last** decade.
5 In the **distant** future, scientists may be able to cure almost all common diseases.
6 Anti-social behaviour is **a problem nowadays** in many big cities.
7 A **series** of events occurred in 1986 which changed the political climate in the country. In **subsequent** years, two new parties were formed which became engaged in **concurrent** attempts to win over voters.
8 Prior **to** 2001, the industry was unregulated. In **recent** years, however, the government has introduced new regulations. (**the last few years** is also correct)
9 In 1968, a monetary crisis coincided **with** a huge budget deficit, and most **contemporary** political commentators warned that the **eventual** cost to the nation would be enormous.

noun	verb	adjective	adverb
eventuality		eventual	eventually
succession	succeed	successive	successively
evolution	evolve	evolving/evolutionary	
emergence	emerge	emergent/emerging	
coincidence	coincide	coincidental	coincidentally
period		periodic	periodically

29.3 is the label for this table.

29.4 *Author's sentences*

Periodically, there are major changes in approaches to language teaching. [from time to time]
Language teaching has **evolved** from focusing on grammar and translation to developing communication skills.
The **emergence** of communicative language teaching **coincided** with far more frequent international travel for both work and leisure.
There has been a **succession** of interesting articles recently focusing on exploiting modern technology in language teaching.

Unit 30

30.1 *Possible answers*

1 Researchers are investigating why chocolate **triggers/induces** headaches in certain people.
2 Wilson's most recent paper has **generated** a great deal of interest among sociologists.
3 The drug **induced/triggered** headaches and dizziness among a number of subjects in the test.
4 Having an end-of-term prize **motivates** students to do well in their class tests.
5 Intensive farming has **contributed** significantly to the decline of bird populations.
6 The missile test **provoked** an immediate and very strong response from adjacent governments and from the United Nations.
7 Astrologists believe that people's lives are (largely) **determined** by the planets and stars.
8 The barrier **inhibits** the flow of water into the area to prevent flooding in the rainy season.
9 A leak in the tank **accounted for** 40% of the fuel loss, and evaporation took away another 5%.
10 The renovated college buildings have wider doors and corridors to **facilitate** the use of wheelchairs.
11 The Minister cut taxes in an attempt to **stimulate** the economy, which was performing poorly.
12 Britain has **derived** many economic benefits from membership of the European Union.

30.2
1 The article explores the origins of the concept of democracy.
2 One small explosion set off a chain reaction, causing massive damage.
3 The confusion probably stemmed from a lack of communication.
4 The proposed new tax could have major consequences for larger families.
5 The disastrous events of 2003 gave rise to a widespread sense of disillusionment.
6 The judge explained that there were precedents for his decision.

30.3
1 De Routa's work in the 1970s influenced the development of computer science. (no preposition after the verb)
2 effect   4 for   6 end
3 to   5 on

30.4 The nouns are:
motivation   facilitation   influence   provocation   trigger   contribution
stimulus (*or* stimulation)   induction   derivation

30.5 1 Byron's poetry **had an influence on** Romantic poets in a number of other European countries.
2 Tree pollen can **be/provide a trigger for** hay fever attacks in vulnerable people.
3 In obstetrics the drug can be used to help **in/with the induction of** labour.
4 The new economic measures were introduced **as a stimulus to** the faltering economy.
5 Tomoko is studying **the motivation of** world-class athletes.

Unit 31

31.1 1 Many educators believe that different learning styles are equally **valid**.
2 In the UK a university faculty is a unit where similar **disciplines** are grouped together.
3 The French impressionists were a key **movement** in European art.
4 The **essence** of international law is the application of a single standard for strong and weak nations alike.
5 Researchers spend much of their time trying to **interpret** their data.
6 Some 19th century artistic styles were a **reaction** to the ugliness of industrialisation.
7 Harvey (2003) **emphasises** that the findings of the study cannot be **generalised**, as only a small amount of data was used.
8 In the late 20th century, intellectual **thought was** greatly influenced by ideas of gender and race.

31.2 1 There **are some interesting PhD theses** on water resources in the library.
2 What **was** your main **criterion** in designing your survey?
3 She was interested in a **strange phenomenon** connected with comets.
4 The **hypotheses were** never proved, as the data were incomplete.

31.3 1 We must never accept the notion that intelligence is connected to race.
2 The task of choosing an analytical framework is an important stage in any research.
3 The book expresses his viewpoint on the role of the United Nations in times of war.
4 Tannen has always made her stance on gender and language use very clear.
5 Consumers have different perceptions of what low price and high quality mean.
6 The report laid out a new model of family healthcare which changed everything.
7 Physicists developed the concept of dark matter to explain certain observations.

31.4 1 autonomy   3 profound   5 moral
2 the humanities   4 thinking, understanding   6 grounding

Unit 32

32.1

noun	verb	noun	verb
implication	imply	description	describe
observation	observe	statement	state
argument	argue	emphasis	emphasise
assertion	assert	explanation	explain
contention	contend	demonstration	demonstrate

32.2 1 **Harkov's contention** that continued population growth will be a more serious problem than global warming is not accepted by many scientists.
2 **'Global symmetry' is a statement** that the laws of physics take the same form when expressed in terms of distinct variables.
3 **The report makes the implication that** no individual government will ever be able to control the internet.
4 **Dudas provides a demonstration of / as to** how dangerous genetic modification might be.

5 **Groot puts an emphasis on** the role of schools in preventing teenage drug abuse.
6 **Lenard's observation** that women use expressions such as 'you know' in English more than men **was** later proved to be inaccurate.
7 **Plana's explanation of** the possible origins of the pyramids in Guelcoga has been disputed by Ruiz.
8 **Wilson gives a description of** the ancient alphabet of the Guelcoga people.
9 **Wu puts (forward) the argument** that daylight-saving time should be extended throughout the year.
10 **The President makes the assertion** that he cares about fighting poverty.

32.3 The words that do not fit are:
1 pinpoints – pinpoint would be used to focus on something much more unexpected and worthy of note, rather than on generally known background information
2 proves (if it's highly controversial he/she can't have proved it)
3 claims – the structure would need to be 'claims that Malwar's figures are inaccurate'
4 asserts – the structure would need to be 'asserts that pilot testing is important'
5 advances – the structure would need to be 'advances the theory that …'
6 description – this would be used about something that is far more detailed than the context suggested here
7 cast doubt – the structure would need to be 'cast doubt on there being a causal link …'

32.4 1 **In my opinion/view**, courses in academic writing should be compulsory for all new students.
2 It has not yet been **proved** that the virus can jump from species to species. / **There** is not yet **any** proof that the virus can jump from species to species.
3 Richardson **emphasises** a number of weaknesses in the theory. (no preposition after *emphasise* – though we do say 'puts' or 'lays emphasis on something')
4 Taylor **refers to / mentions** several studies which have looked at the problem in the past. (no preposition after *mention*)
5 Pratt's **suggestion** that the poet may have suffered from depression is an interesting one.
6 Our latest results cast doubt **on** our original hypothesis.

Unit 33

33.1 1 critical 2 conclusion 3 side(s)

33.2 1 critical 2 conclusion 3 sides

33.3 1 weighing, conclusion, outweigh, disadvantages/drawbacks, insights, variables, take, constitute, points
2 take into, relevant, course, deduce, basis, predict, scales

33.4 1 The hospital announced that the President remains seriously ill.
2 Dixon was asked to write a review giving his/her opinions on contemporary Irish poetry.
3 The writer was imprisoned for his openly negative views on the government.
4 It is extremely important that all measurements are recorded every hour.

33.5 1 A recent survey has <u>unearthed</u> some interesting facts about commuting habits. (it is as if the researchers were digging into the earth like archaeologists)
2 In predicting trends in inflation, economists often look at which direction the political <u>winds are blowing</u>. (this sees change as similar to changes in the weather)
3 Martins published a <u>ground-breaking</u> study of the formation of galaxies. (as if one is digging a new piece of ground to construct a building)
4 By <u>digging</u> into the archives, Professor Robinson was able to <u>shed</u> important new <u>light</u> on the history of the period. (again, as if one is digging into the ground like an archaeologist; new knowledge is seen as a light)

Unit 34

34.1
Dr Babayan: define, terms
Dr Babayan: terminology, transparent
Dr Babayan: glossary, senses
Tomoko: distinguish, subtle distinctions/differences
Dr Babayan: communicating (could also be conveying), coherent (could also be concise), ambiguous, misinterpret (could also be misunderstand), clarify

34.2
1 mistranslated	4 miscalculated
2 misunderstood	5 incoherent
3 unambiguous	6 mispronounces

34.3 The American songwriter Bob Dylan is often considered to be as much a poet as a musician. He **expressed** his political ideas through folk songs in his early period. His melodies were often simple but his words **conveyed** complex messages, often with subtle **nuances**. In one of his songs, he speaks of a 'hard rain' which will fall after a nuclear war. On one level the words **denote** real, radioactive rain, but the **connotations** of the words are many: life will be hard, perhaps impossible. Perhaps the consequences will fall hard on the politicians who started the war too. There are many things we can **infer** from these words. The song is part of the political **discourse** of the Cold War of the 1960s. It **evokes** an atmosphere of fear and hopelessness. Seen from the **perspective** of the post-Cold-War era, it may seem difficult to **comprehend** such fear, but at the time, that fear was very real.

Unit 35

35.1
1 **We must give top priority to** protecting the privacy of our subjects.
2 **We designed the questionnaire with the intention of making** it as simple as possible to answer.
3 **We had as our goal the definition and evaluation of** a new approach to urban planning.
4 **I had no intention of becoming** a scientist when I began my studies.
5 **A hypothesis-based methodology** does not work in some cases.
6 **Our project is located at the interface between** sociology and psychology.

35.2
1 Prof. Li	3 Dr Tadeus	5 Dr Andreas	7 Dr Finstein
2 Prof. Simons	4 Prof. Horza	6 Dr Janeja	

35.3
1 infrastructure
2 a national debate
3 (academic) disciplines
4 the knowledge base
5 the interface between theory and practice
6 (a) meet/achieve an objective (b) reach/achieve/attain a target
7 motive, motivation
8 practice-led research

Unit 36

36.1
1 The views she expressed were totally **irrational**.
2 The committee seemed to be biased **in favour of** (*or* **towards**) applications from younger people.
3 The book is **a subjective** account of life in a small town in the 1920s.
4 The club rules were prejudiced **against** children.
5 The President's daughter was quite **immature** for her age.
6 He has rather **conservative/reactionary** views about marriage.
7 Her views on education are rather **conservative/reactionary**.
8 Supreme Court judges always act in **an impartial** way.

36.2
1 underlying, philosophy/philosophies
2 to adopt / to shift to
3 held
4 ethical
5 deep-rooted, encounter
6 shifted

36.3
1 change (changed)
2 take
3 (a) in my point of view
4 An ideology suggests the beliefs are rigid and more restricting.
5 standpoint

36.4
1 The people of the area hold some unusual views about nature.
2 Most young people seem to have objections to the proposals on student fees.
3 Examiners tend to be biased in favour of candidates with clear handwriting.
4 Girls look at their careers from a different standpoint than their mothers.
5 Let us now discuss the principles underlying this approach.

36.5 *Suggested underlinings*
Academics have traditionally **taken the view** that their discipline is **intellectually independent** from all others. However, inter-disciplinary degrees are becoming more and more common, suggesting that **preconceptions** about what and how one should study may be **somewhat misplaced**. A more **liberal** view of education would **advocate** greater freedom to explore the links between different **fields of learning**, thus **pushing the frontiers of knowledge** in **new and exciting** directions. Many academics now **feel** that the future lies in this **blending of ideas** and the **cross-fertilisation** of **thought** which emerges from it.

Unit 37

37.1
1 We may well discover that the problem was caused by overheating.
2 It would seem to appear from all the findings that the test is reliable.
3 Of course it is true that not all factories cause huge amounts of pollution.
4 We can certainly assume that the exchange rate will continue to fluctuate.
5 It may well turn out not to be the case that all the questions were answered honestly.
6 It could be argued that conflict was inevitable after the events of recent years.

37.2
In all cases, the adverbs may also be the first word in the sentence, except in the case of 'tentatively' and 'conclude', which usually occur next to each other.
1 Russo was **allegedly** a member of a terrorist organisation, but it was never proved.
2 At that time, the population of tigers was **reportedly** widespread in the region.
3 The collapse of the roof **apparently** caused a sprinkler system pipe to burst.
4 To get a better job is **presumably** a main motivation for going on to higher education.
5 We may **tentatively** conclude that water shortages are likely to increase rather than decrease.
6 The students were **evidently** guessing some of the answers instead of using their knowledge of the context.

37.3

noun	verb	adjective	adverb
tendency	tend		
evidence		evident	evidently
	seem		seemingly
likelihood		likely	
perception	perceive	perceptible	perceptibly

37.4
1 **It is not very likely / It is highly unlikely** that everyone will fail the test.
2 Students **have a tendency** to leave preparation for exams till the last minute.
3 **It was evident** that some students had copied each other's answers.
4 **There is a common perception** that older people cannot learn musical instruments to a professional standard.
5 The melting of the polar ice caps **is seemingly** inevitable.

37.5 *Suggested answers*

1 Rats **are generally considered to be** carriers of diseases.
2 There **is (only) limited** evidence to support the opinion that diesel cars cause more pollution than petrol cars.
3 **There is every likelihood** that rail passenger numbers will continue to decline.
4 In the absence of evidence **to the contrary**, we must conclude that right-handedness is not linked to intelligence in any way.
5 **It is undoubtedly** true that engineering graduates are in increasing demand.
6 The area near the river **is liable to flood/flooding** in winter.

Unit 38

38.1 This essay examines the early life of Catherine of Aragon (1485–1536), focusing particularly **on** the period of her brief marriage to Prince Arthur, his death at the age of 15 and her subsequent marriage **to** his brother Prince Henry, later to become King Henry VIII of England. **For** the purposes **of** this essay, I shall pay little attention **to** either the earlier or the later periods of her life. Her eventual divorce from King Henry is, thus, **beyond** the scope **of** this essay. Much more has already been written **on** the subject **of** this later period of her life. The literature **with** reference **to** the period is extensive but my essay is largely based **on** a couple of key sources, which are particularly relevant **to** any discussion of this period, and I shall refer **to** these throughout.

38.2
1 the pros and cons
2 at the same time
3 and so on and so forth*
4 having said that*
5 that's all very well but*
6 the extent to which
7 in addition to
8 as well as

* Note that these are more common in spoken contexts, and are not normally used in academic writing.

38.3 There are a number of **advantages and disadvantages** to take into account when considering the purchase of a hybrid (gasoline-electric) car. Such cars are, **for instance**, undoubtedly better for the environment in the sense that they cause significantly less air pollution. **Furthermore, the degree** to which they rely on oil, a natural resource which is rapidly becoming depleted, is much less than is the case with conventional cars. **Nevertheless,** hybrid cars are not without their problems. Cost may be an issue **as well as** the technical complexity of this relatively new type of engine. **Provided that** you take these factors into account, there is no reason why you should not decide to buy a hybrid car.

38.4   1 B   2 C   3 A   4 B   5 C   6 B

Unit 39

39.1
1 purpose/aim
2 concerned
3 aim/purpose
4 consists
5 address
6 devoted
7 divided
8 focus

39.2
1 War and Peace
2 After
3 No
4 Olaf
5 Before

39.3
1 Take
2 Firstly
3 addresses
4 below
5 following
6 see
7 consider
8 later

39.4
1 **As can be seen** in Table V there has been an increase in the numbers of students in higher education.
2 In Section 3 we take up again some of the arguments from **the preceding section**.
3 **At this point** let us turn our attention to developments in Constantinople.
4 The country **is divided into** six provinces.
5 Let us now **turn to** the issue of the reunification of Germany.

Unit 40

40.1
1 present
2 call on, make/give
3 welcome
4 on the subject of
5 introduce, address

40.2 *Suggested answers*

1 We need to consider family income too, but I'll **come back** to that later.
2 So, **moving on**, I'll **skip** item 4 on the handout and instead talk about number 5 in **more** detail.
3 I'll try to finish by 3.30, but **feel free** to leave if you have a class or other appointment to go to.
4 There is a handout **going round** and I have some **extra/spare** copies too if anyone wants them.
5 I'll finish there as my time has **run out**.
6 We didn't want to make people uncomfortable by having a camera in the room. **Having said that,** we did want to video as many of the sessions as possible.
7 I'd like to **go back** to a point I made earlier about river management.
8 So, I believe our experiments have been successful. **That's all I have to say.** Thank you.
9 **Going back to / To go back to / Getting back to** the problem of large class sizes, I'd like to look at a study **done** in Australia in 2002.
10 I'll try not to **go over time**, so I'll speak for 30 minutes, to **leave** time for questions at the end.

40.3
1 on 2 with, to 3 to 4 to 5 by

40.4 *Possible sentences*

1 I shall present the results of some studies done recently.
2 Dr Fonseca will now take questions.
3 I want to raise another issue at this point.
4 I'd just like to make a comment, if I may.
5 I will begin by giving an overview of the topic.
6 This is the first time I've given/made a presentation, so I'm a bit nervous.

Unit 41

41.1 Scientists disagree as to whether cold fusion, the controlled power of the hydrogen bomb in the laboratory, is possible. In the past, some believed that **experimental study** under **laboratory conditions** using palladium and platinum electrodes could in fact cause heavy hydrogen atoms to fuse into helium and release energy, as the sun does. In carefully controlled experiments, researchers believed they could **manipulate** the **variables** arising from the complexity of the electrodes and other equipment used. In such **controlled conditions**, they argued, cold fusion was possible. However, attempts to **replicate** some of the experiments which claimed to be successful failed, and many now believe that cold fusion is in fact theoretically impossible.

Some linguists believe that we can best **determine** how language is processed by laboratory experiments. However, laboratory experiments are by definition **artificial** and may not **reflect** what happens in the real world. Other linguists believe, therefore, that **empirical observation** is better, and prefer to carry out **field** studies and **case** studies of individuals in **natural settings**. In this way, **in-depth** data can be **collected** by observers without **interfering** with the process in any way, even though this may be a more **time-consuming** method. However, individual studies in real situations may not be **representative** of the general **population** of second language learners. In short, both approaches have their advantages and disadvantages.

41.2 carry out: a pilot study / an experiment / a procedure
employ/use: a technique / a device / (a) methodology
a piece of / to assemble / check apparatus
(NB You can also employ/use a procedure.)

41.3 1 It was a new **piece** of apparatus so we **assembled** it first and then **checked** it before using it (*or* we **checked** it first and then **assembled** it).

2 The team carried out a **pilot study** before conducting the main **experiment** to see if the **methodology/procedure** they were using was reliable.

3 The team needed to employ a different **technique/procedure** for measuring the pressure, so they used a new **device** (*or* **apparatus**) which they manufactured in their own laboratory. (If *apparatus* is used, we can also say 'a new piece of apparatus'.)

41.4 1 It was very difficult to make reliable **inferences** from the data as we had so little.

2 A correlational study is a good way of seeing if one **phenomenon** is related to another in a **systematic** way.

3 The experiment neither proved nor **disproved** Jessop's theory.

4 We had to explain the unusual scores of five of the **subjects** in the sample, who all had totals well below the norm. It was possible there were **inaccuracies** in the data.

5 An **outside** (*or* **external**) observer can often unintentionally **disrupt** the behaviour of the subjects they are observing.

Unit 42

42.1 1 'Computer programming languages usually **fall** into one of four **categories**: imperative, functional, object-oriented and logic. These languages are **distinct** from one another in how they operate. The **structure** of imperative languages is based on commands, you know, "do this, do that thing". Languages such as Fortran and COBOL **belong** to this **type**. Functional languages **consist** of mathematical functions. The **components** of object-oriented languages are commands which are combined with the data to create "objects". The main **feature** of logic languages is that they state facts or relations between things. Now, in the case of human languages, **diversity** is considered a good thing. In the case of programming languages, it suggests we still haven't found the best one!'

2 'For your end-of-year project, you must carry out a survey of consumer preferences for one product or a type of product. You'll need to **devise** a questionnaire, and you'll need to take a lot of factors into account. These include **gender**, that is how many males and/ or females are in your sample, social **class**, and so on. And also different **generations**; will it just be adults, or young people too? And what about **senior citizens**? They may be retired, but they still buy a lot of things. Also, what about **occupational** status? Are you going to separate **blue collar** and white collar workers? Or are you also interested in people who are not in **employment**, such as **homemakers**, but who are often the ones who buy the goods? And in our multicultural society, don't forget **ethnic** background.'

42.2

noun	verb	adjective	adverb
similarity		similar	similarly
difference	differ/differentiate*	different	differently
allocation	allocate		
description	describe	descriptive	descriptively

* *Differ* is intransitive (it does not take an object); *differentiate* is transitive (it does take an object) or can be used with *between* (*differentiate between x and y*).

42.3 1 It is hard to **differentiate** between these two **similar** plants. They hardly **differ** at all.

2 The professor persuaded the university to **allocate** more resources to his department.

3 There are some magnificent **descriptive** passages in the writer's later novels.

4 In your essay please comment on the **similarities** and the **differences** between the two poems.

42.4 Note that in this exercise both the original sentences and those in the Key are equally appropriate in academic English. The purpose of the exercise is just to practise using a range of language.
1 It is difficult to **classify** human emotions as we know little about their **nature**.
2 Sensation and action can both be **subsumed** under the term *behaviour*.
3 Linguists **assign** all languages to a place in the system of language families, based on their grammars and other key **dimensions/features/characteristics**.
4 The atmosphere of the planet **is made up** of different gases.
5 **Urban** and **rural** people often differ in their political attitudes. **Marital status** is also a relevant factor.

Unit 43

43.1 1 The study found links **between** use of the drug and heart problems.
2 Jill's thoroughness is complemented **by** her co-researcher's originality.
3 Musical talent correlates **with** mathematical ability.
4 The sculpture is an unusual combination **of** gentle curves and sharp angles.
5 The conference has brought **together** scholars from all over the world.
6 The researcher is trying to piece **together** information from a range of sources.
7 Peter's study is closely related **to** his previous research.
8 The term 'hacker' used to refer **to** a computer programmer.

43.2 1 There is usually a very strong **bond** between a mother and her child.
2 Salaries have fallen over the last few years not in real terms but **relative** to inflation.
3 In the UK black cats are **associated** with good luck.
4 In the experiment, group A performed best on the manual dexterity test and least well on the memory test whereas for group B the **reverse** was the case.
5 'Malicious' is more or less **synonymous** with 'nasty'.
6 The problems discussed above are all closely **interrelated**.
7 **Taken** together, the studies by Johnson and Mahesh provide very strong evidence that previous theories on the nature of this disease were flawed.
8 The research is original in **that** it approaches the topic from a completely fresh angle.
9 The painter loved to explore the **interplay** between light and shade.

43.3 **Interaction** within a chimpanzee community is the theme of Gavros's fascinating new book. It describes the various different **relationships** between the animals, and **reveals** how an individual's behaviour **reflects** his or her position in the community, showing how the older females in particular offer each other **mutual** support. The book also provides **evidence** to **suggest** that chimpanzees use sounds in systematic ways to communicate with each other. One particular sound, for example, clearly **corresponds** to the human cry of 'Watch out!' while another would seem to be the **equivalent** of 'Help!' Certain gestures also seem to be **associated** with specific meanings.

43.4 *Possible answers*
1 Different universities competed with one another in the chess competition which Alf won. (Note that a hyphen is used here. The rules for the use of hyphens are not very predictable in English – look out for examples and make a note of them.)
2 Highways linking different US states with each other are usually good, fast roads.
3 If two countries are economically interdependent, it means that they are dependent on each other, rather than, say, just one country being dependent on the other.
4 Intermarriage can refer either to marriage between people of different social groups or as in the example sentence to marriage between people of the same family or set of families.
5 Interchange of information conveys the idea that information is going in both directions and not just one. In other words, everyone is both giving and gaining new information.
6 Interconnecting parts connect with and relate to each other. In other words, they are not separate from each other.

Unit 44

44.1 1 as compared 3 compared 5 from/to 7 analogy
2 difference/contrast/distinction 4 comparison 6 comparison 8 In contrast*
* *On the other hand* would also be possible here, but *in contrast* better expresses the sharp opposition between the two scientists' views.

44.2 *Suggested answers*
1 The two groups were **different from/to** each other.
2 **There was a contrast between** the two groups of children.
3 The three liquids **were similar** to one another.
4 The data revealed **differences in/among the informants' responses**.
5 The title of her paper was: 'Male attitudes towards prison sentencing **compared with/to** female attitudes'.
6 The economy of the north is booming, the south is **similarly** enjoying an economic upturn. / The economy of the north is booming. **Similarly,** the south is also enjoying an economic upturn.

44.3 *Suggested answers*
1 **Unlike** the south of the country, which has little in the way of forests, the north of the country is covered with thick forests. / The north of the country is covered with thick forests, **unlike** the south of the country, which has little in the way of forests.
2 **Rather than** a questionnaire, in this case, face-to-face interviews are better.
3 Asian languages such as Vietnamese are quite difficult for learners whose first language is a European one. **Conversely,** European languages are difficult for learners whose first language is an Asian one.
4 **On the one hand,** oil is plentiful at the present time. **On the other hand,** it will run out one day.
5 Boys tend to prefer aggressive solutions to problems, **whereas** girls prefer more indirect approaches. / **Whereas** boys tend to prefer aggressive solutions to problems, girls prefer more indirect approaches. (*While* could also be used in both cases instead of *whereas*.)
6 In the post-war period, public transport enjoyed a boom. Nowadays, **the reverse is true.**

44.4 1 True
2 False; compatible means things can exist together or work together
3 True
4 False; if there are parallels then there are similarities between them
5 True

Unit 45

45.1 1 Students always seem to have difficulty in remembering this formula.
2 Ford pointed out that the methodology had a number of inconsistencies.
3 The need to find replacement fuels poses considerable challenges for scientists.
4 The media continue to focus on the controversy surrounding the President.
5 In the figures he presented several errors were apparent.
6 On their way across Antarctica they experienced many difficulties.
7 The results of the opinion poll raise some important questions for the Party.
8 Problems caused by pollution in this area arose fairly recently.

45.2 1 It is no easy task mediating **between** unions and management.
2 In this lecture I plan to deal **with** the later novels of Charles Dickens.
3 The answer to most problems in agriculture lies **in** the soil.
4 He thought for a long time but was unable to come **up** with a solution.
5 Green tourism may initially feel like a contradiction **in** terms.
6 I wonder what the professor's reaction **to** the article will be.
7 The company has experienced a number of difficulties **with** the computer operating system.
8 Have you found a solution **to** the problem yet?

45.3

noun	verb
solution	solve
reaction	react
contents	contain
error	err

noun	verb
resolution	resolve
response	respond
contradiction	contradict
mediation	mediate

45.4

1 contradicted		3 solution		5 contains		7 resolved
2 err		4 mediate		6 response		8 reacted

Unit 46

46.1

1 environment		3 existence		5 absence		7 context
2 status		4 circumstances		6 infrastructure		8 conditions

46.2

1 unstable		3 infinite		5 maximum
2 Instability		4 absence		

46.3

1 In the 1960s the government **imposed** (*or* **placed**) **restrictions** on the amount of money you could take out of the country.
2 The problem **is confined to** the capital city.
3 All fossil fuels **are finite resources**.
4 In the accident there was **minimal** damage to the car.
5 All research is **subject to the constraints of** funding decisions.
6 **The social instability of/in** the country deters investors.
7 **In/Under normal circumstances** we would not behave in this way. / **If the circumstances were normal** we would not behave in this way.
8 Most small children believe **in the existence of fairies**.

46.4

1 restrict		3 restrain		5 minimum		7 circumstances
2 intrinsic		4 integral		6 imposed		8 restraint

Unit 47

47.1

1 verify		3 supplement		5 step
2 procedure		4 simulation		6 design

47.2

1 consume		3 display		5 insert		7 input
2 advent		4 emerged		6 invent		8 secure

47.3

verb	noun
apply to	application of
behave	behaviour of
simulate	simulation of
select from	selection of
design	design of
ratify	ratification of
insert into	insertion

verb	noun
verify	verification of
utilise	utilisation of
emerge from	emergence of
consume	consumption of
secure	security of
input into	input
display	display

47.4

1 emergence		3 insert		5 application		7 behaviour
2 consumption		4 ratify		6 input		8 design

Follow up

Possible word combinations
painful, difficult, learning, ageing, production **process**
correct, standard, special, official, technical, experimental **procedure**
first, next, final, difficult, crucial, early **stage**

Unit 48

48.1
1 expansion
2 sustainable
3 perceptible
4 increasingly
5 development
6 elimination
7 modifications
8 adjustments
9 acquisition
10 relaxation

48.2
1 If prices fluctuate they go up and down; they change a lot.
2 If a disease is eliminated none of it remains, it disappears completely.
3 If interest in something is diminishing it is becoming less.
4 If there is a marked change in someone's behaviour it is probably a big change. It is a noticeable change.
5 If most people feel that mobile phones enhance their lives, they feel that their lives have become better.
6 If controls on imports are relaxed they become less strict.

48.3
1 recovering
2 converting
3 refine
4 abandon
5 adjust
6 status quo
7 maintain
8 restore

48.4
1 in
2 to (*or* from *or* out of)
3 away from
4 on
5 on
6 to adjust to changes
7 from
8 to

Unit 49

49.1
1 misguided, inadequate
2 ground-breaking
3 important, significant
4 crucial
5 unique

49.2
1 credit, acknowledged, crucial
2 borne, mistaken, evidence, flaws
3 challenged, validity, flawed, limited
4 viewed, seminal/ground-breaking, ground-breaking

49.3
1 By no means is it certain that all the students will pass their final exams.
2 He had never before taught such an outstanding student.
3 Rarely has the country witnessed such a display of public feeling.
4 We will in no way / We will not in any way be able to halt the process of global warming. / We will not be able to halt the process of global warming in any way.
5 Under no circumstances will students be allowed to defer the completion of their thesis longer than one month.
6 Only when we gather a lot more data will we know the answer.

49.4
1 highlights
2 solid
3 compatible
4 comprehensive, key
5 worth recalling, limited
6 underlines

Unit 50

50.1
1 **In conclusion**, the tests suggest the drug has no dangerous side effects.
2 **To summarise**, losing the war was a humiliating defeat for the country on a number of different levels.
3 **In summary**, it is impossible to blame the disaster on one person alone.
4 From the survey we can **draw the conclusion / come to the conclusion** that advertising has a stronger effect on teenage girls than on other groups of the population.
5 **To recapitulate**, there were a number of different reasons why the experiment was less successful than had been hoped.

50.2
1 balance
2 abstract
3 put, eventually
4 provide
5 analysis
6 words
7 points
8 close

50.3
1 at last
2 lastly
3 Lastly
4 at last
5 at last

50.4 *In the end* means 'finally, after something has been thought about or discussed a lot'. *At the end* is usually followed by 'of (something)', and refers to the final point of a thing or time or place, e.g. *at the end of the film, at the end of the month, at the end of the street.*

50.5 This paragraph is a **précis** of *Academic Vocabulary in Use*. **In sum / To sum up**, the book provides 50 units covering key aspects of academic vocabulary. Stated **briefly**, each unit has **attempted** to present and practise the words that all students need. The **overall** aim of the book is to help students not only to understand but also to use academic vocabulary. In bringing the book to a **close**, we hope we have helped you and wish you success in your future academic studies.

Reading and vocabulary 1

1 1 cherished companions   3 prolong   5 concentrated
     2 crucial   4 initiated   6 Study participants

2 1 persons   2 underlies   3 behaviours   4 calamity

3

noun	verb	adjective
convention		conventional
help	help	helpful
expectancy	expect	expectant
pleasure	please	pleasurable

Reading and vocabulary 2

1 1 False: Australia is indeed 'arid', i.e. it has little or no rainfall to support plants, but Antarctica is even more arid
     2 True
     3 False: the species developed because of Australia's isolation from other landmasses
     4 False: seismic (earthquake) activity persists (continues to occur) in the eastern and western highlands
     5 False: the general geological appearance is 'relatively uniform', i.e. all of the same type

2 1 roughly equal   3 the end result   5 seemingly unchanged
     2 massive upheavals   4 common misconception

3 1 lush   2 inhospitable   3 a window   4 theorize

Reading and vocabulary 3

1 1 of   2 by   3 from   4 to   5 along with   6 of   7 to

2 1 Accessing web pages is quite **straightforward**, and people with **virtually** no expertise can use the web.
     2 The browser contacts the **appropriate** server to transmit the document.
     3 The WWW is **essentially** a search system.
     4 The information added to documents **distinguishes** web servers from Internet servers.
     5 Years ago, the Internet was **mainly** used by experts.

Reading and vocabulary 4

1 1 The skin is the largest organ in the human body.
     2 Psychologists disagree as to how exactly memories are stored in the brain.
     3 Humans share almost all of their genes with the other great apes such as gorillas.
     4 As children become young adults they have bursts of growth.
     5 It is important that animals in captivity are given the right diet.
     6 People have approached the problem in a variety of ways.

2
1 complex
2 spread out
3 numerous
4 outnumber
5 amplify
6 partially
7 final
8 specific
9 spread

3 *Possible answers*
Scientists disagree as to how much **matter** there is in the universe. (substance)
Observing safety procedures is a **matter** of some importance. (situation)
What's the **matter** with the baby? Why's she crying? (problem)
Wax and ice **pass** from solid to liquid as you heat them. (change)
The main symptoms usually **pass** after a couple of days. (go away)
Pass me the test tube, please. (give)
The ice caps were **formed** millions of years ago. (created)
The survey **formed** the basis of the report. (provided)
The child **formed** the mud into the figure of a dog. (shaped)
The monks sleep in small, bare **cells**. (little rooms)
When creating a table in Word, it is possible to merge **cells**. (individual sections of a table)
When **cells** split, the DNA goes through a process called replication. (smallest parts of an organism)

Reading and vocabulary 5

1
1 tiny devices – notice also *simple devices* in the fifth paragraph and *novel medical devices* in the final paragraph
2 display properties
3 make use
4 experimental nanotechnology
5 completely different – and notice also *profoundly different* in the second paragraph
6 greatest advances

2 *Possible answers*
1 complex, intricate, strange, special, electronic (and many more)
2 have, exhibit, show, lack, require
3 a suggestion, an offer, an apology, progress, a mistake, money
4 advanced, applied, theoretical, cutting-edge, medical
5 profoundly, totally, absolutely, partly, slightly, somewhat
6 significant, considerable, major, important

3 1 without knowing   2 in the near future   3 from the beginning

Reading and vocabulary 6

1
1 consists of
2 govern
3 concerns itself (only) with
4 In contrast
5 controversies
6 arising out of
7 lines
8 increasingly
9 implicate

2 *Possible answers*
1 fundamental
2 traditional
3 is based on
4 has its origins in
5 with regard to
6 goes against
7 behaviour
8 signatories, countries which signed
9 give

3 *Possible answers*
1 nation: national, nationality, nationalist, international, internationally, nationalise
2 significant: signify, insignificant, significance, insignificance, significantly
3 acceptance: accept, acceptable, unacceptable, acceptably, accepting
4 extent: extend, extension, extensive, extensively, inextensive
5 creator: create, creative, creation, creatively, creativity

Phonemic symbols

Vowel sounds

Symbol	Examples		
/iː/	sleep	me	
/i/	happy	recipe	
/ɪ/	pin	dinner	
/ʊ/	foot	could	pull
/uː/	do	shoe	through
/e/	red	head	said
/ə/	arrive	father	colour
/ɜː/	turn	bird	work
/ɔː/	sort	thought	walk
/æ/	cat	black	
/ʌ/	sun	enough	wonder
/ɒ/	got	watch	sock
/ɑː/	part	heart	laugh
/eɪ/	name	late	aim
/aɪ/	my	idea	time
/ɔɪ/	boy	noise	
/eə/	pair	where	bear
/ɪə/	hear	beer	
/əʊ/	go	home	show
/aʊ/	out	cow	
/ʊə/	pure		

Consonant sounds

Symbol	Examples		
/p/	put		
/b/	book		
/t/	take		
/d/	dog		
/k/	car	kick	
/g/	go	guarantee	
/tʃ/	catch	church	
/dʒ/	age	lounge	
/f/	for	cough	
/v/	love	vehicle	
/θ/	thick	path	
/ð/	this	mother	
/s/	since	rice	
/z/	zoo	houses	
/ʃ/	shop	sugar	machine
/ʒ/	pleasure	usual	vision
/h/	hear	hotel	
/m/	make		
/n/	name	now	
/ŋ/	bring		
/l/	look	while	
/r/	road		
/j/	young		
/w/	wear		

Index

The numbers in the index are **Unit** numbers not page numbers. The pronunciation provided is for standard British English.

battle against 9
be (commonly) associated with 12
be based on 12, 14
be bombarded with 9
be borne out 49
be concerned (with) 39
be made up of 6, 42
be that as it may 16
be united 9
bear out 24
begin /bɪˈgɪn/ 40
behaviour /bɪˈheɪvjə/ 47
bell curve 26
belong /bɪˈlɒŋ/ 42
below /bɪˈləʊ/ 39
benefit /ˈbenɪfɪt/ 33
benefit from 14
beyond the scope (of) 2, 38
biased /ˈbaɪəst/ 36
biased against 36
biased in favour of 36
bit (computer) /bɪt/ 9
blended /ˈblendɪd/ 22
blue collar 42
body of evidence 24
body of literature 23
bond /bɒnd/ 43
book /bʊk/ 15
borrowing rights 21
brainstorm /ˈbreɪnstɔːm/ 21
break off contact 10
brief /briːf/ 40
briefly /ˈbriːfli/ 1, 12
bring to a close 50
bring together 43
bulk /bʌlk/ 7
by chance 13
by far 13
by heart 21
by means of which 16
by no means 49
cafeteria /ˌkæfəˈtɪəriə/ 18
calculate /ˈkælkjʊleɪt/ 3, 25
call for 14, 17
call on 40
candidate /ˈkændɪdət/ 20
career /kəˈrɪə/ 17
carry out 3, 6, 41
case /keɪs/ 2, 15
case study 41
cast doubt on 32
catalogue /ˈkætəlɒg/ 23
category /ˈkætəgri/ 42

cause /kɔːz/ 12, 30
cause-and-effect /kɔːz ənd ɪˈfekt/ 41
century /ˈsentʃəri/ 29
chain reaction 30
challenge /ˈtʃæləndʒ/ 3, 12, 35, 45, 49
change /tʃeɪndʒ/ 12, 15, 48
channel /ˈtʃænəl/ 8
character /ˈkærɪktə/ 1
characteristic /ˌkærɪktəˈrɪstɪk/ 1, 4, 12, 42
charge /tʃɑːdʒ/ 8
check /tʃek/ 24, 41
circumstances /ˈsɜːkəmstæntsɪz/ 46
cite /saɪt/ 23
claim /kleɪm/ 32
clarification /ˌklærɪfɪˈkeɪʃən/ 17
clarify /ˈklærɪfaɪ/ 34
classify /ˈklæsɪfaɪ/ 3, 42
clear /klɪə/ 24
clearly /ˈklɪəli/ 12
clearly demonstrate 12
clearly identify 12
closely /ˈkləʊsli/ 12
coherent /kəʊˈhɪərənt/ 34
coincide with 29
collaborative /kəˈlæbərətɪv/ 22
collate results 10
collect /kəˈlekt/ 24, 41
collect results 10
college /ˈkɒlɪdʒ/ 19
column /ˈkɒləm/ 27
combination /ˌkɒmbɪˈneɪʃən/ 43
combine elements 10
come back 40
come down on one side 33
come into contact with 10
come to a conclusion 33
come to light 24
come up with 45
comment /ˈkɒment/ 32, 40
comment on 14
common /ˈkɒmən/ 4, 11
common ground 11
common knowledge 23
common practice 11
commonly /ˈkɒmənli/ 12
commons /ˈkɒmənz/ 19
communicate /kəˈmjuːnɪkeɪt/ 34
comparatively /kəmˈpærətɪvli/ 5
compared (with/to) /kəmˈpeəd/ 44

comparison /kəmˈpærɪsən/ 44
compatible /kəmˈpætɪbəl/ 49
complement /ˈkɒmplɪmənt/ 43
complex /ˈkɒmpleks/ 4
component /kəmˈpəʊnənt/ 42
comprehend /ˌkɒmprɪˈhend/ 34
comprehensive /ˌkɒmprɪˈhensɪv/ 24, 49
comps /kɒmps/ 19
concentrate on 14
concept /ˈkɒnsept/ 31
concisely /kənˈsaɪsli/ 50
conclude /kənˈkluːd/ 50
conclusion /kənˈkluːʒən/ 33
conclusively /kənˈkluːsɪvli/ 12
conclusively establish 12
concrete /ˈkɒŋkriːt/ 4
concurrent /kənˈkʌrənt/ 29
conditions /kənˈdɪʃənz/ 11, 41, 46
conduct /kənˈdʌkt/ 3
confine /kənˈfaɪn/ 46
confirm /kənˈfɜːm/ 1
conflict /ˈkɒnflɪkt/ 45
conflicting /kənˈflɪktɪŋ/ 24
conflicting elements 10
connotation /ˌkɒnəˈteɪʃən/ 34
consent (to)/kənˈsent/ 14
consequence /ˈkɒnsɪkwəns/ 30
conservative /kənˈsɜːvətɪv/ 36
conserve energy 10
consider /kənˈsɪdə/ 3, 24, 39
considerable /kənˈsɪdərəbəl/ 7, 11
considerable influence 30
considerably /kənˈsɪdərəbli/ 5
considered to be 37
consist (of) /kənˈsɪst/ 39, 42
consistent /kənˈsɪstənt/ 26
constant /ˈkɒnstənt/ 25
constituent /kənˈstɪtjuənt/ 10
constitute /ˈkɒnstɪtjuːt/ 33
constrain /kənˈstreɪn/ 46
constraint /kənˈstreɪnt/ 46
construct /kənˈstrʌkt/ 22
construct knowledge 22
consult a source 23
consume energy 10
consume /kənˈsjuːm/ 47
consumption /kənˈsʌmʃən/ 47
contact /ˈkɒntækt/ 10
contain /kənˈteɪn/ 8, 45
contemporary /kənˈtempərəri/ 29
contend /kənˈtend/ 32
contention /kənˈtenʃən/ 32

elucidate /ɪˈluːsɪdeɪt/ 9
emerge /ɪˈmɜːdʒ/ 14, 24, 47
emerge (of phenomena) 10
emergence /ɪˈmɜːdʒəns/ 29, 47
emphasis /ˈemfəsɪs/ 3, 15, 32
emphasise /ˈemfəsaɪz/ 3, 14, 31,
    32
empirical /ɪmˈpɪrɪkəl/ 24, 41
employ /ɪmˈplɔɪ/ 41
employment /ɪmˈplɔɪmənt/ 42
encounter /ɪnˈkaʊntə/ 36
encouraging /ɪnˈkʌrɪdʒɪŋ/ 10
end /end/ 30
end-of-semester /end əv sɪˈmestə/
    21
energy /ˈenədʒi/ 10
engage in debate 10
English-medium /ˈɪŋglɪʃ ˈmiːdiəm/
    17
enhance /ɪnˈhɑːns/ 48
enormous /ɪˈnɔːməs/ 7, 11
enrol /ɪnˈrəʊl/ 20
enrol on 22
enter your username 22
entitlement /ɪnˈtaɪtəlmənt/ 28
entry requirement 17
environment /ɪnˈvaɪrənmənt/ 46
equal opportunities policy 17
equip with 14
equivalent /ɪˈkwɪvələnt/ 43
era /ˈɪərə/ 29
erase information 9
erasure /ɪˈreɪʒə/ 9
error /ˈerə/ 45
especially /ɪˈspeʃəli/ 5
essay /ˈeseɪ/ 15, 20
essence /ˈesəns/ 31
essentially /ɪˈsentʃəli/ 5
establish /ɪˈstæblɪʃ/ 3, 12, 24, 35
establish contact 10
estimate /ˈestɪmət/ (noun) 25
estimate /ˈestɪmeɪt/ (verb) 25
ethical /ˈeθɪkəl/ 36
ethnic /ˈeθnɪk/ 42
evaluation /ɪˌvæljuˈeɪʃən/ 35
even number 25
even so 38
eventual /ɪˈventʃuəl/ 29
eventually /ɪˈventʃuəli/ 5, 50
evidence /ˈevɪdəns/ 12, 24, 37,
    43, 49
evident /ˈevɪdənt/ 37
evoke /ɪˈvəʊk/ 34

evolve /ɪˈvɒlv/ 29
exact /ɪgˈzækt/ 25
examination /ɪgˌzæmɪˈneɪʃən/ 15
examine /ɪgˈzæmɪn/ 3, 12, 24
exceed /ɪkˈsiːd/ 27
exceeding /ɪkˈsiːdɪŋ/ 7
excess /ɪkˈses/ 7
excessive /ɪkˈsesɪv/ 7
exclude from 14
exist /ɪgˈzɪst/ 23
existence /ɪgˈzɪstəns/ 42, 46
expansion /ɪkˈspænʃən/ 48
expenditure /ɪkˈspendɪtʃə/ 28
experience /ɪkˈspɪəriəns/ 45
experiment /ɪkˈsperɪmənt/ 41
experimental /ɪkˌsperɪˈmentəl/ 41
explain /ɪkˈspleɪn/ 3, 32
explain a phenomenon 10
explain by the fact that 27
explanation /ˌekspləˈneɪʃən/ 32
explicit /ɪkˈsplɪsɪt/ 11
explicitly /ɪkˈsplɪsɪtli/ 5
exploration /ˌekspləˈreɪʃən/ 15
explore /ɪkˈsplɔː/ 3
export /ɪksˈpɔːt/ (verb) 47
expose to 14
express ideas 34
extension /ɪkˈstenʃən/ 21
extensive /ɪkˈstensɪv/ 23
extent /ɪkˈstent/ 38
extra-curricular activities 21
extreme /ɪkˈstriːm/ 26
face-to-face /ˌfeɪstəˈfeɪs/ 22
facilitate /fəˈsɪlɪteɪt/ 30
facilitation /fəˌsɪlɪˈteɪʃən/ 30
fact /fækt/ 24
factor /ˈfæktə/ 12
faculty /ˈfækəlti/ 18, 19
fair /feə/ 7
fair way 10
fall /fɔːl/ 27
fall below 27
falsify results 10
feature /ˈfiːtʃə/ 2, 12, 42
feedback /ˈfiːdbæk/ 22
feel free 40
fees /fiːz/ 17
few /fjuː/ 7
fewer and fewer 7
field study 41
figure /ˈfɪgə/ 25, 27
file (computer) /faɪl/ 9
fill in 17

final /ˈfaɪnəl/ 29, 50
finally /ˈfaɪnəli/ 39, 50
finals /ˈfaɪnəlz/ 19
financial /faɪˈnænʃəl/ 28
financial guarantee 17
find /faɪnd/ 3, 45
finite /ˈfaɪnaɪt/ 46
firmly /ˈfɜːmli/ 12
firmly establish 12
first /ˈfɜːst/ 39
first draft 21
firstly /ˈfɜːstli/ 39
flame /fleɪm/ 22
flaw /flɔː/ 49
flimsy /ˈflɪmzi/ 24
flowchart /ˈfləʊtʃɑːt/ 27
fluctuate /ˈflʌktʃueɪt/ 48
focus /ˈfəʊkəs/ 1, 40
focus on 14
following /ˈfɒləʊɪŋ/ 39, 50
for example 24, 38, 39
for instance 24, 38
for the most part 13, 16
for the purposes of 16, 38
for this reason 16
former /ˈfɔːmə/ 39
forthcoming /ˌfɔːθˈkʌmɪŋ/ 29
fraction /ˈfrækʃən/ 25
framework /ˈfreɪmwɜːk/ 31
fraternity /frəˈtɜːnəti/ 19
frequently /ˈfriːkwəntli/ 5, 12
freshman /ˈfreʃmən/ 19
from the point of view of 16
from then on 13
fundamental /ˌfʌndəˈmentəl/ 48,
    49
further /ˈfɜːðə/ 35, 38
furthermore /ˌfɜːðəˈmɔː/ 38
gender /ˈdʒendə/ 42
general /ˈdʒenərəl/ 42
generalise /ˈdʒenərəlaɪz/ 31
generally /ˈdʒenərəli/ 5, 12
generally associated with 12
generate /ˈdʒenəreɪt/ 1, 30
generate energy 10
generation /ˌdʒenəˈreɪʃən/ 42
get in 17
getting back to 40
give /gɪv/ 3
give a (brief) summary of 50
give a description 3
give an example 24
give credit 23, 49

instability /ˌɪnstəˈbɪləti/ 46
instalment /ɪnˈstɔːlmənt/ 28
instance /ˈɪnstəns/ 24
instigate /ˈɪnstɪgeɪt/ 35
instrument /ˈɪnstrəmənt/ 41
integral /ˈɪntɪgrəl/ 46
intense /ɪnˈtens/ 49
intention /ɪnˈtenʃən/ 35
intentional /ɪnˈtenʃənəl/ 35
interaction /ˌɪntəˈrækʃən/ 43
interchange /ˈɪntətʃeɪndʒ/ 43
interconnecting /ˌɪntəkəˈnektɪŋ/ 43
interdependence /ˌɪntədɪˈpendəns/ 43
interest-free /ˈɪntrəst friː/ 28
interesting /ˈɪntrəstɪŋ/ 24
interface /ˈɪntəfeɪs/ 35
interfere /ˌɪntəˈfɪə/ 41
interim /ˈɪntərɪm/ 10
inter-library loan 21
intermarriage /ˌɪntəˈmærɪdʒ/ 43
intermediate /ˌɪntəˈmiːdiət/ 29
intermittent /ˌɪntəˈmɪtənt/ 10
interplay /ˈɪntəpleɪ/ 43
interpret /ɪnˈtɜːprɪt/ 24, 31
interpretation /ɪnˌtɜːprɪˈteɪʃən/ 12
interrelated /ˌɪntərɪˈleɪtɪd/ 43
intersect /ˌɪntəˈsekt/ 27
interstate /ˌɪntəˈsteɪt/ 43
inter-university /ɪnˈtə ˌjuːnɪˈvɜːsəti/ 43
intrinsic /ɪnˈtrɪnsɪk/ 46
introduce /ˌɪntrəˈdjuːs/ 40
invalid /ɪnˈvælɪd/ 49
invalidate results 10
invent /ɪnˈvent/ 47
investigate /ɪnˈvestɪgeɪt/ 3
investigate a phenomenon 10
investigation /ɪnˌvestɪˈgeɪʃən/ 15
involve /ɪnˈvɒlv/ 3
irrational /ɪˈræʃənəl/ 36
issue /ˈɪʃuː/ 2, 8, 40, 45
it can be argued that 31, 37
it is not surprising that 49
it is noteworthy that 49
it is worth recalling that 49
it may not be the case that 37
it would appear that 37
it would seem that 37
item of data 24
junior /ˈdʒuːniə/ 19
keep to (time) 40

key /kiː/ 27, 49
KISS /kɪs/ 22
knowledge /ˈnɒlɪdʒ/ 22
knowledge base 35
label /ˈleɪbəl/ 27
laboratory /ləˈbɒrətri/ 41
lack /læk/ 15
large /lɑːdʒ/ 7
largely /ˈlɑːdʒli/ 5
largely determine 30
lastly /ˈlɑːstli/ 50
late /leɪt/ 29
later /ˈleɪtə/ 39
latter /ˈlætə/ 39
lay foundations 23
layer /leɪə/ 27
leave (time) /liːv/ 40
leave out 40
lecture /ˈlektʃə/ 15, 18, 20
lecture notes 21
lecture theatre 18
lecturer /ˈlektʃərə/ 18
legend /ˈledʒənd/ 27
less and less 7
liable /ˈlaɪəbəl/ 37
librarian /laɪˈbreəriən/ 18, 21
library /ˈlaɪbrəri/ 18
lie /laɪ/ 45
likelihood /ˈlaɪklɪhʊd/ 37
likely /ˈlaɪkli/ 37
limited /ˈlɪmɪtɪd/ 49
link /lɪŋk/ 22, 43
list /lɪst/ 12
list the main causes/ characteristics/features/ hypotheses 12
literature /ˈlɪtrətʃə/ 23
literature suggests 23
little /ˈlɪtl/ 7
little-known /ˈlɪtl nəʊn/ 24
loan /ləʊn/ 28
lodging /ˈlɒdʒɪŋ/ 28
logic /ˈlɒdʒɪk/ 15
long-term loan 21
look /lʊk/ 15
look back over 6
look for 24
loosely /ˈluːsli/ 12
loosely based 12
lose a battle 9
lose contact 10
lurk /lɜːk/ 22
magnitude /ˈmægnɪtjuːd/ 25

mailing list 22
main body 23
mainly /ˈmeɪnli/ 1, 12
mainly based 12
maintain /meɪnˈteɪn/ 8, 32, 48
maintain a united front 9
maintain contact 10
maintenance grant 28
major /ˈmeɪdʒə/ 11
make a calculation 25
make a to-do list 21
make ends meet 28
make reference to 23
make up 6
manipulate /məˈnɪpjʊleɪt/ 41
marital status 42
marked /mɑːkt/ 48
mathematical /ˌmæθəmˈætɪkəl/ 41
mature /məˈtjʊə/ 36
mature student 17
maximum /ˈmæksɪməm/ 25, 46
means of communication 22
means /miːnz/ 15
measures /ˈmeʒəz/ 8
median /ˈmiːdiən/ 26
mediate /ˈmiːdieɪt/ 45
meet /miːt/ 21
meet deadlines 21
meet objectives 35
memorise /ˈmeməraɪz/ 21
mention /ˈmenʃən/ 32
merely /ˈmɪəli/ 5
message /ˈmesɪdʒ/ 22, 34
method /ˈmeθəd/ 41
methodology /ˌmeθəˈdɒlədʒi/ 2, 41
mind map 21
mind starts to wander 21
minimal /ˈmɪnɪməl/ 46
minimum /ˈmɪnɪməm/ 25, 46
minor /ˈmaɪnə/ 11
miscalculate /mɪsˈkælkjʊleɪt/ 34
misguided /mɪsˈgaɪdɪd/ 49
misinterpret /ˌmɪsɪnˈtɜːprɪt/ 34
misinterpretation /ˌmɪsɪnˌtɜːprɪˈteɪʃən/ 34
mispronounce /ˌmɪsprəˈnaʊns/ 34
mispronunciation /ˌmɪsprəˌnʌnsiˈeɪʃən/ 34
mission statement 35
mistaken /mɪˈsteɪkən/ 49
mistranslate /ˌmɪstrænˈsleɪt/ 34

precise /prɪˈsaɪs/ 4, 25
precisely /prɪˈsaɪsli/ 5
predict /prɪˈdɪkt/ 33
preference /ˈprefərəns/ 15
prejudice /ˈpredʒʊdɪs/ 36
prejudiced against 36
prejudiced in favour of 36
preliminary /prɪˈlɪmɪnəri/ 10
preliminary results 10
present data 27
present study 23
present /preˈzənt/ (verb) 3, 24,
　　27, 40
presentation /ˌprezənˈteɪʃən/ 40
pre-sessional /priː ˈseʃənəl/ 20
presumably /prɪˈzjuːməbli/ 37
primarily /praɪˈmerəli/ 1, 5, 23
primary /ˈpraɪməri/ 1
primary source 23
prime number 25
prime /praɪm/ 1
principal /ˈprɪnsɪpəl/ 4
principle /ˈprɪnsɪpəl/ 2, 15, 36
prior to 29
prioritise /praɪˈɒrɪtaɪz/ 21
priority /praɪˈɒrəti/ 35
probability /ˌprɒbəˈbɪləti/ 26
probability distribution 26
probably /ˈprɒbəbli/ 37
problem /ˈprɒbləm/ 12, 15, 45
procedure /prəˈsiːdʒə/ 41, 47
proceed /prəˈsiːd/ 20
process /ˈprəʊses/ 17
process information 9
professor /prəˈfesə/ 18
profile /ˈprəʊfaɪl/ 17
profound /prəˈfaʊnd/ 31
progress /ˈprəʊgres/ 15
project /ˈprɒdʒekt/ 15, 20
proof /pruːf/ 32
proportion /prəˈpɔːʃən/ 26
propose /prəˈpəʊz/ 32
pros and cons 38
prove /pruːv/ 32, 41
provide /prəˈvaɪd/ 3, 24
provide a (brief) summary of 50
provide a sample 10
provide an example 24
provide an explanation 3
provide feedback 22
provide with 14
provided that 38
provocation /ˌprɒvəˈkeɪʃən/ 30

provoke /prəˈvəʊk/ 30
publish results 10
purpose /ˈpɜːpəs/ 35, 39
put /pʊt/ 3
put emphasis 3
put forward 6, 32, 38
put it briefly 50
qualification /ˌkwɒlɪfɪˈkeɪʃən/ 17
qualitative /ˈkwɒlɪtətɪv/ 4
quantifiable /ˈkwɒntɪfaɪəbəl/ 1
quantifiably /ˈkwɒntɪfaɪəbli/ 1
quantification /ˌkwɒntɪfɪˈkeɪʃən/ 1
quantify /ˈkwɒntɪfaɪ/ 1
quantitative /ˈkwɒntɪtətɪv/ 1, 4
quantitatively /ˈkwɒntɪtətɪvli/ 1
quantity /ˈkwɒntɪti/ 1
quarterly /ˈkwɔːtəli/ 29
question /ˈkwestʃən/ 12, 32
question results 10
quiz /kwɪz/ 19, 22
quotation /kwəʊˈteɪʃən/ 23
radical /ˈrædɪkəl/ 36
raise /reɪz/ 40, 45
raise a point 33
random /ˈrændəm/ 26
random number 25
random sample 27
range /reɪndʒ/ 26
rarely /ˈreəli/ 49
rather than 44
ratification /ˌrætɪfɪˈkeɪʃən/ 47
ratify /ˈrætɪfaɪ/ 47
ratio /ˈreɪʃiəʊ/ 26
rational /ˈræʃənəl/ 36
rationale /ˌræʃəˈnɑːl/ 15
reach a conclusion 33
reach /riːtʃ/ 35
reach a peak 27
react /riˈækt/ 45
reaction /riˈækʃən/ 31
reactionary /riˈækʃənri/ 36
react to 14
reading /ˈriːdɪŋ/ 22
reading speed 21
reason /ˈriːzən/ 15, 30
reasonable /ˈriːzənəbəl/ 7
reboot /riːˈbuːt/ 9
recapitulate /ˌriːkəˈpɪtjʊleɪt/ 50
receipt /rɪˈsiːt/ 28
recently /ˈriːsəntli/ 5
recent phenomenon 10
recognise /ˈrekəgnaɪz/ 49
record /rɪˈkɔːd/ (verb) 24, 41

recover /rɪˈkʌvə/ 48
refer /rɪˈfɜː/ 12, 43
refer frequently/specifically / in
　　passing 12
refer to 14, 38
referee /ˌrefəˈriː/ 17
reference /ˈrefrəns/ 8, 17
refine /rɪˈfaɪn/ 48
reflect /rɪˈflekt/ 24, 41, 43
registration fee 28
reimburse /ˌriːɪmˈbɜːs/ 28
relate /rɪˈleɪt/ 41
related /rɪˈleɪtɪd/ 43
relation /rɪˈleɪʃən/ 15
relationship /rɪˈleɪʃənʃɪp/ 12, 15,
　　41, 43
relative (to) /ˈrelətɪv/ 4, 43
relatively /ˈrelətɪvli/ 5
relax /rɪˈlæks/ 48
relevant /ˈreləvənt/ 4, 11, 24, 33,
　　38
reliable /rɪˈlaɪəbəl/ 24, 26
reload /ˌriːˈləʊd/ 9
rely on 14
remain in the dark 9
replicate /ˈreplɪkeɪt/ 41
reportedly /rɪˈpɔːtɪdli/ 37
represent /ˌreprɪˈzent/ 27
representative /ˌreprɪˈzentətɪv/ 41
representative sample 10
request an extension 21
require /rɪˈkwaɪə/ 17
research /rɪˈsɜːtʃ/ 2, 15, 41
research assistant 18
research is based on 12
research methodology 35
research student 18
resolution /ˌrezəˈluːʃən/ 45
resolve /rɪˈzɒlv/ 45
resource /rɪˈzɔːs/ 22
respectively /rɪˈspektɪvli/ 38, 39
respond to 14
response /rɪˈspɒns/ 15, 45
rest on 14
restore /rɪˈstɔː/ 48
restrain /rɪˈstreɪn/ 46
restraint /rɪˈstreɪnt/ 46
restrict /rɪˈstrɪkt/ 46
restriction /rɪˈstrɪkʃən/ 46
results /rɪˈzʌlts/ 10, 40
résumé /ˈrezʊmeɪ/ 28
retreat /rɪˈtriːt/ 9
return to 40